Praise for

BREAKTHROUGH SUPPLY CHAINS

The last half century of globalization has been characterized by supposedly "efficient" supply chains that were far flung, complex, and fragile. The pandemic, the war in Ukraine, and the potential for conflict in Taiwan have raised the scrim on the myriad problems of this system. These four supply chain experts tell us what we need to do now to create a system that will better serve countries, companies, consumers, and citizens.

—Rana Foroohar
Global Business Columnist, Associate Editor, *The Financial Times*;
author of *Homecoming: The Path to Prosperity in a Post-Global World* and
Makers and Takers: The Rise of Finance and the Fall of American Business

"Breakthrough thinking" is a requirement for retailers and suppliers as they develop new supply chain strategies and innovations that delight customers. As changing economic conditions and uncertainties continue to shape the new era, advanced analytics and technological advances are evolving as solutions that can work through the challenges and support profitable growth. This book discusses these important topics and provides meaningful thoughts and guidelines for developing tomorrow's supply chain strategies.

—Mohan Ram Akella
Senior Vice President, US Omni-Channel
Supply Chain Strategy, Walmart

Breakthrough Supply Chains is the Mount Olympus of supply chain insight. For CEOs seeking to thrive in a world of chaos, it is required reading.

—Sean Ashcroft
Editor-in-Chief, *Supply Chain Magazine*

Breakthrough Supply Chains could not have come at a better time. Increased supply chain and supply chain ecosystem risks due to trade wars, pandemics, and major geopolitical tensions and realignments are all causing reevaluation of the costs and risks of global sourcing and their impacts on both private sector competitive interests and public sector defense, public health, and economic security, while reimagining globalization. *Breakthrough Supply Chains* should be required reading for a variety of audiences—in the private, public, and academic sectors—who need new playbooks for designing and managing the next generation of supply chains.

— Professor Chelsea C. White III
Professor and Schneider National Chair in Transportation
and Logistics, H. Milton Stewart School of Industrial
and Systems Engineering, Georgia Tech

This is an excellent book for everyone who is interested or involved in supply chain management topics. The authors, renowned pioneers and experts in this field, explain in a clear and understandable way *what* supply chains are really and *why* do we need them. The book highlights the key breakthroughs in supply chain management and motivates the reader for innovative thinking to understand and manage supply chains better in an uncertain world.

—Juergen Tinggren
Former President and CEO of Schindler Group, Switzerland,
Chairman of Bekaert SA, and Board Member of Johnson Controls

I highly endorse this book for all those interested in supply chains. I am pleased that the authors reference and build on my book, *The Resilient Enterprise* in the context of what all supply chains need to transform to be successful in the new world era. Their "breakthrough thinking" provides helpful guidance in several critical areas.

—Professor Jossi Sheffi
Professor, MIT, and Director, Center for Transportation and
Logistics, MIT; author of *The Resilient Enterprise* and *The Power
of Resilience: How the Best Companies Manage the Unexpected*

The authors have taken a unique and deeply thought-provoking approach in their explanation of the recent evolution of supply chains as a competitive advantage for companies and nations. The book is a groundbreaking work that dives into the elements of resilience, risk, and supply assurance in the era of ecommerce and heightened political context. As business leaders and political leaders think about the critical role supply chains play in their company's and nation's future, *Breakthrough Supply Chains* is an indispensable playbook that will help all of us plan for the future.

—Tom Nightingale
CEO, AFS Logistics, and 2023 Chairman,
Council of Supply Chain Management Professionals

I highly endorse this book for leaders of supply chains, public officials, and other interested business and public policy makers. The themes are right on—a new world order, new threats and risks, geopolitical risks, exciting new technologies, and sustainability. Today's supply chains need to be reinvented to operate within these new conditions and changing customer requirements.

—Professor Hau Lee
The Thoma Professor of Operations, Information & Technology,
Stanford University Graduate School of Business; author of
Building Supply Chain Excellence in Emerging Economies

The United States and its allies have launched the biggest restructuring of international industrial systems in at least half a century, and this will dramatically affect the operations of every company that builds or sources abroad. The authors of this very important book understand the stakes. Better yet they understand what managers must do to keep their companies safe while staying ahead of the pack. There's simply no better source for mastering the art of building resilient and efficient end-to-end supply chains in a world in revolution.

—Barry Lynn
Executive Director, Open Markets Institute; author of
*Liberty from All Masters: The New American
Autocracy vs. the Will of the People*

The timing for this book is just right. As supply chain leaders have learned from the global pandemic, supply chains were fragile and largely inflexible. The new world era requires innovative thinking for new strategies and network designs to operate under new conditions and goals. Innovative technologies that enable digital transformations are essential for resilience and agility. The book provides breakthrough thinking to help guide business leaders toward supply chains of the future.

—David Anderson
Managing General Partner, Supply Chain Ventures;
former head of Global Supply Chain, Accenture

This book provides important messages about the evolution of supply chains and how supply chains and globalization have enabled great success for businesses. But then the disruptions of the last several years brought many supply chains and businesses to their knees. Readers of this book will better understand supply chains and how to use insight to develop resilient supply chains that beget competitive advantage.

—Dr. Jim Tompkins
Chairman, Tompkins Ventures; author of
Insightful Leadership: Surfing the Waves to Organizational Excellence

Our world and needs are dramatically changing, yet many supply chain challenges remain consistent with the increasing need for core fundamentals. The authors have a great ability to remind us that today's supply chain strategies—large/small/global/local—need resiliency, optionality, proven execution with trusted partnerships. The book's approach is a much-needed "bootcamp" read to help us become more fit and leaner in our thinking and execution.

—Chris Munro
Founder, AVC Partners

Before the Covid-19 pandemic, only experts talked about supply chains. Today, references to global supply chains are ubiquitous, but less understood is how to think about and address their disruptions, weaponization, and the impact their functioning has on society, policy, security, business, trade, and individuals' lives. The authors are experienced leaders that have written a multi-disciplinary book grounded in evidence that is relevant, timely, and accessible, and offers an innovative framework for how to think about and lead on supply chain issues. This will become the go-to resource for leaders, specialists, *and* the public.

—David M. Van Slyke, Ph.D.
Dean and Louis A. Bantle Chair in Business-Government Policy,
Maxwell School of Citizenship and Public Affairs,
Syracuse University, and Member, Defense Business Board

I endorse this book and recommend it to all CSCOs, those aspiring to supply chain leadership positions, and other interested business and public officials. In an ever-evolving business environment, supply chains continue to evolve to maintain competitive advantage. The authors identify the foundational practices combined with breakthrough thinking around the customer value, the use of advanced analytics to create a core set of measures that matter, and sustainability.

—Tom S. Lee
Former Chief Supply Chain Officer at
American Freight, Lovesac, and Spartan Nash

The book *Breakthrough Supply Chains* promises a lot, and builds high expectations, especially given the high profiles of each of the four authors. Yet, the book delivers even more than it promises. For everyone, from the CEO to the supply chain newbie, this book gives a lot of fresh thinking.

—Vivek Sood
Managing Director, Global Supply Chain Group

Breakthrough Supply Chains is unique in its approach; the authors' viewpoint on risk, sustainability, and national policy is not often addressed elsewhere. Just as importantly, it provides a set of guidelines that enable companies to succeed and thrive in the uncertain environment of today and tomorrow. This book will provide valuable inputs in developing strategy, tactics, and national policy. Strongly recommended for supply chain executives and government officials to gain a unique viewpoint on supply chains and evaluate the impact it has on them.

—Anders Karlborg
Senior Vice President, Americas Operations &
Global Channel Operations, VERTIV

The years of the Covid pandemic reminded all of us what a vital role our international supply chains play in ensuring our survival and providing our company—Phillip Jeffries, Ltd., the world leader in high-end wallcoverings—advantage versus our competition. The authors are passionate supply chain leaders and educators with breakthrough ideas in supply chain management. If you care about designing your supply chain to meet your business growth objectives, provide a competitive advantage to your company, and meet your market's sustainability requirements, then you should read and study this book.

—Jeffrey Bershad
CEO, Phillip Jeffries, Ltd.

BREAKTHROUGH
SUPPLY CHAINS

HOW COMPANIES AND NATIONS CAN THRIVE AND PROSPER IN AN UNCERTAIN WORLD

CHRISTOPHER GOPAL · GENE TYNDALL

WOLFGANG PARTSCH · ELEFTHERIOS IAKOVOU

New York   Chicago   San Francisco   Athens   London   Madrid
Mexico City   Milan   New Delhi   Singapore   Sydney   Toronto

1 2 3 4 5 6 7 8 9 LCR   28 27 26 25 24 23

ISBN   978-1-264-98966-9
MHID   1-264-98966-0

e-ISBN   978-1-264-99188-4
e-MHID   1-264-99188-6

Library of Congress Cataloging-in-Publication Data

Names: Gopal, Christopher, author.
Title: Breakthrough supply chains : how companies and nations can thrive and
    prosper in an uncertain world / Chris Gopal, Gene Tyndall, Wolfgang Partsch,
    and Eleftherios Iakovou.
Description: New York : McGraw Hill Education, [2023] | Includes
    bibliographical references and index.
Identifiers: LCCN 2022058681 (print) | LCCN 2022058682 (ebook) |
    ISBN 9781264989669 (hardback) | ISBN 9781264991884 (ebook)
Subjects: LCSH: Business logistics. | Strategic planning.
Classification: LCC HD38.5 .G669 2023 (print) | LCC HD38.5 (ebook) |
    DDC 658.5—dc23/eng/20221215
LC record available at https://lccn.loc.gov/2022058681
LC ebook record available at https://lccn.loc.gov/2022058682

McGraw Hill books are available at special quantity discounts to use as premiums and sales promotions or for use in corporate training programs. To contact a representative, please visit the Contact Us pages at www.mhprofessional.com.

McGraw Hill is committed to making our products accessible to all learners. To learn more about the available support and accommodations we offer, please contact us at accessibility@mheducation.com. We also participate in the Access Text Network (www.accesstext.org), and ATN members may submit requests through ATN.

CONTENTS

Part One

Impacts of Supply Chains on the Global Economy and Society

Part Two

Breakthrough Thinking

ACKNOWLEDGMENTS

As we stated in our first book, *Supercharging Supply Chains*, developing a book with innovative content and practical guidelines that can serve as a "living point of reference" for many years is a significant challenge. In writing *Breakthrough Supply Chains*, we can reiterate this admission, with one qualifier: we believe the timing is perfect to develop this book, as not only are supply chains more visible to the public eye than ever, but they are also now a priority for all companies and public policy officials around the world. While the evolution of supply chain management has spurred many new models, tools, services, equipment, and academic programs, there is not yet a common definition of *what* supply chains really are, *why* they are so important to business, governments, and societies, and *what* kind of thinking these stakeholders need to embrace for their organizations to thrive and prosper in a volatile, uncertain, complex, and ambiguous world.

We want to thank everyone and every organization we have worked and collaborated with over the 25-year period since *Supercharging Supply Chains* was published. All of us learn from others, no matter what the topic, issue, or problem is. Supply chains, with their critical mission and wide scope, can advance only through multidisciplinary contributions and managerial experience.

Each of us has special people with whom we wish to express our appreciation:

- **Chris Gopal** wishes to thank his wife, Sherrie, whose support, inspiration and constant encouragement made this possible; Jennifer Hill, director of the Defense Business Board in Washington and his DBB colleagues, who have made him aware of the supply chain issues facing the nation, and his many colleagues and friends in industry, NGOs, and academia. Finally, Chris wishes to thank his coauthors for their friendship, experience, and the different perspectives they have brought to the book.

- **Gene Tyndall** wishes to thank his many colleagues, clients, and industry friends with whom he has collaborated and continues to learn from each day over his 30-year career. Gene also wants to give a special thanks to his good friend and coauthor Lefteris Iakovou, who kindly joined us for this book. Lefteris has been an outstanding academic and advisor at several well-known universities, governments, and NGOs over his 30-year academic career. He has added special wisdom and thought leadership to this book.

- **Wolfgang Partsch** wants to thank his good friends and coauthors from our bestselling book *Supercharging Supply Chains* in the late 1990s, Chris Gopal and Gene Tyndall, because without our intensive exchange of innovations and experiences across the Atlantic with a view on global supply chain management, we never would have succeeded in launching this project for a desperately needed guideline in the world market. Wolfgang also wishes to thank his son,

Daniel, for his continuous contributions and inputs from his field experiences in operational excellence and supply chain management with his clients, globally leading and well-known manufacturing companies, and the praxis tests of many "breakthrough thinkings" from our think tank. Especially these tests for transformation into actions and reality were and are very useful because at the end of the day it is people who make it happen.

- **Lefteris Iakovou** wants to thank Gene Tyndall and Chris Gopal for their unwavering friendship and support, and an intellectually stimulating supply chain journey that had a profound impact on his academic and professional paths, while further culminating to this book. He also wants to thank all his mentors and friends at Cornell University, the University of Miami, the Aristotle University of Thessaloniki, Greece, and at Texas A&M, along with his collaborators from government and industry across Europe and the United States. Nothing in his life would be possible without the unconditional love and support of his parents, Theodoros and Evanthia. His wife, Maria Polyzoi, and their sons, Thodoris, Nikos, and Loukas, are his true pillars and blessings.

All of us also express our sincere appreciation to two special people who helped make this book a reality. First, to Judith Newlin of McGraw Hill who sponsored us with this superior publisher, and who also understands supply chains and their potential. Judith has provided us insight and advice on writing world-class books. Second, we thank Esmond Harmsworth, of Aevitas Creative Management, who supported us enthusiastically and advised us from the inception on leading practices in writing and promoting a high-impact book for multiple audiences.

And, as always, our views expressed in the book are not part of the official policies of the organizations we are affiliated with.

PREFACE

We published our first book, *Supercharging Supply Chains: New Ways to Increase Value Through Global Operational Excellence* (Tyndall, Gopal, Partsch, and Kamauff, John Wiley & Sons, 1998) over 25 years ago and laid a multiyear vision of high-performing supply chains, focused on a paradigm of end-to-end supply chains, impacts on financial statements, and a justification for action. Several well-respected executives endorsed the book as providing innovative and insightful thoughts on supply chain excellence and its economic value, and many more have credited it with helping them develop their supply chain strategies. Ever since then, we have been asked for a second book that builds on the first. We resisted, partly because we felt that *Supercharging Supply Chains* already addressed the key issues facing companies and supply chain executives.

However, several things have changed. The evolution of supply chains over the past three decades has produced the growth and expansion of complex, multitiered, and interconnected networks that span the globe. The introduction of new rules and the relaxation of others have led to a growth in industry concentration and an emphasis on "financializing" the supply chain—the focus on short-term actions to drive up stock prices and shareholder value. The enormous degree of outsourcing of the Western economies' manufacturing, supply, and product design capabilities to China (the "world's factory") and other low-cost countries has been at the core of this expansion. In essence, "globalization"—the seamless movement of goods, services, and money across national and regional boundaries—has been seen as part of the "anatomy" of corporations, and stakeholders and nations had assumed that it functions in a relatively smooth and predictable manner.

Then came the global Covid-19 pandemic with its multiple variants, and an avalanche of black swan events (the Russian invasion of Ukraine, Chinese aggressions toward Taiwan and their threats regarding the supply of rare earth material, new geopolitical tensions, and massive climate change–related events, among others), bringing to the surface long-existing structural problems of global supply chains and exposing the fallacy of that assumption of smooth global flows. The term "supply chain" was suddenly all over the mass media, a primary topic in corporate boardrooms, and discussed at senior policy and government levels all over the world. The development and distribution of vaccines against Covid-19 was all about supply chains, and the shortage of medical supplies, essential goods, and consumable products was highlighted daily. We realized that many of our supply chains were fragile.

Finally, governments and citizens came to realize that supply chains of critical products and materials, and their resilience, were essential elements of any national defense and security strategy. Indeed, corporations had often offshored supply, manufacturing capabilities, and design for low-cost labor and market access, but often neglected national economic, defense, and social interests.

The globalization narrative has been giving way to new market and political realities, and we now have an international trade environment, a shifting of corporate and national priorities and imperatives working with allies (within spheres of influence of technology and supply controlled by democracies and autocracies), public-private partnerships, and with outsourcing and distribution requiring cross-border movements and new trade agreements. Supply chains, and the global environment they operated in, had changed dramatically over the past several years. We decided at this point (admittedly with some degree of urging) that it was the right time to write this book. It was also time to emphasize that, despite the supply chain "crisis" (some may refer to it as "chaos") and some of the well-publicized economic, social, environmental, and community impacts, these international supply chains delivered some amazing benefits to business, society, and governments. For example, medicines, vaccines, supplies, and food were being distributed throughout the world, and necessary material was provided for recoveries from natural disasters and other major disruptions.

Our intention was to write a book that adopts a "systems thinking" approach to the end-to-end supply chain and addresses several audiences: corporate executives, supply chain leaders across industries, public policy officials, people interested in the issues of global trade and supply chains, and academics. Over the past 20-plus years, we have often seen a focus on "silos" and suboptimization priorities in industry and academia eroding the paradigm of the end-to-end supply chain and long-term business results that we championed in our first book. We have decided "to bring the message back" by addressing the question, "What are supply chains, really?" focusing on the new environment in which they have to operate and the key issues that need to be addressed, rather than on prescriptive details of how to manage specific segments of the supply chain. We provide the "new supply chain basics" and the "breakthrough thinking" necessary to develop new high-performing and resilient supply chains. In other words, we have adopted the Socratic method that is best expressed by the philosopher himself: "I cannot teach anybody anything. I can only make them think."

We believe that this "breakthrough thinking" within the context of the changing environment is a critical and very useful aspect of this book. Each chapter provides innovative and leading practices, suggestions, and principles that contribute to doing the right things, and doing them the right way for the right reasons, in a practical and implementable manner. Equally important, they are addressed in an environment of increased volatility, uncertainty, complexity, and ambiguity, or VUCA (a term first described by Warren Bennis and Burt Nanus in 1985, and later used by the US Army War College early in the 1990s).

The four coauthors are truly global in terms of location and experience. Hence, the challenge of writing this book cannot be underestimated in terms of integrating different perspectives. Although we have each spent over 35 years creating, planning, designing, managing, and improving supply chains, while also teaching and conducting research on a global and national basis, we do not claim to know it all. Our continuing and collective experience, however, has resulted in lessons learned across all industries and all types of private and public organizations. It is within this context that we provide information, insight, and guidance on the following five interrelated sets of questions that form our narrative:

- **Supply chains of yesterday, today, and tomorrow:** What are supply chains, really? Why are supply chains so important to companies and national security, and why have supply chains proved so fragile during the global pandemic and other global crises?

- **Customers, demand, and supply:** Who are the "new" customers, what is their life cycle experience, and how do we manage them? Why are supply assurance and sourcing so important, what are the key issues, and how do we address them?

- **The enablers:** Why are accurate, complete, and timely data, information, and "intelligent" systems so important, and how do we manage them? What talent and skill sets are critical for enterprises and nations in the new supply chain? In a related and vital area, what are the right measures to evaluate supply chain effectiveness in the short and long terms?

- **The new imperatives, resilience and sustainability:** What is supply chain resilience all about, why is it so critical, and how can we cost-competitively build resilience into our supply chains? In addition to resilience, what is supply chain sustainability, why is it so important, and how should companies approach it?

- **The way forward:** What is the right way for executives and policy makers to go forward?

We believe that our breakthrough thinking principles can guide executives and policy makers in developing and honing successful road maps and playbooks for the new supply chains. We also hope that they can provide a pragmatic and comprehensive framework for academics to embed their research and teaching programs, as well as a common platform and understanding of supply chains and the new environment for the interested public. This is a book about the past, present, and future, and the future begins now.

PART ONE

Impacts of Supply Chains on the Global Economy and Society

CHAPTER 1

Defining (and Redefining) the Supply Chain

Difficulties mastered are opportunities won.
—Winston Churchill[1]

Winston Churchill's statement wasn't about supply chains, but it does apply to the evolving story of supply chains, shaped by overcoming challenges and capitalizing on opportunities. Goods and services have required "sequences of activities" to acquire, manufacture, and bring them to market. "The supply chain" is now a high-profile and high-impact term in today's global economic, social, and political environment. Supply chains have taken advantage of opportunities and laws in local, regional, and global trade and have adapted successfully to many difficulties and challenges over the years.

But supply chains and poor supply chain management have also been blamed—often with good reason, but in some cases owing to bad political and government policies—for many of the problems facing society today. These include the shortages of medication and medical supplies, consumables, and building supplies, rising costs and inflation, healthcare problems, and environmental destruction, just to name a few. This raises some basic questions: What actually is a supply chain? What is behind the supply chain issues driving these problems?

In this chapter, we define, from our perspective, the structure and processes of today's supply chains. Subsequent chapters will address the various components, challenges, practices, and the future of supply chains in the new digital, risky, and uncertain world.

In its simplest form, a supply chain consists of a seller and a buyer (a supplier and a customer). As we move closer to the realities of industry and economics, the supply chain usually consists of suppliers of raw materials, who sell to suppliers of semifinished products, who sell to manufacturers of finished products, who, in turn, sell to wholesalers, distributors, and retailers, and so on. The retailers then stock inventory for customers to order online or buy in person at a store, or have product shipped directly to them. For example, Figure 1.1 is an illustration of the supply chain for a ski parka.

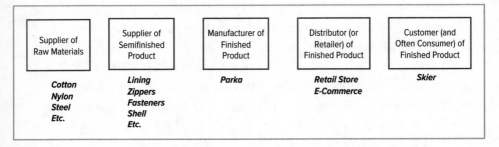

FIGURE 1.1 Supply Chain for a Ski Parka

The supply chain is about matching and reconciling demand and supply in a manner that minimizes risk, ensures liquidity, and maximizes profitability in a sustained fashion. The product must be acquired, made, and shipped (using many and different modes of transportation), warehoused, with inventory planned for and stocked in different places, for the supply chain to work in both fulfilling customer demands and ensuring supply. This applies to online ordering, direct-to-customer delivery, retail store shopping, and a host of variations in order and delivery. Finally, the supply chain must be financed, from the time that cash is paid to a supplier to the time cash is received from the customer. This is the finance and logistics aspect of the supply chain, as shown in Figure 1.2.

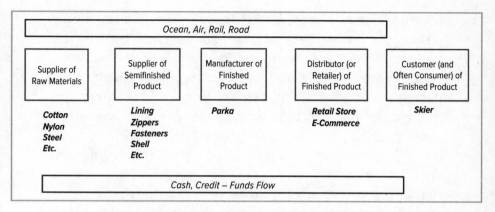

FIGURE 1.2 Extended Supply Chain for a Ski Parka

However, a supply chain is not a straightforward sequential chain of activities, functions, and facilities. It is, instead, really a complex network, even for a relatively simple item like a ski parka. In fact, it looks like Figure 1.3.

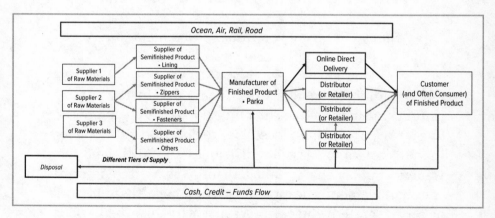

FIGURE 1.3 Supply Chain Network for a Ski Parka

The supply chain structure has multiple suppliers in different tiers and in different countries, multiple modes of transportation and delivery, multiple manufacturing sites, and many channels of distribution—retailers, online, and combinations of both. Every unique product and supply chain has its own set of complexities, vulnerabilities, and uncertainty—consider food in the supermarkets, smartphones, toys, building products, aerospace systems, petroleum products, and others. To round off this introduction, we must include the management and execution aspects of the supply chain. These are all the activities involved: sourcing the supplier, buying from that supplier, contracting, manufacturing the product with high quality, managing transportation and warehousing, estimating and managing the financing of the businesses and the supply chain, assessing demand, planning for supply and inventory deployment, replenishing stocks, and collecting and disposing of returns. All in all, *supply chains and their management are evolving and are complex.*

THE GROWTH OF SUPPLY CHAINS

Study the past if you would divine the future.
—**Confucius**

Our coauthor, Wolfgang Partsch, helped originate this term in 1980 and managed the first modern supply chain project. The term "supply chain" describes the network of suppliers, manufacturers, wholesalers, distributors, retailers, and customers. "Supply chain management" was used to describe the management and practices to manage this network as an integrated whole. In fact, prior to this, the various departments in a company—sourcing and procurement, inbound transportation, warehousing, manufacturing, outbound distribution, and customer fulfillment—were treated in many companies and organizations as independent functions, run in a semiautonomous fashion. Managing in this "siloed" fashion grew increasingly more difficult as companies' operations grew in complexity and length—with sourcing from multiple countries, deploying inventory in different geographical locations, and serving customers on a worldwide basis. Companies began to view the independent business functions as an integrated chain of events and processes that source and bring products to markets and customers, and to see the network of suppliers, intermediaries, channels, customers, and providers as an end-to-end network (Figure 1.4).

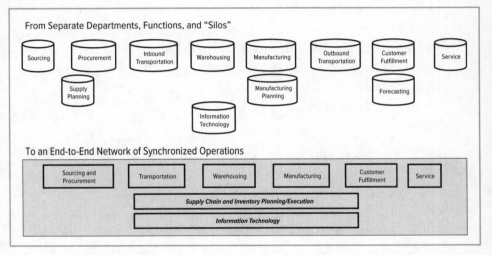

FIGURE 1.4 Management Evolution of the Supply Chain

The result of this ongoing evolution are today's global supply chains: complex, multitiered, and interconnected networks that consist of a large number of suppliers spread across the globe, often supplying raw material, assemblies, and thousands of parts. They often have complex manufacturing systems, making many products and product lines, that include contract manufacturers and plants in different countries. They get these products to the final customer via a variety of distribution channels that include distributors and retailers and encompass both physical and online ordering. Finally, they service a large number of customers and customer types across the globe. These networks span multiple countries and trade zones and require a significant amount of working capital and fixed expense financing. Most of today's supply chains were built on the basis of a global economy, assuming free trade and the seamless movement of goods and services across countries based solely on economic flows. Unfortunately, this assumption could not have been further from the truth.

Today's supply chains, if not structured and managed properly, have proved to be vulnerable to a variety of disruptions—which many companies did not (and sometimes, could not) anticipate, and for which they did little planning. These disruptions have included:

- Extreme weather events and climate change impacts
- Supplier failures and product supply stoppages
- Labor unrest and other issues, including publicity of poor safety conditions, strikes, exploitation of children, and slave labor
- Government trade and tax policies; environmental, social, and governance (ESG) and labor mandates
- Cyberattacks by governments, criminals, and corporate competitors
- Intellectual property thefts by governments and corporate competitors
- Wars, hostile government action, trade conflicts, and regulations
- Pandemics

These disruptions can result in demand spikes and customers ordering far more than they need ("just in case"), massive cost increases, supply disruptions, shortages, and other panicked customers cutting their orders significantly.

While many of these disruptions are not new, recent developments such as geopolitical tensions on a broad scale, serious medical and health events, and climate change–related disasters have amplified their impacts. Furthermore, the supply chains of today are further challenged and stressed by regulators, activists, and activist investors to reduce greenhouse emissions and improve their overall sustainability and social agenda footprint.

In the past, these events and disruptions tended to be regional, sometimes with far-flung but nevertheless local implications. At time of writing, the Covid-19 pandemic, along with the Russia-Ukraine war and the Chinese aggression toward Taiwan, are only the latest in a series of international events with global implications. These are further exacerbated by the increasing tension among the major power blocs—the United States, the European Union, China, and Russia.

As Stephen Hawking is purported to have said, "Intelligence is the ability to adapt to change." Well before the Covid-19 pandemic, technological, geopolitical, and economic forces, along with the perceived need for national security, regionalization, and faster response times to customer orders, had already begun reshaping globalization to what is commonly known as *deglobalization*. The financial crisis of 2008 was an inflection point as multinational organizations began recognizing that the hyperextension of their supply chains had left them exposed to an increasing number of risks. This resulted in the shrinkage of global trade and leveled the myths of globalization and seamless global supply chain integration. As one of our coauthors, Chris Gopal, has said, "Companies don't compete, supply chains compete . . . and industries and countries compete through their supply chains."

We now have an environment that is highly volatile, uncertain, complex, and ambiguous (VUCA), and it has further brought to the surface structural supply chain issues and problems that had gradually developed and accumulated over the past several decades. The pre-2020 supply chains lacked resilience and attention to national security, leading to material and product shortages (empty shelves), rising cost of goods sold, and critical materials and products manufactured in hostile countries, and were clearly inadequate to deal with the new VUCA realities. The supply chains of today and the future must be able to thrive in this environment, one that changes continuously by new technologies, innovations, disruptions, increasing customer demands, and government actions. Designing and managing the new supply chains requires a novel paradigm and road map, one powered by breakthrough thinking.

POSITIVE IMPACTS OF GLOBAL SUPPLY CHAINS

Any discussion of supply chains requires recognition of their impact over the past 40 years on business, society, and government.

Defense and military combat have been changed significantly through the application of new technologies, basic and advanced supply chain management to enable rapid deployment of supplies, medicine, ammunition, and food to the points of consumption; strong and secure supply lines; and the supply and management of spares and equipment service (military logistics).

Disaster response and assistance in the wake of major natural disasters and weather events have created large needs for rapid supply and deployment of recovery products, medicines, supplies, and services to be made available. Supply chains have responded with speed and effectiveness. An example of this is the American Logistics Aid Network, which is composed of many volunteer supply chain and logistics firms that react quickly wherever and whenever people and goods are needed to assist in rapid recovery.

The planning and delivery of medicines and supplies, on a regular and urgent basis, to all countries, and particularly to undeveloped countries, affected by serious public health needs and disease outbreaks. The Covid-19 pandemic, with its global reach, required supply chain companies—from suppliers to manufacturers to distributors to health providers—to work quickly and collaborate with national, state, and local governments to minimize the time to introduce and distribute vaccines and necessary supplies and equipment to every country of the world. Ironically, it was this crisis that finally gave supply chains and supply chain management its overdue recognition as public officials, health directors, heads of state, and news media began using the term in daily briefings and other communications. The world began to hear about supply chains and learn how they work or fail at a high level.

Globalization, through the flow of products, services, finance, and information across countries, has had many positive results. These have included increase of income, jobs, and amenities in different countries, increased supply of food and healthcare to undeveloped countries, access to more markets, and the availability of many products at lower costs around the world.

NEGATIVE IMPACTS OF GLOBAL SUPPLY CHAINS

However, global supply chains have also had some dangerous and negative impacts. Long supply chains, just-in-time, and lean operations have rendered supply chains fragile, and have put national security at risk through indiscriminate offshoring and handing over of intellectual property. There has been increased exploitation of women and children in many offshored manufacturers and suppliers, and the environmental impacts have included increased greenhouse gas emissions, pollution of land and water, and deforestation.

The aggressive national industrial policies of certain countries (coupled with an absence of national policy in others) have intentionally resulted in the concentration of material, technology, and manufacturing capability for certain products in their countries. This is what's often called a "diamond" supply chain, where a few companies control most of the end products and where the number of suppliers (often deeper in the chain—the bottom of the diamond) has been reduced and suppliers are now concentrated in one of a few countries. This structure undermines resilience, national security, and the smooth flow of world trade.

Even more importantly, supply chains evolved over the past three decades with low-inflation growth, relatively stable geopolitics, and rapid technological advances. This was, however, accompanied by rampant outsourcing and offshoring, "financialization" of the supply chain (the management of the supply chain to maximize short-term profits, inventory, and returns on assets), deregulation, and mergers and acquisitions that resulted in monopolization and concentration in industries. In addition, many governments often failed to embrace long-term thinking, a well-thought national industrial policy, or investment in infrastructure, or to undertake necessary reforms. While global supply chains made a few people and companies rich, and raised the standard of living for many, they left behind millions of citizens feeling alienated and worse off. In the Western world, global supply chains provided citizens with a wide selection of products at very low prices, but also with low wages and increased unemployment (benefitting Wall Street but not Main Street). This "income inequality" poses a significant threat to business continuity and international trade, not to mention social cohesion and democratic capitalism.

EVOLUTION OF SUPPLY CHAINS

Winston Churchill's statement that "difficulties mastered are opportunities won" applies well to the evolution of supply chains. Companies that embraced the integrated view of the supply chain sought to overcome the "difficulties" involved, and then exploit the opportunities this presented. Among these opportunities were the relaxation of antitrust laws, a focus on short-term results to drive stock prices (and Wall Street gains and executive compensation), and the "globalization" of trade. This allowed for a relentless search for lowest costs and access to markets, often ignoring the impacts to communities, national security, or the environment. In the process, well-managed and innovative supply chains became very efficient and highly effective.

Disruptions were relatively minor, and a lack of major prolonged crises ensured a reasonably smooth flow of goods and services across international borders. As a result, standards of living in many (especially in developing) countries were raised, healthcare and food supplies were available to much of the world, and several countries acquired the intellectual property and manufacturing capabilities formerly restricted to a few countries.

During this period, the very efficiency and "financialization" of the supply chain ensured that the discipline of supply chain management remained largely invisible to the public. It was only when von Clausewitz's "frictions" began to emerge, with the resultant shortages, high costs, national security crises, and environmental impacts,[2] that the supply chain became a critical and highly public component of the corporate, public, and national awareness. Many politicians and economists had closed their eyes to national industrial policies. This ensured there was no "level playing field" and no such thing as "free trade." Supply chains had to navigate through these challenges on their own.

Our first book, *Supercharging Supply Chains*, was published in the late 1990s. At that time, leading companies such as Dell, Volkswagen, Procter & Gamble, Siemens, and Xerox were introducing innovative new practices in the integrated supply chain. These included disaggregation, direct-to-consumer ordering and delivery, mass customization, collaborative planning, forecasting and replenishment, and a focus on customers. The most important, however, was the perspective of the end-to-end supply chain management of the products, information, workflows, and cash from source to customer, and back.

WHAT ARE SUPPLY CHAINS, REALLY?

Supply chains are quite simple in concept, regardless of how complex their structures and operations may be. Many companies have succeeded in making their supply chains far more complex than they ought to be. A recent survey of executives revealed that nearly half of them felt that their supply chains were "very complex" (we will address supply chain simplification later in this book). Through the evolution of supply chains in terms of form, physical structures, geography, supplier, product, and customer complexity, their fundamental purpose has not changed—which is to acquire, transform, sell, and deliver products and services to customers. The supply chain should be viewed, for maximum effectiveness, from a "systems perspective"—an end-to-end holistic perspective of the entire network. However, there are different definitions of the supply chain based on management level and perspective (like the story of the six blind men and the elephant, each of whom feels one part of the elephant and perceives it as something different, with no holistic perspective). Some erroneously continue to define the supply chain as solely the procurement and supply of products; others define it as the manufacturing of products; still others as the delivery of products. As supply chains evolved, specialization and functional (siloed) thinking by practitioners and academics has further distorted the concept. This has had serious repercussions on effectiveness, efficiency, resilience, and long-term success for corporations and nations alike.

Supply Chains Have Two Primary Characteristics: Process and Structure

Supply chains were originally defined as being composed of five end-to-end processes (sometimes called "mega" processes in the trade)—*plan, buy, make, move,* and *deliver.* We then identified the four major elements from source of supply to the customer—materials/products, cash, information and data, and workflows. The issue of returns and the reverse supply chain (encompassing products that are returned or discarded and their journey to recovery, refurbishing, reuse, or the landfill) was folded under the *deliver* process.

Since then, however, supply chains have evolved in several major ways. The complexities caused by international and cross-border trade, product proliferation, supplier complexity, and the increasing demands of customers, all coupled with the rapid development of e-commerce, have expanded the original set of mega-processes to include a sixth—*sell*. The *sell* mega-process includes new and innovative ways of analyzing customer needs, delivering to individual consumers ("the final mile"), managing the deployment of inventory to enable fast delivery, and the new competitive aspect of customer returns. It is now well recognized that supply chains are the major driver of customer satisfaction across the customer experience life cycle, and therefore a critical component of revenue generation and loyalty. The "deliver" process has been reimagined as "distribute" to account for the increased complexity of logistics networks, intercompany collaboration, and the increased complexities and scope of international and domestic shipping by ocean, air, road, rail, barge, drone, and various combinations.

The six major processes can now be described as *plan*, *buy*, *make*, *move*, *distribute*, and *sell*, with the same four flows of materials/products, cash, information and data, and workflows (Figure 1.5).

These mega-processes reflect the fact that forward supply chains start with suppliers and conclude with the end customers, while the reverse supply chain starts with the consumer and concludes with the disposal. This has given rise to the increasing need to view, understand, and manage supply chains as an end-to-end network, or, as some companies refer to them, "from the supplier's suppliers to the customer's customers" (Figure 1.6).

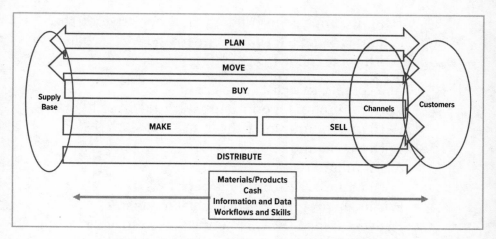

FIGURE 1.5 A Process View of the Supply Chain:
The Six Mega-Processes and the Four Flows

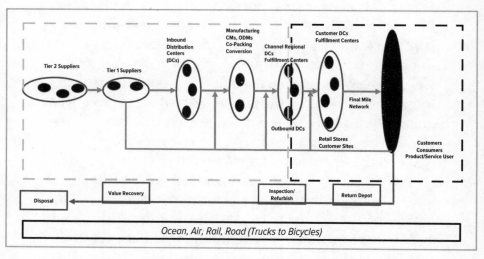

FIGURE 1.6 The End-to-End Supply Chain Network

Putting it simply, the fundamental objective of the supply chain is to match customer demand with product supply within the following guidelines:

- At a competitive cost
- With minimum (or optimum) working capital
- With maximum supply assurance
- With the required quality
- At minimum risk
- With national security considerations
- Within environmental and social mandates
- Delivered when the customer wants it, to where the customer wants it

Customers are dissatisfied with out-of-stocks or late or delayed deliveries; on the other side of the ledger, businesses are harmed by overstocks through reduced margins, excess working capital needs, and scrap. These demands have been amplified and made more pressing by the increasing growth of e-commerce, personalization, information requirements, and delivery. Despite this mission-critical set of objectives, supply chains have historically been regarded as a "back-office" set of functions, until something goes wrong.

Several factors have contributed to the emergence of supply chains to a front-and-center driver of business success—and failure. As an executive put it recently, "The supply chain, together with sales, is the enterprise, except for support functions such as human resources, legal support, and marketing." These factors include:

- The global Covid-19 pandemic and resultant product shortages of everything from medical supplies to paper goods, building materials, semiconductors and food
- The geopolitical threats surrounding rare earth materials, driven mainly by China's current

control of the rare earth mineral supplies, their
increasingly belligerent attitude toward Taiwan
and the West, and their "conflict minerals"
mining issues
- The Russia-Ukraine conflict and threats of conflict
in Asia
- The increasing publicity given to sustainability—
the ESG impacts of global supply chains
- The understanding that corporate tax rates, "short-
termism" and national policy are a prime driver in
sending jobs and capability to other countries
- The over 30-year offshoring of manufacturing and
design that has cost jobs, disrupted communities,
put national security at risk, and lost hard-
developed intellectual property for Western
countries
- The realization among the public and in political
circles that we don't exist in a "free trade" world
with any sort of level playing field, probably to the
chagrin of executives and others whose success
and compensation are vested in propagating that
narrative

As we define and attempt to "demystify" supply chains,
we must note that the media and some trade journals often
articulate and cultivate several myths about supply chains.
Understanding the supply chain involves addressing some
of these common myths.

> **Supply chain** is synonymous with **logistics.** *Logistics*
> refers to physical products and materials and deals
> with the transportation, delivery, and warehousing
> functions. Supply chains are far broader and deal
> with the entire spectrum, from supplier to customer
> and back, including all the major processes and flows.

As a senior executive put it recently, "Supply chains are all about the sale of a product."

No one person can be responsible for the supply chain. While some companies view the scope of the supply chain to be too broad, cross-functional, and geographically distant to be managed by a single executive, an increasing number of companies are now having their supply chains managed by a chief operations officer, a senior vice president of supply chain, or a chief supply chain officer. More than 50 percent of large corporations now have a chief supply chain officer. However, the same cannot be argued for the government . As the role of government is becoming increasingly important for managing specific supply chains critical to public health and national security, a "one-stop" agency overseeing supply chains is often lacking.

Supply chains are only about cost and expense control. In the past, the perception linking supply chains to frugality was owed to the high costs of freight, warehousing, and inventory storage. Today, however, supply chains are a source of competitive advantage—a powerful instrument to drive sales and customer loyalty, ensure supply and national security, minimize risks and maximize cash, and minimize, in a cost-effective way, the impact on the environment. It is far more than cost and expense control.

Advanced technology, artificial intelligence, robotics, and digitalization will replace people in an automation of the entire supply chain. There are always certain dislocations when technology is introduced; however, people will always be needed to make decisions on strategies, service levels, and customer satisfaction. Repetitive tasks often can be done by automation, but supply chain management requires smart managers to plan, design, organize, and adapt to market changes and execute everything effectively. More importantly, managers are needed to make the crucial trade-off decisions in terms of the environment, sourcing, security, customer service, profitability, and resilience. Flexibility in the face of multiple choices, dictated by different priorities and changing conditions, is a critical skillset in today's environment.

As a wider audience develops an interest in supply chains and supply chain management, it is important to understand the evolution of supply chains over time in order to start sketching what future supply chains will look like.

Figure 1.7 highlights the evolution in global (and domestic) supply chains from the "cost optimization" period to the advanced (and tomorrow's) "intelligent" supply-aware and customer experience (CX)–centric supply chain.

The first stage, operational cost optimization, featured low costs, with some emphasis on the trade-off between customer service and the costs of meeting customer needs. Buying or producing the lowest-cost product, shipping it from its origin to its destination, and storing it for future sales were all direct costs. Labor, administration, and technology were also components of the total costs. Companies still operated in terms of functions and departments, and global sourcing was used as method of obtaining hard-to-get materials. It was often a "one size fits all" set of solutions.

The next stage, cost and working capital optimization, saw the advent of globalization, with an emphasis on

OPERATIONAL COST OPTIMIZATION	COST AND WORKING CAPITAL MINIMIZATION	CUSTOMER EXPERIENCE LIFE CYCLE–CENTRIC
• Push-based systems, little customer focus	• Just-in-time systems, customer obsession— all customers	• Customer experience life cycle— centric and supply aware
• Transaction technologies	• Enterprise resource planning systems	• Understanding customer buying patterns, needs, and emotions
• Build-to-stock	• Build-to-order/forecast	• Intelligent and robotics-driven systems
• Inventory is a hedge against uncertainty	• Enterprise perspective	• Postponement
• Functional/ departmental perspective	• Inventory reduced to a minimum and kept moving	• Ecosystem perspective
• Control over operations/vertical integration	• Variability restricted to demand and lead times	• Adaptive: high sense and respond—the extended supply chain
• No visibility	• Outsourcing of peripheral ("noncore") processes—soon to assume all core processes—for lowest costs	• inventory used strategically
• Ignore variability		• Simultaneous focus—profitability, liquidity, growth, capability, cash-to-cash—total supply chain costs
• Focus on cost per unit		• National security parameters
	• Links in the chain thin and vulnerable to disruption	• Actively manages risk— redundancy, national security, ESG
	• Focus on total landed costs	• Customers segmented, with costs-to-serve
		• High end-to-end visibility
		• Supports distributed, adaptive operations

FIGURE 1.7 The Evolution in Global Supply Chains

enterprise resource planning (ERP) software systems to address supply chain planning and specific execution practices, such as warehousing and transportation. This stage coincided with the emergence of China in the global supply chain landscape, with its inclusion in the World Trade Organization in 2001 and its aggressive national trade policies and practices. It also coincided with the relaxation of antitrust regulations (especially in the United States), and the change in executive compensation policies. This led to the "financialization" of the supply chain—"engineering the balance sheet" with supply chains driven by lowest product cost and just-in-time systems—always with the assumption that the seamless flow of goods would continue. The increase in complexity and variability of these chains also led to the development of new technologies to plan and manage demand and supply.

The third stage, and the one we are now entering, is all about the customer life cycle experience, risk management, and supply assurance. The end-to-end supply chain now encompasses and must manage the supply ecosystem, manage risks and environmental impacts, consider national security, and use advanced technologies to enable processes and decisions. The focus is now on total cost, cash-to-cash cycle, and cost to serve, with total visibility, greater flexibility, and resilience.

More recently, deglobalization has been trending. Offshoring has lost much of its appeal, owing to increased shipping times and costs, geopolitical concerns, national trade policies, national security, and the increased need for control and proximity to customers. Given this, regionalization, or "friend-shoring" of supply, manufacturing, and final assembly relocations are inevitable. We have entered the age of "post-globalization regionalization," where the regions are individual supply chain zones.

The supply chains of tomorrow will likely increase in complexity, with pressure from multiple stakeholders and the government—driven from business, activist, and ideological viewpoints. Digitalization of processes and business models, risks, increased customer demands, and advances in technology will drive analytics and data-driven decisions, trade-offs, innovation in financing and business models, and new strategies for differentiating services for customer benefit.

HOW THIS BOOK IS ORGANIZED

We have organized this book to reflect the current trends and environment, and to outline a set of practices in a structured manner to help readers develop a road map for supply change management. Figure 1.8 provides a snapshot of what led us to this point—"why we are where we are."

We will discuss the core practices and ideas for thriving in an uncertain world, the way that executives and policy makers should approach this challenge, and, importantly, the relevant breakthrough thinking for the end-to-end supply network, as well as for each major component. Our structure addresses the end-to-end supply chain and its impacts; the two ends—"customer and demand" and "supply"; the core elements that are critical to its success—data, technology, knowledge, and measurement; and the competitive imperatives of the supply chain—risk management and resilience along with sustainability. We then pull them together in the final section, "The Way Forward," and demonstrate how companies, organizations, and nations can tackle these challenges through "breakthrough thinking."

Let us first define "breakthrough thinking." It is not a fuzzy term like "innovation," which can be, and often is, used to describe almost anything. Breakthrough thinking encompasses three major categories:

- Innovative thinking and constructs
- Structures and concepts that many have been aware of, but very few have tried and operationalized
- "The basics"—concepts that form the foundation of supply chain management and, unfortunately, have largely been ignored by many executives and academics over the past few decades

A Long Time Ago, in a Galaxy Far, Far Away... (The US and Europe in the '70s and '80s)	Regulations, Trends, National Policies (and Lack of...)	Resulting in Companies and Executives Acting on...	And Making Decisions to "Engineer" the Balance Sheet and Reduce Competition	Resulting in Fragile Supply Chains That Are "Built to Break"
Stock price driven by • Earnings per share • Profit margins • Cost trends • Sustainable revenue	Stock options and grants as part of executive compensation	Opportunity to drive concentration, monopolies, and oligopolies, and eliminate competition	• Acquisition of competing and startup firms • Foreign acquisition of critical US/EU firms and technology • Control over platforms and distribution channels driving anticompetitive policies • "Big Tech" shutting out conflicting opinions on trade and country news • Companies giving IP to foreign governments and going silent on social policies	• No inventory to withstand temporary disruptions in the supply chain • Single sourcing • Smaller suppliers at risk • Overly complex, stretched supply chains, perceived as deterministic, functional • Little formal risk monitoring and management • Loss of visibility of components sourcing lower down in the BOMs
Monopolies kept in check by enforcement of Sherman Antitrust Act	Globalization made large foreign markets attractive	Shareholder, investor demands for short-term profits Stock price driven by: • Low working capital • Low inventory • High payables • High return on net assets • Low labor costs • Free cash flow from operations	• Outsourcing to reduce asset base • Offshoring for low labor costs and getting entrance to foreign markets • Just-in-time supply chains to reduce the inventory in the pipeline and downstream • Pressure on suppliers to hold inventory and increase payables • Ignoring source of products • Lowest-cost supply including sole/single sourcing	• Reliance on a few suppliers controlled by a few (and some hostile) governments—"diamond" supply chains • Jobs shipped overseas with reduction in manufacturing and supply chain capability • National security at risk • Little pressure or oversight on labor and environmental issues leading to exploitation and damage • Companies exert power on governments to maintain status quo
	Lack of enforcement and government bypassing of the Sherman Antitrust Act			
	Increase in corporate taxes and national regulations	Companies giving major concessions in hopes of market access		
Clear understanding of the national interest	Lack of national industrial security policy, coupled with national policies by other countries			
And so on...	Stolen (or given away) IP-driven product competition	Cost increases Order cancellations Cyberterrorism/hacking	Supplier disruption Customer disruption Logistics disruption	Hostile government actions Pandemics Natural disasters

FIGURE 1.8 Why We Are Where We Are

This new thinking will define the successful supply chains of tomorrow.

We wrote the book in order to return the discussion about supply chains to its fundamentals, and then to bring it to the next level to deal with today's and tomorrow's challenges. In addition, we believe that our combined experience in the United States, European Union, and Asia across multiple industries, policy-making bodies, academic environments, and NGOs provides a unique perspective on this complex topic. It is because of this conviction that we have adopted a rather unique strategy in writing our book.

Several books have been, and will be, written either going over the same "traditional" functional ground or detailing the use of data science, analytics, optimization tools and technologies, and other innovative methods for redesigning and redefining the supply chain and performance. While we are convinced that it's all about "doing the right things at the right time and doing them well," we decided to focus on "what" supply chain leaders, public policy officials, and influencers should be considering and putting into practice.

The breakthrough thinking and road map process will enable senior executives, managers, policy makers, and academics to develop a vision of the future state and a plan to implement. Readers can contribute by further honing and building upon this plan. We hope that this thinking will be of value to all supply chain leaders and policy makers as they negotiate the cycle of high-level strategic imperatives driving execution and structure, which, in turn, drives strategy.

CHAPTER 2

How Supply Chains Have Enabled an Evolving World

When it is a question of money,
everybody is of the same religion.
—Voltaire[1]

In the first chapter, we described supply chains, the core flows, and their fundamental purposes. We discussed their evolution from a back office and support function to an enabler of the business strategy, then to a critical part and main driver of business success (or failure). Alongside this was the development of the end-to-end supply chain construct driven by the clear need for business process and ecosystem integration.

In recent years, two types of events have changed supply chains in dramatic ways. The first was an avalanche of global "black swan" events—the Covid-19 pandemic, the Ukraine conflict, and massive climate-fueled droughts and floods. The other consists of nationalistic policies such as the increasingly overt Chinese hegemonial designs on Taiwan and the Far East, the Chinese exploitation of supply and capacity through "diamond" supply chains, and the weaponization by Russia of its vast energy stores. The confluence of these events has highlighted the importance of supply chains in world trade, exposed their weaknesses and vulnerabilities, and increased their awareness by business CEOs, public policy leaders, and the society at large. In this chapter we will discuss how supply chains have contributed to societal and national development and enabled world prosperity and health. However, it has also generated some adverse environmental and social impacts and has been "weaponized" by some countries.

Success in this new uncertain environment demands that "breakthrough thinking" be adopted by executives and policy makers, and this is an integral part of the discussion in this book. It is our intention that these actions and perspectives be used by executives and policy makers to sketch, design, and implement new supply chain road maps and playbooks for resilience and success in a world where risk and uncertainty promise to be defining and ongoing characteristics.

We summarize the Breakthrough Thinking actions and perspectives at the end of every chapter and, to provide a more holistic perspective, we have compiled them in the Appendix at the end of the book.

THE DESIGNS AND IMPACTS OF SUPPLY CHAINS

It is well established, but perhaps not well recognized, that as global supply chains have developed over the last four decades, they have opened up the world. Companies have globalized their design, sourcing, and/or production, penetrated new markets, offered a wide breadth of product selection for customers, and enabled the rapid delivery of goods and services across the world. This has led to reduced costs to customers and reduced costs of goods sold for companies, and increased customer service levels while keeping inventory and working capital low. The international trade of intermediate goods (used to make finished products) has been driven by a series of trends and policies, including tariff and tax changes, structural reforms, relaxation of national and anti-monopoly trade regulations and government trade policies, and probably the most important, advances in technology, mobility, and end-to-end supply chain visibility. Companies were able to invest and outsource to offshore factories and suppliers, with great financial benefits for some, but with supply chain fragility, community, and national interests being secondary conditions at best.

This, however, has come at a price. Many of today's supply chains are complex, lengthy, multitiered networks, and as such, they have become highly vulnerable to a variety of disruptive events. These include extreme weather events, supplier and transportation disruptions, hostile government actions, financing issues, labor stoppages, public health crises, cyberattacks, and trade conflicts. The impact of the global Covid-19 pandemic, one of the most high-profile of all global risk events, has exceeded the scale and duration of all disruptions since the financial crisis of 2008. Supply chains' lack of resilience was exposed, leading to product and material shortages, customer dissatisfaction, increasing costs and needs for working capital, and the realization that national security was at risk.

Many of the global supply chains of 2020 were clearly inadequate to deal with the challenges that confronted them. During the pandemic, the world witnessed dramatic surges in customer demand in several product categories, including essential medical and healthcare products and equipment, basics such as paper goods, technological products such as semiconductors, and, of course, food. These inadequacies were driven by panic buying (and hoarding), the media, changing buying patterns from remote working, and supply chains that were dependent on inherently risky sources of supply, relied on low inventories and "just in time" practices, and had been built to handle conditions of stable demand. In the initial phases of the pandemic, corporate demand forecasts did not reflect demand spikes, and it soon became apparent that supply chains lacked the redundancy of supply and capacity, the management capability to handle the new demands and pressures, or the flexibility to shift production to different products in the same category. This resulted in several high-profile supply chain breakdowns, confusion about causes and solutions, and consequently, supply chains were labeled (rightly so, in many cases) as the main culprits behind much of the healthcare, food, and material shortages. As this began to sink in, people also realized that supply chain offshoring had led to the loss of jobs and destruction of communities in developed countries, increased national security vulnerabilities, and loss of industrial capability in many areas critical to national security. However, these developments also led the world to realize that supply chains were the platform of global trade and critical for healthcare and economic prosperity.

Over the past several decades supply chains have helped expand the quality of life in many parts of the globe, improved healthcare, and enabled a significantly higher level of prosperity. They have influenced and changed customer behavior, altered corporate strategies, and driven national behavior, policy, and expectations.

Factors Driving International and Local Supply Chains

International and local supply chains have been shaped by several institutional and structural factors, driven by a host of government policies (or lack of), the almost universal acquiescence to the concepts of the neoliberal political order, corporate supply chain decisions, and international events, and they have had tremendous positive (and some significant negative) impacts on the global economy, the environment, and society at large. These factors and impacts are illustrated in Figure 2.1.

The factors that have driven the growth of global supply chains include:

- **Relaxation and lax enforcement of laws and regulations** dealing with antitrust, unions, and the environment (for example, the relaxation of anti-monopoly laws in the US and Europe, and

PROVING TREMENDOUS PROGRESS AND POSITIVE IMPACTS

- Increase in international standards of living
- Employment opportunities across the globe
- Lower costs to customers
- Increased market access for many companies internationally
- Normalization of expectations and "consumerism" across the world
- Access to healthcare, vaccines, pharmaceuticals, and related supplies for needy countries
- Increase in food supplies and food security for needy countries

AND SOME VERY SIGNIFICANT ADVERSE IMPACTS

- Adverse environmental impacts
- Worker exploitation (including women and children)
- Conflict minerals mining fueling wars or human rights abuses
- Companies implementing their own and their government's social agenda
- Supply disruptions and shortages to critically affected and needy areas
- Elimination of small local competition and increases in prices
- Monopolistic control of supply, giving rise to single points of failure in many supply chains
- Loss of manufacturing and design capability, destruction of local communities, and loss of local jobs
- Formation of "diamond" supply chains that concentrate supply in a few countries

FACTORS THAT HAVE DRIVEN SUPPLY CHAINS

- Monopolies and oligopolies
- The lack of national industrial policies
- Collaboration with hostile foreign governments
- Weaponization of the supply chain by certain national governments
- Global conflicts that disrupt supply chains
- Global sourcing to countries with fewer or lax laws regarding the environment or labor
- Natural disasters and extreme weather patterns, often fueled by climate change
- Globalization and consolidation of the supply chain
- Relaxation and nonenforcement of laws and regulations dealing with antitrust, unions, and the environment
- Short-term stock prices as the basis of executive compensation

FIGURE 2.1 Driving Factors and Impacts of Global Supply Chains

35

the Environmental Protection Act laws in the US), leading to the rise of monopolies and oligopolies. This has created concentration in several industries in terms of products, supplies, and distribution channels, while leading to cooperation with sometimes adversarial foreign governments.

- **Industrial policies** by some national governments to "weaponize" the supply chain and to corner supply and capabilities and ensure that the playing field is not level. This goes hand in hand with the lack of concerted national industrial policies in Western countries, particularly those involving critical capabilities and materials. This has been exacerbated by *corporate executives of multinational corporations working with foreign governments (sometimes inadvertently)* to drive low costs and obtain market access. This has led to some countries becoming consolidated centers of manufacturing, with control over the global supply of important commodities.
- **Global risk events such as conflicts,** natural disasters, and extreme weather patterns, often fueled by climate change, that unexpectedly disrupt supply and supply chains.
- **Global sourcing** to the lowest cost sources in countries, which may have fewer or unenforced laws involving the environment and labor, coupled with "just-in-time" structures that minimize inventory and erode resilience.
- **Financialization** of the supply chain, leading to practices that emphasize short-term financial results and stock prices, often used as the basis of executive compensation.

Positive Benefits to Society

Supply chains have had several positive impacts on economies and societies, and some of the more significant include:

- Employment opportunities across the globe, with the resulting increase in international standards of living.
- Lower costs and increased availability and selection of products, food, and supplies to end-customers and end-consumers.
- Increased market access for many companies internationally.
- Normalization of expectations and "consumerism" across the world—consumer buying preferences, speed and response in fulfillment expectations, shopping convenience, to name a few (sometimes called the "Amazon effect").
- Acquisition, storage, and distribution of healthcare, vaccines, pharmaceuticals, and medical supplies to countries in need.
- Food and supplies for countries that cannot feed themselves—thereby ensuring food security.

Significant Adverse Impacts

Global supply chains have also had several detrimental impacts on society and the environment. These include concentration and monopolies, allowing companies to dictate pricing, terms, and social agenda; adverse environmental impacts; and worker exploitation.

- Environmental impacts, such as increased greenhouse gas emissions across the end-to-end supply chain, deforestation, water and land pollution, plastics in the ocean, massive landfills, and, in general, overexploitation of common resources.

- Worker exploitation (including women and children) and forced slave labor, lack of safety standards, and conflict minerals mining (which fuels wars and leads to human rights abuses).
- Companies attempting to use their power to implement their own (and sometimes their governments') social agenda on both a national and global basis.
- Supply disruptions and shortages of consumables, food, healthcare supplies, and pharmaceuticals to critically affected and needy regions.
- Elimination of smaller local competition leading to increases in prices, reduction of local availability, and the monopolistic control of product and supply. This has further given rise to single points of failure in many critical supply chains.
- Loss of manufacturing and design capability, destruction of local communities and loss of local jobs, and a factor that cannot be ignored, the loss of small to medium enterprises.
- Formation of "diamond" supply chains, which have concentrated supply and capacity in the hands of a few countries.

THE SUPPLY CHAIN CHALLENGE

The supply chains of today were designed, built, and have evolved under a number of assumptions, which can be summarized into three broad categories:

- **The continuation of the status quo,** where governments would continue relaxing, or not enforcing, rules against monopolies and toward promoting workers' well-being, and where compensation schemes based on short-term stock prices would continue to be the prime business objective.

- **Low-probability risks that were believed to be minor could be ignored.** These included risks to national security, government trade policies, mercantilism and the "weaponization" of the supply chain, environmental and public health crises, and war.
- **A completely false set of assumptions** on the existence of a "level" playing field (the "flat world"), and that free trade and international trade would incentivize countries to embrace liberal democracy, human rights, and theoretical "globalization."

Objectives of Supply Chains

Supply chains designed under these assumptions were structured to achieve several objectives, with the three primary ones being *financial*—achieving the lowest possible costs, working capital, and cash-to-cash cycles and high return on assets; *speed and velocity in the supply chain*, while balancing demand and supply; and *access to markets* (or the promise, anyway), even at the costs of national security and loss of intellectual capital.

The Results: "Built to Break"

When confronted with the realities of international and cross-border trade, nationalist policies, major risk events, the "frictions" and "fog" of war, it became obvious that many global supply chains were "built to break." The Covid-19 pandemic and geopolitical tensions generated by the Russian invasion of Ukraine and China's aggressive stance toward Taiwan and the West brought the structural weaknesses of supply chains to the forefront of governments' and the public's mindset and scrutiny. The lengthening of the supply chains, just-in-time policies, global supplier selection in the lowest cost but high-risk areas or adversarial countries, and reliance on supply in countries that had developed "diamond" supply chains for material and capability control all contributed to a lack of resilience. This resulted in some of the worst shortages we have seen for a long time in the areas of medical supplies, pharmaceuticals, food, semiconductor chips, building supplies, and equipment. These impacts far exceeded the various issues we had run into prior to the pandemic, and they manifested themselves in terms of pharmaceutical and consumables' quality, banned materials, governments threatening to withhold materials from other countries to suit political ends, and governments, competitors, and nefarious agents engaging in economic espionage and cyberterrorism. These developments culminated in the shocking realization in Western economies that many of their critical materials and capabilities were controlled by adversarial nations (or strategic competitors), while some of the components and software employed in high-tech and defense equipment were developed by unfriendly countries.

We have reached an inflection point in the evolution of supply chains. While supply chains have impacted the global economy and society in several very positive and profound ways, they have also resulted in several significant negative impacts and have left companies and nations alike vulnerable to serious threats and risks. The "weaponization" of the supply chain by some countries has put national security in the US, the UK, the EU, and several allied countries at risk. This is a new supply chain landscape characterized by a number of new risks, threats, and challenges, not the least of which include:

- **Supply:** A shortage of supply and minerals to meet ever-increasing demands. This often is coupled with an overdependence on certain countries for commodities, material, and critical manufacturing capability, as well as practices of single sourcing with small, specialized, and large suppliers (sometimes state-owned enterprises, SOEs) in risky countries.

- **Perspective and structure:** A lack of an end-to-end perspective of the supply chain—it is a connected network rather than a set of functional "silos" operating and measured independently. One outcome of this is the overly complex and thinly stretched chain.
- **Risk management:** Inadequate risk identification, risk management, and risk mitigation policies. Even more, a lack of accountable executives for supply chain risk management.
- **Talent:** Lack of talent and critical worker skills and training in science, technology, engineering, mathematics (STEM), manufacturing, advanced technologies, and supply chain management.
- **Financialization:** Continuing financialization of the supply chains and "engineering the balance sheet" as opposed to engineering the supply chain, a set of practices largely driven by "short-termism" and ongoing executive compensation systems.
- **National security and intellectual property:** A lack of national security guardrails that still permit collaboration, export of critical technologies, and investment with adversarial countries at the expense of national security. One result of this is the continuing loss of intellectual property and trade secrets to other countries.

It would be naive to assume that the major risk events we have faced are all one-offs. They are a series in a train of such events that we must plan for. Supply chains will need to be reimagined and redesigned going forward in order to address the new realities that corporations and nations are facing.

A BLANK SHEET: RETHINKING THE SUPPLY CHAIN

So, how do companies determine how their supply chains will look and operate in the short-term and in the longer-term future? Terms such as "transformational thinking" and "innovative thinking" are thrown around, but these are often just consultants' terms for doing something different. It is true that companies need to rethink their supply chains in terms of structure, priorities, objectives, and operations. They must do so within financial, environmental, and national security guidelines and guardrails. These guardrails are briefly discussed later in this chapter. As a point of note, some consultants and analysts recommend starting with a "blank sheet" of paper to design the supply chain of the future. In our experience, this results in a lot of "ideal" designs and wishful thinking.

A far better strategy than a blank sheet would be to focus on specific conditions and capabilities (such as existing structure, major critical suppliers, guidelines, and guardrails) and then develop tailored supply chain strategies. One such set of conditions is the type of supply chain—and there are two types to consider. One, a *producer-driven* supply chain (e.g., for semiconductor chips and electronic equipment), which requires high capital investment, significant product and manufacturing technology capability, and, as such, is typically restricted to large companies, either physically or virtually vertically integrated; and two, *buyer-driven* supply chains (e.g., textiles and agrifood products), characterized by relatively low product and manufacturing technology requirements (ideal for outsourcing and requiring a core competency in design and inventory management). These two types of supply chains demand different physical networks, priorities, cost and financing structures, and demand-supply and inventory management approaches.

Size

It is no accident that the "top" supply chain companies identified by several institutions are all very large and exercise a great deal of power in their extended supply chains. Furthermore, their rankings are often based on people's opinions and on somewhat irrelevant metrics on the environment. Such companies can get over problems through brute force—for example, by forcing suppliers to hold inventory, extend payment terms, and provide preferred supply, and obtaining best rates. Using the "leading practices" employed by these companies may not be the best strategy for smaller companies—smaller companies cannot always do what these behemoths do.

Financing Ability

Companies' strategies are constrained by their ability to finance investment, operations, and working capital. Large and dominant companies can usually obtain better financing rates and more financing. The key question is, what sort of financing is realistically available, and how can this be increased through innovative supply chain financing deals with institutions, suppliers, and customers?

Basis for Competition, Customer Needs, and Channel Demands

A core question needs to be addressed: *Who are our customers* (home-based consumers, for example) and *what do they need*? We must take into account our channels and what the competition offers (for example, low cost, two-day delivery for which we can charge them, free five-day delivery, selection, order tracking, returns). Importantly, *what does each channel demand* (trade spend, inventory, returns, etc.), *and how much does it cost?*

Product Characteristics

Product characteristics are typically looked at in three distinct ways: the *type of product*—"functional" with high volume, predictable demand with cost efficiency being the prime driver, or "innovative," for which time to market *is* critical—defined by factors such as cost, proprietary technology or design, product "clockspeed" (the speed at which technology and components change), product changes, and manufacturing complexity; the lead time for replenishment—long, short, with its associated variability; and the customer demand patterns—predictable, stable, variable.

Government Environmental Mandates

A lot of this depends on the company's senior executives, its board of directors, and actual government mandates in the country of operation. The guardrails range from the altruistic "I believe in doing good" to "it's mandated by law, so I must comply." But always, it comes down to cost (and its impact on margins and working capital) and return on investment. After all, a company's obligations are to its shareholders first, then to its workers and the community, and then to the nation (all are stakeholders). The decisions encompass sourcing, transportation, product design and materials, and manufacturing.

National Security Requirements

Historically, national security requirements have long been ignored in many Western economies but are now increasingly becoming the most important. This involves an analysis of bills of material, reducing sourcing in currently or potentially unfriendly and risky countries; restricting obtaining financing from, and developing partnerships with, companies that are controlled by adversarial foreign governments; and supplying certain types of products to these countries. We must adopt what other countries have long realized, a "whole of country" approach to supply chain management and product development. Contrary to what many seem to believe, shareholder value and executive compensation do not trump national security.

Current Contracts and Investments

Many companies have made large capital investments in facilities and supplier networks. Many of these decisions and investments have been made in hostile and risky foreign markets, while contracts have been inked with other suppliers who may prove to also be risky because of environmental or illicit labor issues. Moving away from these facilities and suppliers will require planning and time.

Working within these guardrails requires trade-offs in terms of increased short-term costs, access to markets, certain business priorities, and impacts on certain countries. But every company must deal with these trade-offs in order to ensure national security.

BREAKTHROUGH THINKING

The breakthrough thinking that is critical for corporate executives and policy makers to adopt for success in this new environment deals with the perspectives from which the supply chain is viewed, structured, and managed.

CORPORATE EXECUTIVES AND POLICY MAKERS

- View, structure, and manage the supply chain as an end-to-end network from the point of first supply to the end consumer and back (returns and reverse logistics), in terms of product, spares, materials, data, costs, and cash.
- Adopt a balanced time perspective, avoid "short-termism" and make risk an integral part of the management process.
- Globalization is, and always has been, a myth. International trade has always been about international supply chains, cross-border trading, and national interests.
- Nothing will go as planned; always plan and manage for risk—supply, demand, national and company security, infrastructure and logistics, environmental.
- National security must be an integral part of the supply chain—novel public-private partnerships and a "whole of country" approach should be adopted. Guidelines and guardrails for industry, government organizations, and NGOs must be developed at the senior policy level.
- In designing the supply chain, start with reality: focus on specific conditions, "gateway" elements, sources, and capabilities, and then develop supply chain strategies and designs that fit the company.

This chapter addressed the supply chain, its impacts, changes, and challenges in the new environment. It sets the context for what follows. The next chapter will address one of the critical elements of the supply chain—where it all starts—the customer and customer demand.

PART TWO

Breakthrough Thinking

CHAPTER 3

The Customer

Managing Demand

We focus on the customer.
We are customer-centric.
We are customer-driven.
Our obsession is the customer.
—Various executive and company
statements over the years

How many times have we heard or read these statements from companies across industry sectors or public officials in various governmental departments? The reality is that most of the time these leaders' actions do not align with their words. Corporations focus on shareholders and executive interests, while public officials focus on public employee unions and politics (driven by short-term thinking owing to quarterly reporting, union support, and reelection cycles). This becomes even more obvious in times of challenge—whether they be crises, industry or societal disruptions, or competitive threats.

An anonymous business executive recently highlighted the differences between words and actions: "I traveled to Europe recently on a major international airline. Following canceled flights, lost baggage, and an inability to get through to customer service for hours, we came to realize that customer obsession meant 'obsessed with avoiding the customer.'"

WHO IS THE CUSTOMER?

It is imperative that organizations listen to the "Voice of the Customer," to understand their customers, what drives them, and their needs. Without this the focus and priority of supply chains (and sales and marketing) become an issue of guessing. There are five basic questions that companies must ask themselves about the customer and the product:

1. Who is the customer?
2. What is the customer's demands and needs across the entire customer life cycle experience today and tomorrow?
3. How much does the customer want? And when?
4. How will we deliver this today and tomorrow?
5. How much will it cost? (Can we make money at it?)

The first and core question is, "Who is the customer?" In terms of the supply chain, it is extremely important to define this clearly. The customer could be the original equipment manufacturer, the wholesaler, the distributor, the channel, or the end consumer, or some combination of these. The old definitions of business-to-business (B2B) and business-to-customer (B2C) are morphing into business-to-business-to-customer (B2B2C), where the customer is both the company supplied to and the customer who buys from that company. For example, a company that supplies to a retailer has two customers—the retailer and the consumer. A third-party logistics company that supplies on behalf of the retailer has two customers—the retailer and the consumer to whom the product is delivered. Both of these parties have different needs—some critical ones are outlined in Table 3.1.

The needs of these different players in the supply chain require different supply chain capabilities and design, including inventory deployment, warehousing networks, transportation constructs, order management systems and processes, forecasting, and more. None of these are trivial, and all require investment, working capital, and talent. Hence, listening to the "Voice of the Customer," defining the customer(s) and their supply chain needs and demands, is critical.

TABLE 3.1 Customer Needs That the Supply Chain Must Fulfill

RETAILER	CONSUMER
• Attractive, easy-to-stock packaging • Delivery in bulk to distribution centers • Delivery to individual stores in specific windows • Quick replenishment to store level • Advanced shipping notice and reliable delivery	• Convenience of carrying product • If delivered to the home after in-store ordering, then deliver to individual homes "online-to-offline" or support "buy online, pick up in-store" • Rapid delivery in agreed time frame • Delivery of individual items and small parcels • Shipment tracking in real time • Information about delivery times

Supply Chains Drive the Customer Experience (CX)

Supply chains have substantial influence on customers' perceptions of a company or organization, and they strongly influence brand equity in several ways. While marketing builds brand awareness and sales commits to customers, the supply chain delivers on the promise through sourcing, procurement, manufacturing, packaging, making the goods available for purchase, responding to orders, providing information, and delivering the goods—on time, in full, with the right quality, the right packaging, and available as necessary. Brand equity is dependent on the customer experience and emotion, and the customer experience begins with a customer browsing or being interested in a product or service. CX spans all the way to the point when the product is returned or disposed of and the customer purchases again and becomes an advocate. The focus of the company must, therefore, be on the entire customer life cycle experience, measured by a series of appropriate metrics, including cost to serve, revenue, margins, liquidity, and customer profitability. This is by no means a straightforward process, as can be seen in Figure 3.1.

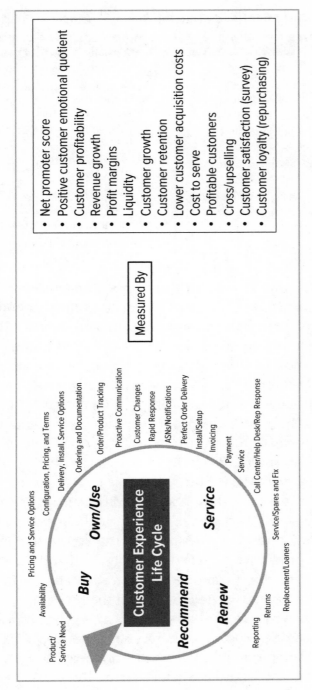

FIGURE 3.1 The Entire Customer Life Cycle Must Be the Focus of the Supply Chain and the Integrated Business

The customer experience life cycle is similar for the individual consumer in a home, to a business manufacturing plant, to a retail store, or to a government military depot.

Insightful knowledge and data about the customers of the company, or the users of the supply chain, has never been more important in designing supply chains to meet customer expectations and requirements of service, cost, convenience, and quality. Several key factors have contributed toward—indeed, driven—this over the past several years, namely:

The natural evolution of all types of customers in terms of knowledge, behaviors, choices, and the widespread availability of robust product and consumption information—the whole customer experience. This has led to increasing demands and expectations on a worldwide basis and to the shift in emphasis from just the supply of products to both supply and fulfillment of customer demand.

The morphing of business and consumer demands and expectations of service. Businesses (and governments) are now expecting the same terms of low cost, speedy delivery, small order lots and individual shipments, and real-time online tracking ability that consumers are getting. For example, a well-known footwear and apparel company transformed its global supply chain to optimize customer demand, both for its retail outlets and its direct-to-consumer (DTC) business. Focusing its investment and attention on customers, the company upgraded its ordering and fulfillment operations to provide easy shopping and buying, along with rapid fulfillment capabilities that exceeded those of other footwear and accessories companies. The company continues to maintain its position as a premier brand, and these supply chain initiatives are enabling high levels of customer profitability, satisfaction, and retention.

Customers are starting to look at more than the "traditional" aspects of product, cost, ease of doing business, convenience, and service and are now examining the overall profile of the company they are considering buying from. This includes environmental record and actions, labor issues, exploitation and slavery, gratuitous social messaging and virtue signaling, and national security considerations (such as doing business with and pandering to adversarial countries). A critical aspect to this, and one that is fast becoming recognized as a key driver, is the emotional quotient of customers when viewing a company and its products—how customers feel emotionally, at any given point in time, about a company, its image, and its products.

Concentration in many industries has adversely impacted customers' prices and product availability. However, this has created opportunities for more nimble competitors to enter and compete on cost, service, and value-added differentiated service offerings.

The growth and expansion of e-commerce. Companies are now reaching customers and selling products through multiple channels (omnichannel management). The highly competitive environment has driven organizations to seek in-depth knowledge and understanding of their customers and strive to obtain and retain their loyalty. This has fueled innovation not only in products and their design and packaging, but also in services that involve getting the product to the customer and handling returns much more efficiently.

The realization that all customers are not equal.
While all customers may be important, we can paraphrase George Orwell's *Animal Farm*[1] in saying that "some customers are more important than others." Customer segmentation in terms of buying and service requirements, profitability, and cost to serve is important for a company to focus its attention and resources on its most valuable customers. Equally important is to provide different service levels to different customer segments. These can include all aspects of service, ranging from overnight delivery for some to three-day delivery for others, dedicated customer service representatives ("high touch") for some to web-based services ("no touch") for others, and even to specific product availability programs.

The integration of the supply chain and marketing.
Net promoter score (NPS) essentially asks customers if they would be likely to buy again from the company or recommend the brand to others. This is based on the customer experience—a large part of which is driven by the supply chain. To be effective, NPS must be combined with advanced analytics to ascertain true customer satisfaction, how a company can address key issues that may pose problems, and, importantly, how to build on positive feedback. Even more advanced methods and approaches are being developed to understand customers and what they want. These methods combine NPS with digital

empathy and the customer-focused supply chain services that use them to drive revenue, margins, and retention. This is the new frontier in understanding the customer—and integrating the supply chain and marketing to take fast and positive action.

The hallmark of this approach is, as Peter Dorrington of Anthrolytics said, that "competence is not a differentiator—competence with compassion is."[2]

Perfect order fulfillment is a major driver of customer satisfaction, but as more companies make it their focus, it is no longer the main competitive differentiator that it once was. The Covid-19 pandemic and the disruptions from conflicts, climate change, and hostile countries' actions have resulted in a rise in e-commerce transactions and a greater percentage of business interactions occurring digitally. These digital interactions, coupled with the accompanying order transparency and rapid service, have resulted in a situation that, for many brands, it is difficult to not be perceived as a commodity. In the "experience economy," having a great product or service is necessary but not enough; a company must deliver a standout overall experience.

In today's e-commerce "experience" environment, companies must understand what customers value and how to integrate that with the supply chain to deliver a differentiated experience—one that meets both the functional and emotional needs of customers. Ongoing research continues to demonstrate that empathy is now a critical aspect of customer loyalty. Study after study shows that customers are prepared to pay a significant premium for being listened to, understood, and treated like human beings, rather than just a case number.

This is the new and exciting science of "digital empathy"—which turns the Golden Rule on its head. Instead of:

"Treat customers the way you want to be treated yourself," it says, "Treat customers the way they want to be treated themselves."

This is changing the role of the supply chain in customer life cycle management. The emphasis is now on high availability, speed of response, end-to-end visibility and transparency, communication of status, and, importantly, the integration of the supply chain with marketing. At the heart of digital empathy is not the traditional customer survey, but predictive behavioral analytics—an innovative way of combining data science with behavioral science to understand and predict human behavior—to predict, for example, customer decisions when one of the major events (late or wrong delivery, incorrect order, quality issues, poor communication, or, on the plus side, excellent service experience) occur, and then respond quickly and appropriately.

Europe-based Anthrolytics is one such company that addresses the empathy component by using data gathered from a mix of sources and then using its analytics engine to predict what individual customers are feeling, why, and what they are likely to do next. These behavioral insights are then used in customer service to integrate the supply chain with marketing to execute a range of proactive and reactive tasks, including journey orchestration, campaign management, communications with customers when necessary, and, of course, offering of special deals—all to cement brand loyalty and generate increasing revenue. It also bears noting that this approach is applicable to an organization's employees, their satisfaction, and retention.

For example, a telecommunications company using this solution in an emerging market identified an empathy-based segment of customers it felt were ready, willing, and able to buy more. Focusing the integrated supply chain and marketing to this group increased the average revenue per user from that segment by over 70 percent within a month, an effect that was still in evidence months after the campaign ended. This takes the analytics-driven supply chain to a new level in terms of its focus, investments, and response to the customer, moving from the physical to the emotional.

THE CUSTOMER INFLUENCE ON SUPPLY CHAIN DEVELOPMENT

While the supply chain is critical in its impacts on the customer life cycle, it is the customer who has impacted the development of the supply chain. Supply chains have evolved over a thirty-year period, from optimizing costs and meeting broad service requirements to today's "supply-aware, customer-centric" designs. They have progressed through several broad stages.

Initially, the objective was cost minimization, particularly in manufacturing, transportation, and warehousing. These common processes were defined to a granular level, analyzed, and relevant cost models were developed, sometimes down to the activity level. The focus was on the minimization of costs for domestic operations.

This was then followed by an expansion of international trade, government policies, changes in the methods of executive compensation, and a relaxation of trade regulations. As a result, the next phase of supply chain evolution was characterized by outsourcing of manufacturing and design, along with the relocation of manufacturing and sourcing offshore to low-cost countries, in order to reduce material and production costs while increasing balance sheet returns on assets. The expanded need for data on suppliers and manufacturing turned the attention of supply chain executives toward data-driven designs.

Software systems were developed to collect and manage data and to help design supply chain physical networks, forecasting, and demand-supply management. While the end customer was not forgotten (or was certainly given lip service), customers' individual service requirements were represented by the channels and supply chain players— retailers, wholesalers, distributors, and the creativity of the business marketing and sales departments. This led to increased sophistication of systems and data to manage and design supply chains.

The next phase of supply chain evolution was (and is) being driven by the customer to an extent unlike ever before. The rapid development of e-commerce has revolutionized the focus on the customer and customer service—not only in the speed of delivery (from five days or more to next-day or same-day delivery) and convenience, but in many other services as well. Customers now expect their services from other companies to be comparable to the overnight delivery they expect from Amazon, without any extra costs. This is true of both consumers and business customers alike.

Finally, we have reached the stage of the "supply assured, customer driven and shaped" supply chain, where supply assurance is a key component, and customer needs are driven by customer demands and are shaped by companies. For instance, a major company shapes customer demand by analyzing both customers' buying habits and the availability and shortages of products and key components. They then provide special offers in terms of specific configurations of products, rapid delivery, complementary products, and price deals based on the results of this analysis, while promoting certain products that give them higher margins. This demand shaping is an ideal vehicle for integration with digital empathy to cement the buying and brand relationship with customers.

Customer life cycle–driven supply chains are the new objective and are part of the executive suite and board of directors agenda for reporting, focus, and investment. While companies such as Amazon have led the way in setting and delivering to these new expectations of service, sometimes losing money in the effort, all companies are facing the reality that this scope and level of service is now "table stakes" for competition and success in the global environment. Both discussions and the downstream part of the supply chain today are focused on the customer experience. These trends are illustrated in Figure 3.2.

OPERATIONAL COST OPTIMIZATION	COST AND WORKING CAPITAL MINIMIZATION	CUSTOMER LIFE CYCLE–CENTRIC
• Basic customer needs	• Customer needs from sales and channels	• Customer life cycle experience
• Logistics costs minimization	• Outsourcing	• Supply chain as key factor in customer experience
• Manufacturing process and costs reduction	• Offshoring to low-cost countries	• National security considerations
• Build-to-stock	• Product cost minimization	• Cost to serve
• Push system	• Little emphasis on cost to serve	• Friend-shoring and near-shoring
• Supply control		• Environmental considerations
		• Cost to serve minimization
		• Total fulfilled cost minimization

FIGURE 3.2 Trends Toward Customer Life Cycle–Centric Supply Chains

DESIGNING THE SUPPLY CHAIN BACK FROM THE CUSTOMER

The key to CX life cycle centricity is to design the supply chain from the customer back *and* from supply forward. Regardless of whether the supply chain is international or domestic, this can involve changes and practices in every corporate function, supply chain process, and all links in the supply chain—trading partners and service providers. The integrated supply chain–customer experience (ISC-CX) objectives should be comprehensive and include the main drivers of customer loyalty, satisfaction, retention, and profitability. These objectives should include the following:

- Total acquisition cost (price) and total cost of ownership
- Convenience in ordering, changing orders, tracking, receiving, and returns
- Ease of doing business
- Costs to serve and customer profitability
- Speed, response, and reliability (assurance)
- Perfect order fulfillment
- National security and cybersecurity considerations
- Customer help desks
- Some degree of personalization
- Management attention (in case of problems of emotional dissatisfaction)
- Value-added services

This is by no means a simple list, but we can never lose sight of the fact that the customer pays the bills. Equally important is that, in today's world of social media and ubiquitous computing, customers share experience across their CX life cycle, and this can impact sales and brand equity—positively or negatively. The profitable and supply-assured customer experience is fast becoming the primary driver of supply chain designs and operations.

For example, a leading electromechanical manufacturer in Europe focused on developing a clear definition of customer requirements and expectations. This allowed it to redesign its forward supply chain and eliminate a complete warehouse echelon (layer) in its network, resulting in better service quality and inventory reductions.

Committing to such a focus and set of strategies will require a change in organizational mindset, metrics and measurement, process execution, investment, and information technology capability. For example, sales will now need to be measured on profitability and adherence to corporate contract terms, not just on pure revenue and sales. Marketing would need to be measured on the effectiveness of its marketing spend on the customer, without the false consideration of efforts to put a social message across. Finally, product development would need to be measured on design for logistics, packaging, ease of use, and other market-related metrics.

Differentiated Service Offerings

The new operating model will require that customer needs and preferences be targeted by products and services directed toward specific groups and segments. Customers have more information available than ever before on alternative suppliers, products, and services. Companies, on the other hand, have a great deal of information on different customers and segments, their profitability, cost to serve them, their willingness to pay for certain services, their propensity to buy from the company, and increasingly, their emotional attitude toward companies. It is critical that profitable personalized solutions be created and employed on a consistent basis to the right segments. For instance, organizations should ask themselves which combination of differentiated service offerings should be offered to which groups of customers, and in what geographies? Examples of these differentiated services include communications and incentives based on emotional quotient and service history, delivery times, specialized deals, and how much (if at all) customers should be charged for them—all on as personalized a level as possible.

A key development is the growing potential for increasing collaboration among supply chain network entities and stakeholders to understand customer needs, forecast demand, and develop and deliver targeted differentiated products and services profitably. Such collaboration can include visibility into order and shipment status, product availability, and shared advanced analytics, all of which can have powerful impacts on customer buying, loyalty, and price premiums.

Planning for Demand

Predicting customer demand for many products or services has always been a challenge for both sellers and buyers. In many industries and for many products, demand has always been uncertain and volatile; additionally, today's customers have changed their buying patterns and behaviors, driven by information availability and e-commerce. Retailers and manufacturers depend on multiple channels for sales, which further complicates the demand management process. A new channel is the Metaverse, where brand owners can acquire space in virtual showrooms and consumers can use virtual reality to shop by viewing products in 3D and in optional colors. This innovative new technology is currently designed primarily for shoppers, as opposed to focusing only on sellers.

This is not all one-sided. In recent years, while advancements in technologies, digital analysis, and strategies have succeeded in transforming the shaping of customer demand, they have also impacted supply chain planning. Forecasting is one aspect of supply chain planning, and estimates indicate that soon 50 percent of all supply chain forecasts will be using artificial intelligence (AI), improving accuracy by up to 5 percentage points. Using supply chain planning to meet a forecast is not a "leading practice" in these volatile times—the focus is instead on responsiveness to demand. Supply chain planning now includes resilience (redundancy and hedging to address risk factors), inventory deployment and management, capacity, equipment, and labor availability and is driven by advanced analytics to predict demand, supply, and trends.

Historically, the much-used and taught economic order quantity model (EOQ) for ordering inventory has been about trading off inventory holding costs (the costs of carrying inventory) and fixed ordering costs to meet forecasted demand. Additional factors, such as variations in lead time and in demand, were incorporated into this formula, as were safety stocks based on preset service levels or fill rates (percent of time an order can be filled based on stock, or percentage of demand that is satisfied based on stock, respectively). But recent events, interest rates, risks, and disruptions—the variable, uncertain, complex, ambiguous (VUCA) environment—have altered all these assumptions.

The costs of capital are now the working capital finance costs (and costs of the product can change depending on the supply chain finance arrangements with suppliers) across the end-to-end supply chain. Uncertainty and variability involve risks of different types for different products and materials, as well as for lead times. Risks today range from low-probability and low-impact types of risk to those that can be catastrophic, and these must be considered in determining order quantities and safety stocks. Some companies use a weighted index of risks depending on source location, material type, scarcity of supply, and other risks of disruption. In some instances, certain components demand nearly 100 percent service level (scarce materials, risky sources, healthcare, defense), and these risks can be mitigated by redundancy and diversification. In other words, the game has changed, and the traditional algorithms have become more complex, beyond the "few sizes fit all" approaches that have been used.

A critical part of the supply chain planning process is sales and operations planning (S&OP) or, in the new consultant jargon, integrated business planning. Figure 3.3 illustrates the various components and process of sales and operations planning. While the process is important, a critical element of effective supply chain planning is the education of the people involved in the concepts and trade-offs (addressed in Chapter 6) and their thorough training in the tools and technologies used.

Historically, a key weakness has been the separation of planning and execution. S&OP has now been integrated with sales and operations execution (SOE) to respond rapidly to changing conditions. "What-if" analysis and scenario planning are critical for assessing risk factors and supply chain resilience (addressed in Chapter 7).

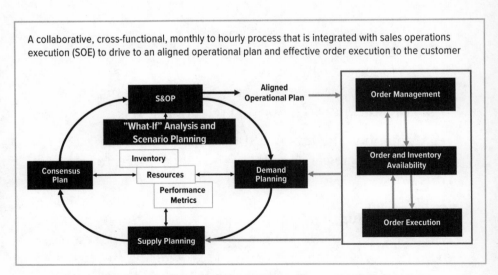

FIGURE 3.3 Enterprise-wide Sales and Operations Planning and Execution

Fulfilling Customer Demand

While improved supply chain planning is helping companies better understand their customers and channels and plan efficiently to match supply with demand, the demands on order fulfillment have increased dramatically, whether it be direct to business or direct to customer. On-time delivery is no longer enough—speed of response, product availability, full order fulfillment, and cost to serve are now the competitive factors. Innovation in getting products to customers, collaboration, and costs of the "final mile" are part of the design of logistics networks and management decision-making. An example of such innovation includes retailers leveraging their stores for customer pickup and ordering and shipping points with "micro fulfillment centers," while brands determine how to deliver direct to customers without creating channel conflict. These are among the trade-offs that companies must make, based on analysis, and most of these trade-offs (but not all) involve:

- Cost versus service
- Working capital versus service
- Cost versus speed of response
- Working capital versus product availability
- Status information and tracking costs versus customer satisfaction and retention

Planning must be integrated with execution, using creativity, collaboration, and thorough cost analysis to make this work.

Making It Happen

There are certain challenges that must be addressed to become more customer-centric and provide differentiated service offerings around the customer experience life cycle. In our experience across several companies and organizations of all sizes, we have found these challenges to include:

1. **Defining the value proposition** for such initiatives around revenue, growth, loyalty, and increased margins.

2. **Phasing in change** in a measured, minimum viable product manner, while focusing on change within the organization. Trying to make the changes overnight is doomed to fail. Customers are less likely to buy based on heavy marketing, more advertising, or social messaging than on actual results and services. Loyalty must be earned.

3. **Gaining insights into the customer journey across the life cycle.** Spontaneous buys are becoming fewer as customers grow in product knowledge and share service experiences.

4. **Creativity in providing value to customers.** Ineffective creativity is often a limitation to customer centricity—particularly in the business-to-business sector. Smart customers want new ideas, new information, and new reasons to buy.

5. **Involving the entire organization in customer centricity.** Customer centricity becomes the responsibility of a sole coordinating function—whether it be the integrated supply chain, sales and marketing, or even a customer experience officer.

6. **Simultaneously addressing the issues around supply assurance.** After all, a company cannot sell what it doesn't have, and as bad, supply shortages will affect a customer's perception in the organization's ability to keep its promises.

7. **Focusing on business basics**—working from the customer back involves defining the operations strategy, focusing on cost to serve, managing through multiple channels, optimizing working capital, and designing the supply chains for cost-competitive resilience.

This evolution of customer centricity has changed business and supply chains. However, it is not a dramatic change, as many of the supply chain basics are still critical. The primary metrics used to measure customer focus, satisfaction, and profitability of today (and tomorrow) include:

- Speed of response to customer orders
- "Perfect orders" (on-time, in-full)
- Ease of doing business
- Communication based on order status, customer needs, history, and emotional quotient
- National security considerations
- Costs to serve
- Working capital
- Customer and product profitability

Whether customers are individuals, businesses, institutions, or the government, this is the business imperative of both today and the future. Satisfying demand is critical to designing and operating effective and efficient supply chains. However, a customer-focused organization is only half the story. In order to satisfy customers across the customer experience life cycle, we must also focus on supply assurance, inventory and product availability, cost, and working capital.

BREAKTHROUGH THINKING

Addressing the issues of the customer and managing demand have resulted in several breakthroughs in thinking and approach that have changed how leading supply chains operate. We have gone beyond treating customer service and satisfaction as something to be outsourced to call centers, virtue signaling, and occasional "feel good" communication. The new and uncertain environment dictates new approaches, which are summarized in the following list.

CORPORATE EXECUTIVES AND POLICY MAKERS

- Focus the supply chain on the customer experience life cycle and measure what the customer wants; understand the customer's tangible supply chain needs. Invest in technologies to understand the customer.

- Use ordering policies based on risks, lead times, and service levels—not just on trading off costs of holding inventory with ordering costs.

- Adopt and institutionalize an integrated, multifunctional sales and operations execution (SOE) process with a member of the executive staff as the sponsor.

- Focus on the information needed for real-time and quick reaction to changing demand and conditions.

- Don't just identify demand—shape it to maximize margins and exploit product and component availability and shortages.

- Use "what-if" analysis and scenario planning, stated in terms of revenues, costs, and working capital, to analyze risks, changes in demand and supply, and disruptions.

- Invite key suppliers and channels/customers to be part of the process.

- Focus on the customer, but also on cost to serve (all customers may be equal, but some are more equal than others) and supply assurance. Segment customers to determine cost- and revenue-effective services and strategies.

- Design the supply chain from the customer back and supply forward.

- Ensure that the customer's emotional state and attitude toward the company are considered, and take action to maintain a high level of satisfaction.

- While forecasting is important, focus on speed of customer response and product availability.

- The customer is both the entity or person ordering a product or service as well as the consumer.

- Address the concentration issues in the various industries that adversely affect customers' price and choice, and undermine the business continuity critical for communities and the government.

- Assign top people in a multifunctional effort to enhance the customer experience.

This discussion of the customer journey to determine demand and service must be balanced by the process that provides supply at the right availability, right time, and at a competitive cost in a resilient manner to satisfy demand and service requirements. The evolution of supply chains has progressed to where customer centricity is the focus, and supply assurance is the backbone enabler. The next chapter addresses the critical supply side of the equation.

CHAPTER 4

Managing Supply

*The enemy of a good plan is the
dream of a perfect plan.*
—**Carl von Clausewitz**[1]

The end-to-end supply chain has two major components: supply and demand. Spanning both is operations. While both supply and demand must be integrated, planned for, and strategized in a holistic fashion, each necessitates different skill sets, perspectives, and strategies. While the supply chain must be directed at demand (after all, the customer pays the bills), it must also be supply-aware—it is the supply that drives policy (and reversely, it is increasingly being driven by policy), garners headlines, encompasses a lot of the risk, and contains the largest portion of the costs. While the jargon of the day is the "demand-driven" supply chain, effective supply chains must be both demand-driven and supply-based.

This chapter deals with the supply part of the supply chain. A point of note: there is a tendency in the media and by people to confuse "supply management" with the entire supply chain and "supply chain management." The "supply" component, critical as it is, is a part of the supply chain, and deals with strategizing, structuring, and managing the supply base to ensure supply availability, cost minimization, and working capital and fixed asset optimization, while dealing with ESG considerations, risk mitigation, and national security implications.

One of the major misconceptions and myths about supply and, indeed, about the entire supply chain, is that it's global and based only on economic factors—a myth that academics adore and many politicians, the media, and globalists love to promote. Despite the attractive notions that goods flow seamlessly across borders and that flow and sourcing are driven solely by economic forces, the reality is quite different. The supply chain is not truly global in nature (even though we use this term throughout our book)—it never has been and probably never will be. It is instead international and cross-border. Countries and regional trade groups have their own tariffs, taxes, incentives, regulations, ownership restrictions, environmental mandates, antidumping mandates, laws protecting local industry, and national security–based restrictions governing intellectual property, jobs, and labor. Indeed, different states in the United States have their own unique taxes and environmental, labor, and business laws.

OUR SUPPLY LINES HAVE BEEN "BUILT TO BREAK"

What has resulted in the state of supply chains today? A good part of it is the supply part of the equation. Figure 4.1 illustrates the various parts of the end-to-end supply chain. In focusing on the supply side, every node, facility, and link is a potential breaking point. Over the past few years, in several industries, we have seen one or more of these points break under stress. The results have been obvious and very public—shortages of medicine, medical supplies, baby food, furniture, semiconductor chips, and paper products, to name a few. Of course, there will be more and different sets of shortages as we go on. Many of the root causes for this breakage lie in the decisions that we, as executives (often under constraints and incentives defined by policy makers), have made in supply management.

The offshoring of supply has often been conducted with a focus on product unit cost, with a short-term outlook and little consideration given to longer-term capability, sustained financial success, national security, or exposure to

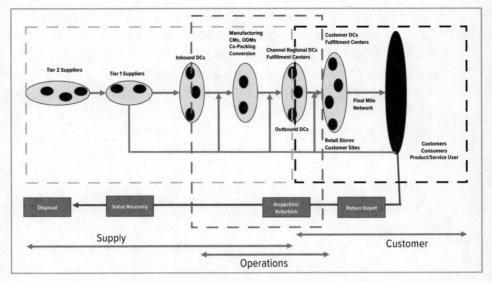

FIGURE 4.1 The End-to-End Supply Chain Network

Every node, facility, and link is a potential breaking point.

risk. Equally flawed was the assumption that we could rely on a "global" world, where goods and services flowed seamlessly across boundaries, driven by economic factors alone. We ignored von Clausewitz's "frictions"—"the concept that differentiates actual war from war on paper," those surprising things that happen during wartime that make "even the simplest thing difficult."[2] To add to this, we implemented "just-in-time," lean supply chains, which required very little safety stock (the inventory employed to absorb variability of demand, lead times, and supply), or risk-mitigation additional inventory, and depended on smaller delivery (order) sizes.

The global supply environment today is impacted by a host of factors ranging from government policies and actions to variability to natural disasters. The dynamics of supply have changed from a relatively pure and traditional cost per unit decision to a more strategic role encompassing a number of criteria—managing vulnerability and risk, ensuring supply assurance, total acquisition costs (the total costs from time of acquisition through maintenance and use, to the end of useful life) and total landed costs (the total costs from procurement through manufacture and logistics to our local warehouse or distribution point), increased control through shortened regionalized supply chains, environmental performance, national security, resilience, agility, and flexibility. These changes have been driven by a number of factors:

Loss of capability and capacity. Large companies have introduced just-in-time systems, outsourced design and production, given away their intellectual property (IP), and exported jobs and skills to offshore locations, often in adversarial or strategic competitor nations, in exchange for low costs, tax breaks, promised access to markets, and the ability to keep their margins and balance sheets attractive. It has become increasingly obvious that "engineering the balance sheet" does far more harm in the longer run to the company, the region, and the host country than does "engineering the supply chain."

Concentration and weaponization of the supply chain. Several countries have realized that there is no thing as a seamless, fair global trading system and that countries now compete on their domination of key supply chains. As a result, "chess player" nations with lengthy planning horizons have successfully embarked on a series of mercantilist strategies and industrial policies that include trade regulations, cost and tax incentives, tariffs, dumping, low-cost labor and anti-strike laws, and building the infrastructure to support the concentration of critical parts of the supply chain of certain key industries. This has resulted in "diamond" supply chains (see

Figure 4.2) where key technologies, capabilities, and materials have often been deliberately concentrated in a particular country, thus giving it tremendous economic, geopolitical, and often military leverage. Additionally, the lack of enforcement of antitrust regulations has resulted in monopolization on an industry basis—most major industries are now heavily concentrated, giving enormous supply chain power to a few companies. (Is it any wonder that most of the top 25 supply chain companies are all very large, powerful, and dominant in their industries and supply chains?) The danger of diamond supply chains in critical industries, products, and materials cannot be underestimated. Large, dominant companies can dictate social policy to communities, smaller companies can be starved of material and put out of business, and hostile countries can bring their adversaries to their knees very quickly through control of supply. Indeed, we have seen signs of this happening all over the globe.

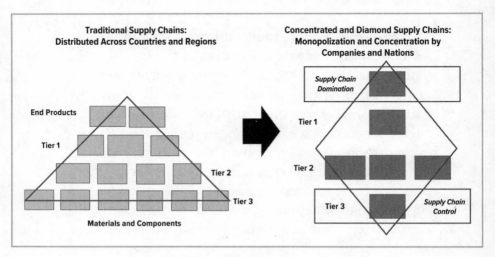

FIGURE 4.2 Supply Chain Structures

"Bundles" of products, data, and services are sourced and purchased. The business environment now reflects integrated and complex products with increasingly shorter life cycles (e.g., the impact of Moore's law on all products employing semiconductor chips), finished goods outsourcing (where the supplier sometimes designs and builds the product, and often has more expertise and design experience than the buyer), and products that are now "bundles" of products, data, and services. The traditional methods of costing and coordinating at the customer are now inadequate and pose new challenges.

Supply chain financing is becoming increasingly important. The supplier-buyer relationship has become more complex—with factoring and financial institutions, varying agreements and rates of financing, and deals involving payables, receivables, margin points, schedule changes, varying lot sizes, and inventory holding. As a result, supply chain financing has become a larger part of the equation.

"Traditional" supply tools and methods are increasingly irrelevant. The days of the traditional material "should" costs, standard supply market analysis, and price per variance are in the rearview mirror, while instruments such as the standard letter of credit (LOC) have been reduced in scale and importance. (However, given the increasing lack of trust among international trading partners, LOCs appear to be making a comeback.) Suppliers are increasingly likely to be in multiple businesses and industries, products are bundled with software and services, price per unit is a small component of the total landed cost, and very few companies buy base commodities—the products are far more likely to be assembled, integrated, or processed.

Supply management talent requires a new breed of supply manager. Supply decisions today demand business acumen, multidisciplinary awareness, and data-driven analysis. Supply management is no longer only about "procurement" or "supplier selection," but rather it requires business acumen—awareness of the impacts of sourcing and procurement decisions on the balance sheet and income statement, as well as on the end-to-end supply chain and on other parts of the business (see Chapter 6). Supply management also requires knowledge of manufacturing, transportation, sales and marketing, government regulations and environmental mandates, legal issues, national security, and, of course, the customer. The new sourcing manager can now be thought of as a business manager for a commodity or product or business unit or company with additional environmental and national security perspectives.

Technology and the connected supply network. New technologies have changed the equation of supply management. Whereas the basics of good modern supply practices apply more than ever, technology has been enabling end-to-end visibility of the supply chain, providing "intelligent" tools for critical areas such as risk monitoring, cost trends, supplier identification, data integration, advanced analytics, and multiparty collaboration. This is being done in a way that would not have been possible before and is changing the latency, speed of response, risk mitigation, and ability to manage total costs. The dream of true end-to-end visibility, management, decision support, and collaboration is gradually being realized—assuming, of course, that companies across the supply chain actually want it.

Risks are increasing in diversity, scope, and impact. The supply chain risks that companies and countries face are external, regulatory, and internal. They range from natural disasters to hostile government actions, and from supplier problems to material and shipping shortages, rising costs, and internal IT breakdowns. Supply managers must assess these risks, their likelihood and impact on the business, and the costs and times to recovery while making sourcing decisions and assessing the necessary trade-offs (see Chapter 7)—all this with a far greater degree of complexity than what they faced just a few years ago. Two relatively new aspects of risk are environmental, social, and governance (ESG) issues and cybersecurity. While we deal comprehensively with sustainability and ESG in Chapter 8, it bears emphasizing that lack of compliance with government regulations, as well as some activist group expectations, can result in adverse impacts on revenues, costs, and the brand. Supply chains today involve many more players in the network, all of whom are vulnerable to cybersecurity breaches—whether by competitors, hackers, ransomware players, governments, or even their own employees.

A new realization of the importance of supply management. It has now become obvious that supply and sourcing decisions drive key business areas such as product costs and supply assurance, impact risk mitigation and environmental performance, and play an important role in ensuring national security. It is the stuff of presidential and prime minister speeches, news headlines, and breathless newspaper pieces. Supply management is of strategic value and is no longer the sole purview of the traditional purchasing manager.

A NEW SUPPLY PARADIGM

These factors have resulted in the need for a breakthrough in thinking about supply management—a different perspective, new and multiple goals and trade-offs (the "whats"), an enhanced set of enabling factors (such as people, technologies, suppliers, and core capabilities), methods, and approaches (the "hows"), as illustrated in Figure 4.3.

THE CORE

First, the core of supply is setting the supply strategy, targets and metrics, and the analytics and organizational parameters for determining trade-offs. Supply management is no longer linear—it involves a series of trade-offs based on the benefits of the expected outcomes and the costs. The different strategic options and decisions must be looked at with a reasonable and structured analysis and an examination of the underlying assumptions. This requires an understanding of financial analysis, the impacts on the company's financials and other functions, and the capability to quantify the impacts of different strategies and actions. Figure 4.4 illustrates some of the key benefit and cost trade-offs that must be made.

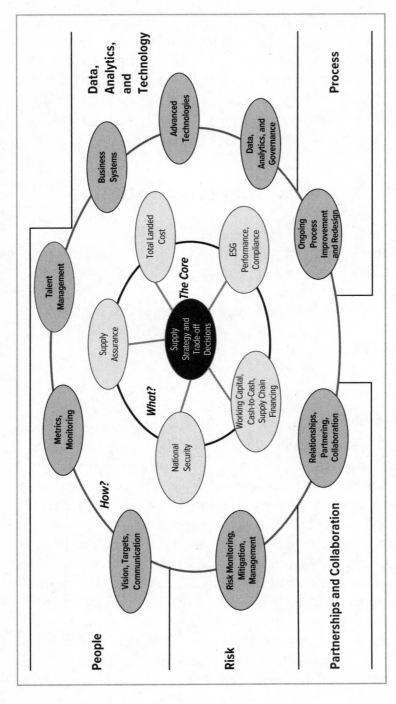

FIGURE 4.3 A Different Supply Paradigm: The Core, the "Whats," and the "Hows"

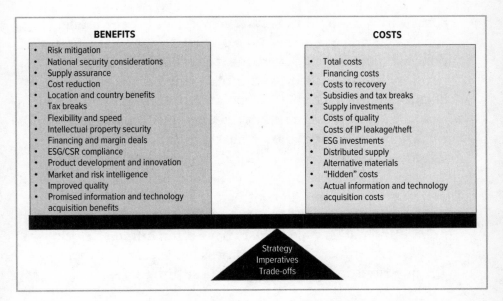

FIGURE 4.4 Benefits and Costs Trade-offs
of Supply Management Strategy

THE "WHATS"

Moving on from the strategy, imperatives, and trade-offs structure, we address the "whats." We've found that a good way to explore these is to pose a few questions for each.

National Security

It must be borne in mind that defense and government supply chains are quite different from commercial supply chains, although many of the principles, methods, and breakthrough thinking are equally applicable to both (for instance, risk monitoring and mitigation, talent management, and technology application). Commercial supply chains were designed and are operated to acquire, make, move, distribute, and sell products to a variety of customer types, with their imperatives and parameters focused on cost, working capital, customer service, and speed (under constraints and incentives often provided by governmental policies). Defense and government supply chains, and particularly the acquisition and contracting processes, have been designed to conform to parameters of high product availability, new systems and technologies, competition requirements, a focus on big purchases and systems and (often bureaucratic and political) socioeconomic quotas and set-asides. These supply chains have to integrate with private supply chains (of contractors found in the defense industrial base), and this poses significant challenges as private and public stakeholders have often different clock times ("government time"), business models, and IT tools. The questions in Box 4.1 address these differences.

BOX 4.1

Questions for National Security

- Have we identified the critical products, materials, and diamond supply chains that have concentration, with an assessment of the real economic, employment, and social impacts?
- Have we studied the cascading effects of a disruption of supply for critical products across industries, the national economy, and security?
- Are any of these suppliers located in adversarial or potentially hostile countries? Can we friend-source? Can we distribute/diversify our supply?
- Have we examined all levels of the bills of materials (BOMs) to determine concentration and national security risk?

- Have we given away, or are we in the process of giving away, core intellectual property that would help an adversarial country?

- Have we done all we can to ensure that our critical intellectual property stays at home or with friendly countries?

- Do we employ contractors who could take our IP or critical information with them to other companies that may be controlled by or beholden to adversarial countries?

- Do we check our suppliers and technology providers as to who finances or invests in them?

- Do our sourcing and acquisition processes explicitly consider these issues?

Supply Assurance

Traditional sourcing and procurement focused on unit cost, delivery performance, and treating suppliers as "arms-length" vendors. Recent events have shown us that this set of priorities is very short-term focused and exposes the supply chain to risks, disruption, and product shortages that result in lost sales, reduced customer loyalty, and, importantly, shortages of critical products. To remedy this, the stratification of suppliers is an imperative: for example, relationships with type A suppliers (following a Pareto/ABC analysis) have to be cultivated based on trust, collaboration, and lengthy win-win relationships. The new and changing environment demands supply assurance, risk minimization, and a longer-term perspective of costs and supplier relationships. Some of the key questions that must be asked are listed in Box 4.2.

BOX 4.2

Questions for Supply Assurance

- Do we assess risks, monitor risks, and have a risk mitigation strategy?
- Do we have both cybersecurity and physical security programs in place?
- Do our metrics include costs to recovery and time to recovery in case of disruption?
- Do we have end-to-end visibility in our supply lines, covering products, orders, and materials?
- Do we have flexible, option-based contracts with our suppliers and providers?
- Do we have capacity-reservation contracts we can employ for adding capacity in case of a crisis?
- Do we have distributed supply sources?
- Are any of our suppliers, at all BOM levels, in potentially risky areas or countries?
- Have we cultivated solid long-term collaborative relations with our key suppliers? Do our sourcing and procurement managers nurture these relationships?
- Do we maintain enough hedge inventory to cover for variability and reasonable disruption?

Total Delivered Cost

One of the focus areas of traditional sourcing has been unit cost. However, in today's international, and at the same time increasingly regionalized, fragmented, complex, and variable supply chain environment, the costs of a product are far greater than just the unit cost—they encompass all direct and indirect costs. This is particularly important in this era of e-business where direct-to-customer delivery is a major aspect of many supply chains, and total landed costs are one piece of the total delivered cost (TDC). TDC includes the costs of inventory and working capital, planning, logistics, and warehousing; costs of quality and governance, compliance, customs, trade costs and tariffs, and taxes; and the costs of sourcing and procurement—in other words, the total delivered cost from supply to the point of distribution, fulfillment, and to the end consumer. Box 4.3 highlights the key questions that must be answered for total delivered cost.

BOX 4.3

Questions for Total Delivered Cost

- Do we consider all relevant costs when costing a product and/or evaluating a supplier?
- Do we monitor cost trends and project costs?
- Do we allocate overhead costs appropriately based on activities?
- Do we assess these total delivered costs periodically, evaluate our assumptions, and take action?

Environmental, Social, and Governance Performance and Compliance

We cover the ESG aspects of the supply chain in greater detail in Chapter 8. It must be borne in mind, however, that supply chains exist and are managed for business, public, and national security results. Some ESG requirements are the outcome of government regulations, laws, and reporting due diligence mandates (often different in different countries and often not harmonized with mandates imposed by international bodies) and must be adhered to as a cost of doing business in those countries. Other ESG demands, compliance, and needs must be addressed with a perspective that covers business, competitive position, brand equity, financial results, and available resources. Box 4.4 lists a set of the questions that executives must ask themselves about ESG performance and compliance.

BOX 4.4

Questions for ESG Performance and Compliance

- What are the laws we must comply with in the different countries we operate in? What are emerging regulations locally and globally?
- How much further than these laws and regulations do we want to go as a company?
- Are any of our suppliers in violation of these standards? Do we monitor these?
- What will be the impact on our business (revenues, costs, brand) if we get caught up in an ESG issue with our suppliers? Have we done a cost analysis on this? Do we have a "Plan B" for supply if a scandal of this type erupts at one of our suppliers?
- Do we require self-reporting? Do we have audit capabilities?
- Are these compliance standards part of our supplier evaluation and selection process?
- What extra costs will we be incurring as a result of such compliance? Are our new ESG features "nice to have" or "necessary"? Have we done a reasonable return on investment analysis?

Working Capital, Cash-to-Cash Cycle, and Supply Chain Financing

Supply chain financing is what makes the supply chain operate efficiently and effectively. It involves funding working capital and short-term operational costs and managing cash flow. In the past, this focus often got lost in the chasms between organizational silos and in the connections among supply chain partners. Risk events and the post-Covid-19 increased inflation have shown us that this is one of the most important aspects of supply chain management. The key questions to ask are listed in Box 4.5.

BOX 4.5

Questions for Supply Chain Financing

- Do we monitor our days payable outstanding (DPOs; both contracted and actual) on a regular basis for our suppliers?
- Do we use this as leverage to get improved prices and volume deals?
- Are our DPOs on par with those of the industry? What are the trends?
- Is our procure-to-pay process efficient so that we maintain our days payable contract commitment?
- Do we monitor and measure the inventory we hold as a result of doing business with a particular supplier? What are the trends?
- Do we look at innovative ways of supply chain financing that reduce our costs and further tie our suppliers closer to us?

THE "HOWS"

These questions are leading to breakthrough methods of supply strategy, assessment, and execution. Several of these factors will be addressed in more detail in later chapters. Let's take a brief look at these factors.

People

Talent management, including acquisition, development, tracking, reskilling, and upskilling, is now a strategic function on its own. Supply management talent (or the lack of it) is the Achilles' heel of many companies but also of key relevant governmental agencies. Leading companies recognize this and have put in place several practices to get the best talent. These include hiring based on diversity of perspective, expertise, and experience; the ability to work in a remote-onsite hybrid fashion; incentives for development and increasing skill sets; and, often ignored, structures that provide challenging and fulfilling work. Leaders have realized that, more than ever, the distributed and uncertain business environment demands the setting and clear communication of a crisp vision, targets, objectives, and accountabilities. While metrics are as important as ever, today's supply complexity demands a different type of end-to-end set of metrics tied to outcomes in supply management.

Process

There is now an increased focus on process, and particularly the "back-office" processes of supply. The key supply processes of strategic sourcing and selection, supplier relationship management, contracts management and adherence, monitoring, and procure-to-pay processes are critical. While strategic sourcing is the most visible and prominent, the back-office processes that support supply must be monitored regularly for performance and the underlying assumptions evaluated. Companies today have adopted systems of ongoing process management and process redesign to increase efficiency, effectiveness, and simplicity and reduce costs. Accelerating this trend is the use of new technologies such as blockchain to drive new "smart contracting" processes and methods—these are contracts on a blockchain system (based on a distributed, immutable ledger assuring that only trusted supply chain stakeholders have access to the system) that are executed when certain conditions are met. They automate the execution of a supply contract so that all participants can be immediately certain of the outcome, without any intermediary's involvement or time loss, while further ensuring that only authorized participants can access information. Blockchain has the potential and the capabilities to address systemic challenges in global supply chain management for both industry and government.[3]

Figure 4.5 provides a thumbnail sketch of the overall process of supply management. Sourcing starts with product, component, material, or service requirements and extends through supply strategy, supplier selection, and innovative contract management. Following that is procurement, the execution and day-to-day management of supply. Last but not least is supplier relationship management, the monitoring of supplier performance, taking corrective action, and cultivating and nurturing collaborative relationships with supplier executives.

This focus on the back-office processes has been coupled with new approaches to ordering product and materials. These include "options theory"–based ordering and planning methods borrowed from financial trading using probabilities, contracting, and a portfolio approach. The objective is to minimize risk of stockouts and excess

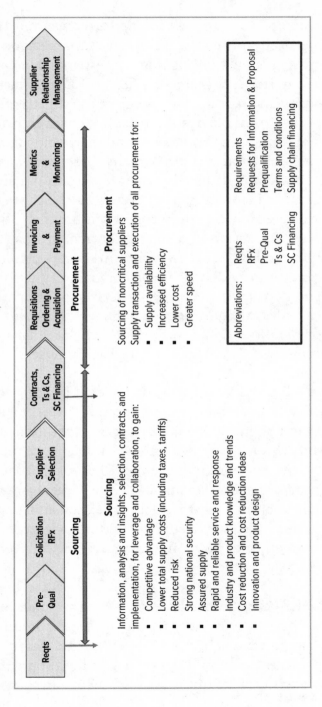

FIGURE 4.5 Supply Management

Sourcing and procurement form the supply management continuum.

inventory, while mitigating the effects of variation in forecast accuracy.

Supply chain financing is a critical aspect of working capital and operating the supply chain. New methods of supply chain financing driven by financing and factoring houses, fintech applications, and technology are now making it possible for companies to obtain working capital funds at every stage of the supply delivery process.

Finally, companies are adopting socially responsible but economically viable sourcing approaches, balancing ESG initiatives and returns with profitability, conducting comprehensive return on investment (ROI) analyses with realistic assumptions testing, and trading off multiple stakeholders' needs. As one executive put it to us, "We are a socially responsible supply chain that reflects national security, generates cash, and makes good margins in a sustainable fashion. We are not in the business of saving the world!"

Risk

Risk—of all types—is now an explicit and critical part of the supply equation and encompasses supply assurance, national security, and ESG considerations. Breakthroughs have included the development of new methods and intelligent systems for evaluating, assessing, and quantifying risk. Companies are also rising that provide services to conduct supply market analysis, financial viability, and risk assessment, as well as continuous risk and event monitoring. Among these new methods are new approaches in holistic ways of evaluating the true ROI of offshoring considering national security, cyber- and IP security, and supply chain agility and flexibility along with risk mitigation. Among the most important of these new methods are novel metrics for managing risk based on time and cost to recovery and time to survival.

A most interesting development in managing risk and supply assurance is a return to the old, maligned strategy of vertical integration. Today's volatile and uncertain environment is quite similar to the one that gave rise to the vertical integration phase in the nineteenth century. At that time, upstream (or "backward") integration through the acquisition of suppliers and their factories ensured the steady supply of materials, while forward integration ensured that distribution and sales networks could deliver to the customer at the right quantity, right time, and right quality.

Owing to the increased overall supply chain risk of today, some large multinational corporations are trending away from the "buy" decision toward the "make" decision, producing more vertically integrated supply chain designs for greater visibility, control, and resilience. In many instances, this takes the form of "virtual vertical integration," where companies exercise control upstream and downstream through investment and their overall power.

Examples of this trend for integration over the 2020–2023 time frame include:

- Walmart invests upstream in a meat producer to assure proper supply.
- Honda partners with LG (to share costs) to build a $4.4 billion electric-vehicle battery factory in the United States.
- Ford and other auto manufacturers are investing in semiconductor chip manufacturing capacity, emulating Tesla.
- Tesla avoided chip shortages during the Covid-19 pandemic by designing its own semiconductors and in-house production of microcontrollers.

- Maersk moved downstream in the supply chain ("forward") by expanding its reach across the business-to-consumer market with the acquisition of warehouse and distribution, e-commerce, and last mile logistics providers and of air cargo planes to provide integrated services and freight transportation flexibility for its customers.
- Amazon adopted a similar strategy with the expansion of its own delivery capabilities.

It is time that companies start exploring such strategies—rather than relying on the traditional mantras of "core competencies, return on assets, changing fixed-to-variable costs"—and look toward supply assurance, control, and synchronization of their supply chains.

Data, Analytics, and Technology

The currency of today's supply chains is data. Historically, executives have understood the importance of accurate and timely data presented in the right format but have often assumed that this takes care of itself. The need for transparency, analytics to drive decision-making, interoperability, and multiple types of reporting has changed this. Leading companies focus on data accuracy and ownership, implementing new methods and approaches to the endemic problem of multiple systems, lack of integration, and inaccurate data. The focus on the data and not the systems drives advances such as data lakes and other means of collecting, aggregating, and analyzing data. A significant and critical part of this is governance and the role of the chief data officer with, often, the collaborative decision role of a business-led data council in setting standards, policies, metrics, technology, and, of course, the requirements of talent needed (see also Chapter 5).

Partnerships and Collaboration

We have long been proponents of the guiding principle "in the future, our clients won't be companies, they will be industries,"[4] namely, companies don't compete, supply chains compete, and countries compete using supply chains; this has never been truer. For supply chains to compete effectively, supply chain stakeholders must collaborate with each other and, occasionally, with the government. This demands the alignment of objectives among the different players and the exchange of information to provide a degree of transparency (based on the comfort level of the organization). For leading companies today, collaboration is much more than exchanging production schedules. It includes collaborating with suppliers and providers on supply chain financing, costs and working capital, design, technology, manufacturability, ESG compliance, and speed and assurance to market. An effective way to accomplish this is to treat suppliers as "knowledge and design engines" and simply ask them (and if possible engage them actively in issues) about design, products, supply, and trends.

For example, a major chemical manufacturer in Europe was struggling to manufacture the right color mix for car paint for their automotive manufacturing customers. A study revealed that customers claimed to never have been asked by the supplier for detailed forecast numbers. Since that point, the companies began exchanging production plans with the types and quantities of colors, and the problem to address the right production mix was solved with minimal inventory levels.

It is now recognized that concentration in "diamond" supply chains at the product, component, material, and capabilities levels poses significant risks and can have devastating effects on national economies and national security. Policy makers often consider only the immediate industry impacts of a critical product and component supply disruption. Figure 4.6, however, illustrates the cascading impacts (also known as ripple effects) that, for example, a semiconductor disruption can have on the economy, affecting multiple industries and potentially bringing the economy to a standstill while further eroding national defense capabilities. This underscores the "burning platform," demonstrating the need for breakthrough thinking by both executives and policy makers alike, to assure supply.

Innovative, forward-thinking companies are starting to partner with like-minded organizations in noncompeting industries to share warehousing, transportation, manufacturing facilities, and supply volume. Supplier relationship management today is more than establishing personal contacts and relationships with supplier executives. Governments are starting to invest in capabilities and manufacturing, developing local sources of supply, embark on private-public partnerships, using private executive expertise, and working with allies and trusted trading partners to address the supply issues and risks.

Supply management today (and tomorrow) is very different from the supply management of the past years. Figure 4.7 illustrates some of the key differences. The result is a shift from supply lines that are "built to break" to supply lines that are engineered to be cost-competitively resilient and agile and to thrive, thus benefiting all the end-to-end supply chain stakeholders.

Managing supply from the point of the first supplier to the customer is replete with serious challenges. The functional aspects from sourcing to storing and reordering, the risks of disruption, cost and revenue erosion, climate change impacts—all have serious impacts on supply availability, resilience, profitability, speed, and quality. However, the component of the end-to-end supply chain that pulls it all together is data and information. Data is

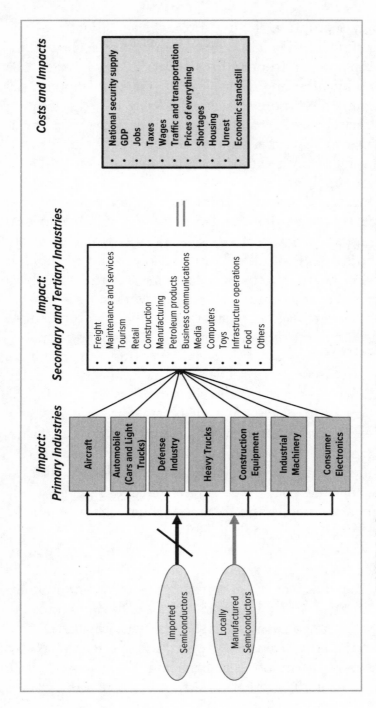

FIGURE 4.6 Semiconductor Supply Disruption Causes Cascading Industry Effects

"Built to Break" → **Engineered to Be Resilient and Agile and to Thrive**

The Old Normal	The Ever-Changing New Normal
Focus on cost per unit and volume	Focus simultaneously on supply assurance, national security, risks of all types, and now ESG
Supplier selection on cost, volume, capability, financial viability	Supplier selection on total cost of acquisition, flexibility, risk, capability, financial viability, and reliability
Minimum inventory—"just-in-time"	Inventory used as a strategic and risk management tool
Talent based on procurement tactical knowledge	Talent management, end-to-end, including business acumen, risk management, procurement, finance
Financing and cash inflow at the end of the process	Innovative supply chain financing through the process
Measurement based on purchase price variance and market prices	Measurement based on total costs of acquisition, reliability, speed, ease of doing business, risk, and ESG
No measured and process-based approach to risk	Structured approach to identifying, assessing, and quantifying the impact of risks, continuously monitoring them, and putting in place mitigation strategies and structures
Should cost and supply market analyses based on simple products and "single industry" supplier business models	Assessing product-information-service "bundles" and complex supplier environment and business models
ERP transactions and manual processes, with systems and technology acquired on costs that always increase and promised benefits that often don't materialize	Digitalization and transformation of the process, contracting, continuous risk monitoring, and visibility; hard ROI analyses for technology acquisition, with emphasis on frequent milestones for costs and benefits

FIGURE 4.7 The Changing Face of Supply Management

sometimes called the currency of the supply chain and the base of warfighting. In Chapter 5 we address the critical (and ever increasingly important) issues of data, information, and governance.

BREAKTHROUGH THINKING

Strategic sourcing, procurement, and approaches to managing the supply base and risk have undergone major changes in the last few years. The challenges caused by serious disruptions in international supply chains have raised procurement and manufacturing to the C-suite and national policy levels everywhere. The new necessary principles, strategies, and guidelines that need to be adopted by corporate executives and policy makers are highlighted in the following summary breakthrough thinking principles.

CORPORATE EXECUTIVES

- Partner with suppliers for demand-supply matching, technical developments.
- Shorten supply chains and/or make them much more robust through a diversified portfolio of onshoring, nearshoring, or friend-shoring.
- Focus on hiring the right talent with business acumen and supply chain knowledge.
- Diversify suppliers, nurture the supplier ecosystem, and build redundancy into the supply base.
- Know and develop personal relationships with key suppliers.
- Abide by national security guardrails—for example, source only noncritical components or manufacturing from adversarial countries; be wary of accepting financing from companies that are based in or controlled by hostile nations; carefully vet critical technical hires from such countries.
- Focus on the "back-office" processes—source to settle, procure-to-pay.

- Examine bills of material for supply sources.
- Strive for real-time information and status—as much as is necessary and financially feasible.
- Plan for hedge stock and capacity with suppliers to cover potential risks and system variability.
- Build risk identification, monitoring, and mitigation into the sourcing and acquisition process.
- Use options-based flexible supply ordering and planning.
- Use simulation for scenario planning and "what-if" analysis.

POLICY MAKERS

- Monitor the acquisitions process to incorporate strict national security parameters and conflict of interest rules.
- Evaluate demand-supply management to include major risk, disruption, and "black swan" type of events.
- Identify nationally critical products, materials, and supply chains; design and implement risk-mitigating strategies.

These guidelines, while relatively simple to conceptualize, are a bit more difficult to plan and execute. They involve capital, relocation, partnerships, diversification, change management, and talent management. More than that, they will require executive action, perseverance, and political will. Many companies and nations have initiated such strategies, while others appear to be adopting a "hope it will go away" attitude based on a lack of understanding of the supply chain, concentration, and impacts. However, planning and executing to these new realities and practices demands *knowledge*—information, data, and analytics, using new and existing technologies and processes. The next chapter addresses this critical area of the supply chain.

CHAPTER 5

Information, Data, Governance, and Analytics

Scientia potentia est.
—Thomas Hobbes[1]

The Latin saying *scientia potentia est* perfectly sums up our argument in this chapter: "knowledge is power." Add to this power the capability of intelligent systems to develop insights, know the status of supply chain assets in real time, and make decisions, and one can easily state that data is the new currency of business and supply chains.

DEFINING DATA

First, let's define the terms *data*, *information* (given the two are often used interchangeably), and *analytics*.

- *Data* is individual facts, quantitative and nonquantitative, that can be related or unrelated. Data forms the base of any decision-making and insight.
- *Information* is data that has been aggregated and processed in some way, and coupled with experience and insight provides knowledge.
- *Analytics* (which has a great overlap with information) is the analysis of data that reveals insights, patterns, and trends.

Data and its intelligent use, management, and governance are critical for running supply chains and for business survival and success in today's VUCA (volatile, uncertain, complex, and ambiguous) environment—for corporations, governments, military, and global health organizations alike. This becomes even more important given the speed of events, advances in technology, and the increase in rates of change in trends, behavior, and regulation.

Today's supply chain provides a core of data bundled with a service and wrapped in a product, and these cannot be handled separately. To be successful and thrive on a sustained basis, an organization must view itself as, and become, a *data-driven organization*. Data-driven organizations have several characteristics: major decisions are fact-based and analysis-based (which could include non-fact-based risk factors); data is always available in the shortest time possible (which might be in real time), easy to use, and accurate; and data is owned and managed as an asset. Equally important is the role of the chief data officer (CDO)—responsible and accountable for data, governance, storage, and analytics. Data is a corporate asset—far more than just bits, and much too important to be left to individual functions or the IT department. Just like any valuable organizational asset, it must be managed effectively. However, this is often easier said than done.

OBSTACLES TO EFFECTIVE DATA MANAGEMENT

There are many obstacles to the effective management of data to drive the best supply chain results, and they range from lack of trust in the IT systems and refusal to share information to the core of data accuracy and timeliness. We will discuss these obstacles next, with some relevant examples drawn from our experience.

Personal Behavior and Lack of Trust in IT Systems
Data and information are sources of power, and some executives, managers, and governmental officials don't want to give them up and prefer to keep them private. Data is

often maintained on "off-the-network" local databases and spreadsheets. One particular company in the electronics industry decided to embark on an assessment of its supply base to ascertain total supply spend, supplier concentration in key commodities, supplier performance and adherence to contracts and terms, level of competitive prices paid to suppliers, and total acquisition costs. The executives discovered, to their surprise (and horror), that much of the most important data did not reside in their enterprise resource planning (ERP) systems, but on the computers of their sourcing and purchasing managers. Collating this data and assessing the true supply picture was a painful process.

On the other hand, much of this company's analysis was done on spreadsheets. This was viewed as "poor practice" and was derided by the IT department and executives who had invested very heavily in the corporate ERP system. However, they failed to recognize that the sourcing and purchasing managers used the spreadsheets very well, were familiar with them, and found them simple to use and manipulate, and thus they were effective. The tools brought in by the ERP system were exactly the opposite—complex, "simple" only to the IT group, required changes in format and use, and in general proved ineffective. The company returned to using spreadsheets, with a difference—the data is now centralized.

Data is often inaccurate and is not trusted by managers in the organization. Executives and frontline operators in a major organization had long known that the accuracy of their inventory data and status was poor. Rather than addressing and resolving this issue, employees merely made decisions and took action to compensate for inaccurate information. In one instance, planners ordered far more inventory than needed to make up for the expected shortfall. As a result, inventory piled up and periodically had to be disposed of—scrapped, sold at deep discounts or for salvage value and thus wasted—even if it could have been used in other business units or locations.

Organizational and Cross-Organizational Issues

A huge organization could not articulate who owned the data, or even its accuracy, in the field. As a result, the response was "the CIO is responsible." After a chief data officer was appointed, it became "the CDO is responsible." This reflects a number of pervasive problems:

- Data is not always viewed as an organizational asset.
- Data in an organization is often spread across many unintegrated systems.
- Data in the organization is often not owned by anybody, and nobody is held accountable for its accuracy and timeliness.
- Other organizations in the supply chain ecosystem are often reluctant to share their data—for fears of loss of privacy and sensitive corporate information or allowing themselves to be exploited.

Data Accuracy and Timeliness

Many organizations often have problems with data accuracy and timeliness:

- The right data is sometimes not collected at the point of generation.
- Different processes and habits of data entry mean that data in the systems is often not timely.
- Senior executives often pay no attention to the accuracy and quality of data.

For example, we were asked to advise on developing a road map for a company on supply chain planning and execution from the current state (using existing tools, ERP systems, and spreadsheets) to a future artificial intelligence and machine learning (AI/ML)–powered integrated end-to-end supply planning and execution state. Ten minutes into the discussion, the director of worldwide inventory admitted that their inventory accuracy was only 80 percent. The vice president in charge of the initiative suddenly realized that unless they addressed inventory accuracy and quality first, they would only make mistakes much faster with more sophisticated systems.

Finally, we are in the age of "big data," where there is a danger of having too much data and, sometimes, not the right data. This can result in overload and too much information to make good decisions.

A STRUCTURED APPROACH TO MANAGING DATA

Data in the supply chain comes from multiple sources and is used for several different supply chain decision-making points and activities. Figure 5.1 illustrates this point for a typical supply chain. For the data-driven organization, each of four levels demands a tailored approach, mandate, or strategy: the core data, collecting data, the uses of data, and data presentation that enables decision-making.

The Core Data
Identifying the data needed and locating where it resides in the organization and across organizations.

Collecting Data
Collecting the data into a centralized location. This is not systems integration or a common system; this is about getting the data into a common base where it can be used for analytics and reporting. Many leading companies use structures such as data lakes to achieve this.

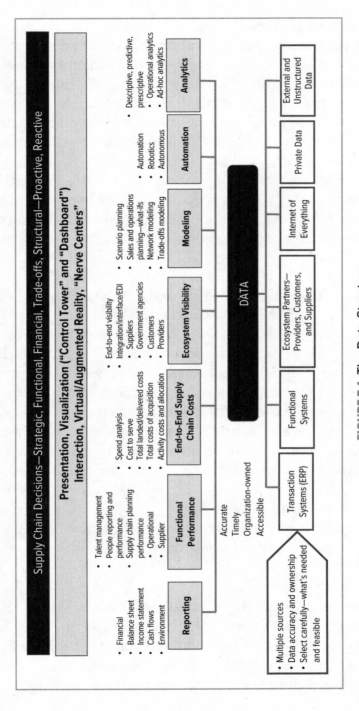

FIGURE 5.1 The Data Structure

The currency of supply chains—business and national

The Uses of Data

The uses of data need to be mapped out and defined. They can include standard reporting of functional performance, supply chain status, modeling, and analytics using multiple types of data across the ecosystem. It's not simple, but it should not be unduly complex, either.

Data Presentation That Enables Decision-Making

The intelligent use of data requires analytics, presentation, and visualization. Some leading companies utilize a "control tower" to monitor and execute key aspects of their end-to-end supply chain from different locations (physical, virtual, or both). The information, display, and interactive capability can range from the strategic and overall supply chain planning to the functional and is often extended to partners in the ecosystem. The control tower concept moves large organizations closer to the "holy grail" of end-to-end supply chain information integration—providing transparency, rapid response, reduction in costs and working capital, and a reduction in the dreaded bullwhip effect (the distortion of information upstream in the supply chain; see also Chapter 7). Presentation and visualization have expanded to the use of virtual and augmented reality in simulation, training (e.g., Amazon has been actively pursuing these for training of workers in its fulfillment centers), and scenario planning. In today's Internet of Things—or as some call it, the Internet of Everything—world, there is plenty of data but far less insight and knowledge-based decision-making.

IMPLEMENTING AN EFFECTIVE DATA STRATEGY

Implementing a data strategy requires an organizational emphasis, a focus on the right things, and often a change in some aspects of long-standing cultural practices. Figure 5.2 further illustrates these aspects.

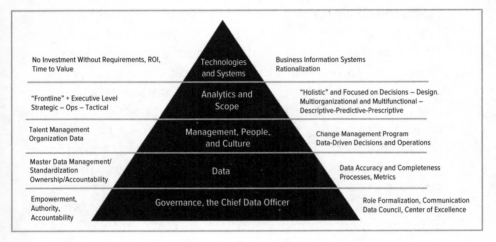

FIGURE 5.2 The Management of Data

Governance

It bears repeating that, in today's environment, data must be treated as a corporate asset (and, in the case of the country, as a national and defense asset) and is far too important to be left to individual functions or departments, even the IT department. Data governance is, essentially, the organizational design of data—the processes, ownership and roles, standards, metrics, quality, security, and structure of the data in the organization. It ensures common definitions, accuracy and completeness, and the ability of the different functions and business units to be flexible in their analytics and use of data. The strategy specifies (or understands) the location in the organization and eco-system and ensures the "single version of the truth" (to raise an age-old business phrase)—referring to the lack of duplicate or conflicting data. Equally important, data governance specifies the consistent approach and method to address master data management (MDM)—a critical step in ensuring common data structure, description, and nomenclature (after all, a "nut" is a "nut," isn't it?) and ensures the integrity of the structure and data accessibility. Governance strives to achieve six major objectives: security, accuracy, compliance, reporting, communication, and data-driven decision-making (further discussed in Chapter 7). It involves everything surrounding data collection, governance, categorization, storage, analytics, and use.

Two critical breakthrough developments in the past few years have shifted the discussion from information systems and architecture to data and the data-driven enterprise. One is the emergence of the CDO, distinct from the CIO or CTO, to drive the governance and management of data in the organization. The CDO, in many instances, reports to the CEO. The other is the recognition of data as an organizational asset to support end-to-end cross-functional and cross-organizational analytics and decision-making. These developments have been transforming business and the supply chain.

Data

Data, as the currency of the supply chain (and the currency of modern, often hybrid and asymmetrical warfare), has certain characteristics. First, it must be treated with the same diligence as talent management and commodities. It must be defined (supplier, customer, logistics, etc.), and someone must own it and be accountable for it—preferably the people who enter it into the system. The data must, to be effective and lead to a competitive advantage (or enable mere survival), be all-encompassing in scope. In other words, it must be multifunctional, multiorganizational, supported by interoperable systems, and extend to the enterprise and (where possible) the entire supply chain ecosystem.

Second, there needs to be a focus on *overall data quality*—an attribute that encompasses several factors: there must be only one point of entry and modification, the "single version of the truth," and the organization must implement "Class A" initiatives defining and measuring data accuracy, timeliness, and integrity. In many companies, executives and managers often assume their data is correct or, if they know it's not, don't admit it. A 2017 *Harvard Business Review* article highlighted the fact that "only 3% of companies' data meets basic quality standards."[2] This is a composite score of various data attributes. This statistic is far more terrifying than issues with demand and supply planning; in any company with such an abysmal level of data quality, those issues would already be bad. There are different ways of computing the financial impacts of poor data quality, and all of them show that the impact is significant—sometimes even "make or break" significant.

Third, data entry and monitoring must be made easy for the people doing it. Having experts work on artificial intelligence applications to supply chain planning is probably useful, but having experts work on ensuring convenient, error-free, and easy data entry and maintenance is far more important. The best way to do so is to invest in tools that can "cleanse" data, freeing up the experts to explore "supply chain intelligence" tools and analytics.

Fourth, we need to differentiate the data needed for planning, whose periodicity can be weekly or greater, and execution. In certain high-speed and volatile industries with very variable demand, the execution of real-time accurate data is fast becoming an imperative.

Finally, we need to ask ourselves, What is the value of data? Do we need, or can we afford, end-to-end, real-time data that supports real-time visibility, status, and performance across the supply chain? Small, medium-sized, or even some of the larger companies may not be able to afford to obtain and use real-time data; others may want it selectively (for example, not real-time and only for certain suppliers and providers in the supply chain), while extensive visibility may be a competitive necessity for others. After all, real-time visibility can be expensive, requiring software, integration with systems, process design, aggregation, and analysis. Worse, would a lack of good aggregation, analytics, and presentation for decision-making result in a "highly nervous" organization? Therefore, even for those who have such visibility, the follow-up questions are, Do they know what to do with it and do they really need it?

Data is valuable as it is the currency of the supply chain, and in certain circumstances it can be monetized. For example, customer data and buying patterns can be sold (or used as components in supply chain financing or trade deals) to upstream supply chain partners or to non-competing companies for use in their marketing, supply chain services, or product development programs.

As an example of investing in tools and data, Walmart, the world's largest retailer, has invested billions of dollars in e-commerce, supply chain technologies, and new fulfillment options. It has leveraged its technological and data science talent to provide its e-commerce and supply chain leaders with data-driven options for new initiatives in planning and execution. Advanced network design, for example, is now a continuous planning process.

Similarly, PepsiCo has been investing in digital tools and advanced technologies, along with data integration and sophisticated data analytics, at levels beyond others. Its use of advanced planning systems has contributed to the profitable growth of its food and beverage brands worldwide.

Management, People, and Culture

Knowledge and data are corporate and national assets to be guarded and made secure, enabled by functional experts, data scientists and translators. Unlike the traditional historical perspective, data today does not just originate from an ERP system—it is both unstructured and structured, from multiple sources, including social media (data from social media is unstructured and requires artificial intelligence to make sense of it). As such, it is complex and, in today's "big data and Internet of Everything" environment, somewhat daunting. As a result, it must be carefully managed to provide the necessary intelligence for its specific business purpose. Nobody knows better what they need, or what they trust and don't trust, than the frontline employees, functional executives, and supply chain executives. They are the core of transforming the company into a data-driven organization. The main principles that should support a data-driven organization are the following:

- Decisions and trade-offs are made and justified with data.
- Data is accurate, has integrity, and is trusted by the organization.
- Data must be across the end-to-end supply chain, encompassing both structured and unstructured data.
- Data has owners and a process for generation and entry.
- There is a "single source of truth" for data.
- Data gathering and storage must be focused on data accessibility, maintenance, and flexibility.

- Hiring must focus on data scientists, translators, and experts.
- Data must be secure.
- Data must be controlled by the company, not by consultants and contractors.
- Standards and architecture must be set by the chief data officer, preferably with the oversight of a data council.

While this appears to be a lengthy list, most of it is common sense. Data needs the same attention that is placed on sales, working capital, and costs.

Additionally, data is the base for digital transformation. Digital transformation is not merely the automation of a process; it is the data-driven and system "intelligence" that drives changes in the supply chain model, structure, and processes.

For example, Amazon expects that its new delivery route algorithm will help it to avoid millions of miles driven per year after deploying it across the entire United States, according to a post on the Amazon Science website in 2022.[3] The Customer Order and Network Density Optimizer (Condor) algorithm assesses customer orders before they leave a fulfillment center to identify the most effective shipping options. It was introduced in a few Amazon delivery stations in January of 2022, before going live nationwide. The company plans to deploy it in other countries as well. This initiative will be enormous in impact—leading to more deliveries, higher customer fulfillment, fewer emissions, and lower costs, while easing the burden on the drivers.

Digital transformation must be undertaken carefully. When does digital transformation stop being a vendor and consultant buzzword and start being an integral part of business strategy and structure? When it is driven by the business. Aligning the strategic and supply chain goals requires an emphasis on strong and comprehensive ROI evaluation, with serious and realistic assumption testing. Technology acquisition certainly should not be based on journal articles or analysts' opinions.

Finally, a critical part of the equation is people and culture. It is people who collect the data; enter it into systems; share it with colleagues, other departments, and supply chain partners; aggregate and analyze it; present it; and make the necessary decisions. It is the organizational culture that makes this happen. Change management is an integral part of the data strategy. This should include programs to educate executives, managers, and frontline personnel on the reason change is needed; the necessity for data accuracy, ownership, completeness, and timeliness and for data sharing; the process of data management; and, of course, the critical importance of standardization and the "single source of truth"—the imperative that everyone in the organization uses the same data from the same source, with no exceptions. Without this, no data strategy can be successful.

Analytics and Scope

Analytics, simply put, entails the analysis, presentation, and visualization of data for informed and intelligent decision-making. Analytics must be multifunctional and multiorganizational, with the metrics of tomorrow driven from a bottom-up user perspective. This last one is particularly important; a key component of effectiveness is to ask those who use the analytics in decision-making what they need to enhance their decision-making. Corporate IT cannot do that. Analytics must address the four inputs to decision-making: descriptive (What happened?); diagnostic (Why did it happen?); predictive (What is likely to happen?); and prescriptive (What should be done?).

Equally important as the analytics themselves are their periodicity (how often the data is refreshed and the analytics updated), their presentation, and visualization (for ease of understanding, clarity, ability to manipulate and change, and assimilation). Many companies use both flexible "executive" and "functional" dashboards—carefully designed and specified—as well as sophisticated and interactive control towers and supply chain nerve centers to help manage their supply chains. When coupled with technologies such as virtual and augmented reality, analytics can be very powerful and game changing. Of course, in order to realize this end point, analytics cannot be left to IT. It is a business function and should be driven by those with supply chain knowledge and business acumen. It must span the supply chain and its ecosystem by being multifunctional, multi-supplier, multi-provider, multi-geography, multichannel, and multiorganizational. Carl von Clausewitz perhaps said it best. His succinct words about war are equally true about global supply chains:

> I shall proceed from the simple to the complex. But in war more than in any other subject we must begin by looking at the nature of the whole; for here more than elsewhere the part and the whole must always be thought of together.[4]

For example, the cost of shipping a product by a particular transportation mode (say, an ocean carrier) and provider is not often relevant unless it is matched with transit and delivery lead times, ship and destination locations, history and variability of performance, what others are paying and benchmark rates, and aspects of consolidation and trade-offs. Moving on, it becomes important to have an idea of what will happen in the future in terms of shipping capacity, shipping costs (for example, owing to various ESG mandates, including the upcoming monetization of CO_2 emissions in the shipping industry, or to dramatic upheavals in the global maritime freight transportation as the ones experienced during the Covid-19 pandemic), government source risks, and other trends. Leading-edge companies adopt this approach in addressing their analytics program.

Analytics must be directed at outcomes, performance, and trends, spanning various operational levels from strategic to tactical. However, a lesson learned from leading companies is that one can get carried away with enthusiasm—too much analysis can be as bad as too little. One organization, for example, has hundreds of key performance indicators (KPIs) or critical success indicators (CSIs)—somehow, the words "key" and "critical" have been misunderstood.

Major organizations, from governments to large companies, have embarked on efforts to define, structure, and implement data, governance, and analytics programs and are finding out that it takes a great deal of up-front thinking and design. A good way to start or enhance the analytics program is to define what we intend to measure, at what level, and to what end. Figure 5.3 demonstrates an example of such a pragmatic framework that has been used to define the analytics and focus on the key elements. It's simple and can provide a guide to implementation— but it requires some hard thought on strategy, operations, success, and the future.

Technologies and Systems

For the purposes of this discussion, we will focus on the key management and performance aspects of technologies and systems.

The management of technology and systems for the supply chain (or the organization) comes down to five aspects: how we buy it, how we implement it, how we use

TYPE	FOCUS/ TARGET AUDIENCE USERS	PERIODICITY	TYPES OF KPIs/CSIs/ DATA—CORE	TYPES OF KPIs/ CSIs/DATA— ADVANCED	DESCRIPTIVE DIAGNOSTIC	PREDICTIVE	PRESCRIPTIVE
Strategic	• Enterprise Business Unit • Strategic imperatives • Shareholder and reporting metrics • Government-mandated (e.g., ESG)	Monthly Weekly Daily	Examples: • Performance • Cost • Status	Examples: • Major accounts performance • Risk monitoring and early warning signals	• What happened yesterday and today? • Why did it happen? • Facts • Analysis	• What will happen and impacts given current trends and other factors: • Internal/local • Other organizations • External • "What-if"/ interactive options	• What should we do given the data and trends? • What are our options? • "What-if"/ interactive options
Operational	• BU/unit functions • Major projects and programs	Monthly Weekly Daily Real-time					
Tactical	Local	Daily Real-time					
Data Sources			• Transactional: Local • Organizational: Functional	• Cross-organizational • Cross-functional • External			
Measurements	Customers. suppliers, operations, inventory, channels, risks, people, cash and working capital, costs, trade restrictions, government mandates, etc.						

FIGURE 5.3 Framework for Design Analytics

it, carefully monitoring all three of these, and then deciding if and when we should build on it or cut it. A few of
these deserve some further explanation.

Too many companies and organizations appear to close
their eyes and jump when acquiring systems and technology. Often, acquisition is based on trade press accounts,
analyst opinions, practices of competitors, consultant
pitches, and vendor promises, and these include everything
from ERP systems to blockchain to artificial intelligence.
The very large companies can sometimes afford to experi-
ment and try out these technologies, but others cannot and
must keep a watchful eye on out-of-control IT spending.

The ROIs conducted often use unrealistic assumptions
and rely on sources that are biased at best: the IT department, vendors, consultants, analysts, and a few selected
customer references. Often, in our experience, the benefits
are overstated; they address areas that have little relation
to the system being evaluated, ignore the fact that much
of these benefits would be realized in the normal course of
operations improvement anyway, and are often projected
to start far into the future. Equally dangerous is the fact
that the costs are often understated, don't include the total
costs of acquisition, and use overly optimistic, unrealistic
assumptions. A final aspect that is often missed is that
data cleansing can cost a lot of money and take time. As
a result, many systems and technology acquisitions are
doomed to disappoint.

Another important aspect that's often overlooked is
the measurement and monitoring of milestones, costs and
benefits to the projected ROI, and implementation time-
line. Rarely do the people who put the ROIs and timelines
together suffer any consequences, and worse, many acquisitions stay beyond the "expiry date." Few companies are
willing to cut a program even if it is taking far too long
and is not meeting costs, benefits projections, and targets,

though it is probably doing more harm in terms of effectiveness, efficiency, waste of money and resources, frustration among the employees, and, ultimately, business results.

THE DIGITAL SUPPLY CHAIN

While there is an increased focus on the role of the digital supply chain in driving revenue and transforming the business, there is a lot of confusion, often brought on by the indiscriminate and interchangeable use of the terms involved, as to what digital supply chains are and how to approach the topic. There are several definitions and terms here—used differently and addressing different issues—and this can be confusing to supply chain executives and policy makers alike. There are three distinct aspects (and stages) of the digital supply chain, and we have endeavored to define them as simply as possible:

Digitization: Internally focused—automating paper-based and analog processes into digital processes and workflows.

Digitalization: Encompassing the supply chain ecosystem—the development and execution of digital end-to-end processes using data collection and intelligent devices, such as the Internet of Things, sensors, robots, and wearables, integrated with advanced technologies such as artificial intelligence/machine learning and cognitive computing, 3D printing, blockchain, and virtual and augmented reality.

Digital transformation: The transformation of the supply chain to develop and execute new business and operational models.

The journey of the digital supply chain starts by moving from internally focused digitization to embracing the supply chain ecosystem and, ultimately, to changing and transforming the entire business and business model. Executives who want to embark on this process should start by:

- Automating processes: defining and automating processes and workflows and ensuring commonly defined and accurate data
- Then moving on to using all forms of data (structured and unstructured) from inside and outside the enterprise—indeed, from the network and beyond—to transform the supply chain in terms of speed, reaction, risk management and mitigation, cost, working capital, customer growth, and decision-making
- And finally, using technology and the digitalization of the supply chain to create and redefine new forms of business, operations, and value

The high-impact segment of this journey is the middle stage—the "digitalization" of the supply chain. This is where companies of all sizes, in all industries, and those part of the national security domain should set their targets. Digitalization, with its emphasis on the end-to-end (and beyond) supply chain network, while using both structured and unstructured data, opens up new possibilities for high-speed decision-making, rapid revision of direction when necessary, faster transaction speed, and, importantly, collaboration. Digitalization has a huge potential to improve supply chain resilience (as discussed in Chapter 7) and will allow for rapid evaluation and action based on the status of risk and supply for nationally critical supply chains. Supply chain digitalization can decrease the time and increase the accuracy of major processes;

enable each network partner and provider to operate on a single, consistent, and accurate version of data; and lead to lower total supply chain costs, improved working capital, better planning, replenishment, and deployment of inventories, and higher levels of customer service. In the national security area, it will help to ensure the availability of critical material, the assurance of supply, and the management of the risks of supply and operating status of equipment. This hard commercial value proposition, the resilience and national security benefits, and the competitive advantage it provides (along with the advantages that competitors will obtain if they are ahead) are what motivate enterprises to move toward the digitalization of their supply chains.

Most consultancies and analysts have espoused a similar approach toward supply chain digitalization. The relevant steps are quite obvious and easy for any executive or policy maker to obtain. We discuss some of the critical issues in planning and implementing a digital supply chain journey from digitization to digital transformation. These include the following components.

Master Data Management
A centralized dictionary with definition and knowledge of data sources that ties data into a commonly defined and accessed corporate asset. This is important for aggregating data from across the supply chain network. Further, it would be a great advantage to have common and consistent terms for all items across the enterprise (and, if feasible, across the entire supply chain network).

End-to-End Visibility
The capability to see, in real-time, near-real-time, or periodic fashion, the status and events of the global end-to-end supply chain, including customers' orders, products,

materials, manufacturing status and schedules, costs, suppliers' order status and schedules, location of customers and their products, and, importantly, the ability to connect all these to obtain a complete picture of the business. This necessitates that each partner in the supply chain provides the most recent updates or reports that can be accessed or read by electronic data interchange (EDI, the computer-to-computer exchange of business documents in a standard electronic format between companies) or automatic communication—the ability of different computer systems to communicate with each other using a software interface called an application programming interface (API), which can get "near real-time" data and actual real-time data from supply chain partners' systems (see also Chapter 7). Some of these APIs are executed using the Global Positioning System (GPS).

Relationships with Partners in the End-to-End Supply Chain

While envisaging end-to-end supply chain network information integration is comparatively easy, obtaining the information from supply chain partners and providers is not. This requires an understanding of the partner's business and business acumen, crafting a convincing "win-win" value proposition, and collaborating to get it done. It must be part of a plan that focuses on phases and priorities.

The Human Element, or "Who Puts the I into AI?"

Technologies such as artificial intelligence are sometimes billed as the ultimate solution for the supply chain—one where machines make the decisions in an "intelligent" self-learning supply chain. Not long ago, experts were predicting that AI would turn supply chains into autonomous self-regulating entities that would optimally manage end-to-end flows with very little human intervention. However, this vision has not yet materialized. A 2022 study by the Boston Consulting Group found that the root cause of this unfulfilled potential stems from companies not having pursued using AI to make recurring decisions, taking into account patterns in big data that humans cannot recognize.[5] While AI does have a place in the supply chain, and will have a more prominent place as it evolves, it is unlikely to replace the quick-change, fast-pivot, juggling of multiple priorities human aspect. At some point in the future, AI will probably replace supply chain planning, and its future uses further encompass retail store inventory, strategic sourcing, and responses to changing business conditions. Companies have announced AI-driven tools that leverage deep learning, massive amounts of data, videos and images to manage manufacturing and warehouses, help track, plan and order inventory, predict demand and understand customer needs, and plan to match it, source, track and flag risks, and develop predictive insights. This is just the beginning of the march towards the Spatial Web 3.0 and the "intelligent", information-driven, self-managed supply chain of the future.

There are three aspects to the interface of humans and technology, as discussed here:

- Humans set guidelines and controls by which machines operate and make decisions. This is the issue of "who puts the I into AI" and who (or what) puts in the guardrails—it needs to be supply chain experts rather than the third-party programmers and their managers.
- The human-computer interface (this used to be called "user interface," but it is far more than that

now) is the means (hardware and software) by which humans and computers communicate with each other. The next phase is human-technology integration, or HINT, integrating humans and computers—a powerful concept in managing the future generations of supply chains.

- Humans make quick-change decisions in an uncertain and rapidly changing environment. Direction change, on-the-spot reaction, and supply pivots are best done by experienced and expert humans who can absorb a large amount of nontraditional information and make decisions. The age of complete machine control of global supply chains is still some distance away, not to mention the days of "technological singularity" where the growth and advancement of technologies will become much faster (and ultimately beyond our control), resulting in dramatic changes to supply chains and their overall environmental and social footprints. It is imperative that digitalization strategies and plans take into account the human element.

Looking at the "Edges"

The edges are the areas of connection in the supply chain—the physical locations where data connects with supply chain assets, whether they be people, robots, trucks, drones, machines, or sensors. In other words, it's where the action takes place and where data is generated. As such, edge systems allow for decisions to be made at or close to sources of information. The impacts of these systems will be further amplified as communication technologies develop. This is where the action will be and will result in a combination of centralized and decentralized decision-making, all aligned and integrated, with as close to zero latency as possible. This is a powerful and highly promising vision, indeed, and one within our sights. Unlike many supply chain practices and investments that favor big companies, edge systems will gravitate toward "software as a service," thus making them affordable to smaller companies.

Developing a Vision (or Description) of the Future State of the Supply Chain

This requires an approach that looks at the end-to-end supply chain in a holistic manner and discards the traditional perspective that strategy drives process, which in turn drives technology. Too many digital initiatives are developed in functional or geographical silos independent of an enterprise plan, and as such result in redundancies, high costs, and an erosion of the value and power of supply chain integration. Furthermore, the traditional "strategy-process-technology" sequence has been outdated by the development of systems and technologies, the expertise designed into some of them, and the capabilities of the technologies themselves. This implies that starting with the capabilities of technologies, while considering national security and risk (both cyber and physical) can drive the development and improvement of business models and processes.

Maintaining a Clear Focus on the Overall Objectives

Conferences and trade and scientific journals are full of discussions regarding AGI/ML (artificial general intelligence/machine learning; machine learning is a part of artificial intelligence where machines can perform tasks and learn without human intervention), visibility, supply chain integration, robotics, drones, and virtual and augmented reality. However, the hard objectives and value propositions are often ignored or forgotten. AI/ML should be looked at not for its own sake but in the light of an overall vision with specific business goals and objectives and return on investment criteria. Far too many companies fall into the "vision trap" painted by analysts and consultants. These tend to describe maturity models, various stages of development, sophistication, and process, and are often targeted at the very big companies where mistakes can easily be absorbed. However, most companies cannot afford this, and so they must keep a clear focus on their business objectives. These objectives must include:

- Zero-latency decision-making in response to different events and situations. This means taking the time from an event to an actionable decision to as near zero as possible—at maximum speed.
- Targets that include revenue and margin growth, total cost, and working capital.
- The customer experience life cycle.
- The hard benefits to the enterprise and to its customers (and there are many), from across the end-to-end supply chain network, that can be targeted, obtained, and measured. These benefits are outlined in Figure 5.4 and constitute a powerful narrative for embarking on the digital supply chain journey.

Management Actions

Finally, the development of the digital supply chain vision and execution to these objectives must include some simple (but again, commonly ignored) management actions:

- Clear and complete return on investment analyses, considering both quantitative and qualitative issues, timelines to implementation, and benefits,

Stages	Enterprise and National Security Benefits	Benefits to the Customer
Digitization *(Internal Process Automation)*	Process efficiency Speed Cost reduction Inventory reduction	• On-time, in-full delivery • Resilient and secure critical supply chains, capabilities, and intellectual property • Improved product availability (lack of shortages) • New products and models • Improved pricing, lower costs • Improved service and speed of response • "The promise to customers," service and product reliability—"no surprises" • Environmental, social, and governance improvements
Digitalization *(End-to-End Supply Chain Ecosystem)*	Shareholder value Revenue Costs and margins Risk monitoring and mitigation National security Resilience E-procurement and "smart" contracting Acquisition and contracting process—fast, strategic, with integrity Digital freight management Agility Pipeline velocity and speed of response Service levels, fill rates, and material availability Supply assurance Increased customer retention and lower customer acquisition costs Customer knowledge—preferences and emotional quotient Customer profitability "Mega-process" speed and cost: order-to-delivery, source-to-settle	
Digital Transformation *(Operations Models, Business Models, New Paradigms)*	New innovative and bundled products New differentiated services New operations models New business models	

Critical Elements in Evaluating Initiatives and Projects
Realistic Assumptions, End-to-End Supply Chain Return on Investment, Analyses of Costs and Benefits
Phased Planning

FIGURE 5.4 The Digital Supply Chain Journey

based on realistic assumptions of costs and benefits, and scenario planning
- Minimum viable product–based planning with go-no-go milestones
- Strong relationships and agreements with supply chain partners to collaborate and to share data and benefits
- The "best of the best" team in the enterprise for vision development, planning, and project team
- Accountability—the people who are responsible, accountable, and rewarded for successfully executing this vision to plan

THE NEXT PHASE IN THE SUPPLY CHAIN: THE SPATIAL WEB

The Spatial Web builds on Robert Metcalfe's law, which states that the total value of a network is determined by the number of other users connected to the network: the greater that number, the greater the network scale. The visionary Spatial Web is essentially Web 3.0, created in Eindhoven in the Netherlands. It is the true Internet of Everything and All Things, connecting and digitizing everything. It is the first major step toward the true "intelligent" learning supply chain. This connection, or "convergence," brings together the human, physical, logical, and business environments using the latest technologies. These technologies include AGI/ML, robotics, global positioning and location, end-to-end transparency, network and product status, actual physical location, events and trends, priorities, and imperatives. All of these come with the promise of producing the true "intelligent" supply chain.

Leading companies and government agencies must start examining the possibilities and potential of the Spatial Web in terms of competitiveness, operations, national security and investment. It will be difficult for companies and countries to recover from being left behind in the curve. The pieces are there; what's lacking is the intersection of three things: (1) a firm understanding of the supply chain; (2) a good understanding of what a set of technologies can achieve (this does not mean knowledge of programming or systems integration); and (3) creativity and a good imagination. A recent "vision of the future supply chain" session illustrated that, among a senior group of executives, the first two existed, but the third was noticeably missing. In such cases, a structured design session would probably be the most powerful step to develop a map of the future.

BREAKTHROUGH THINKING

Data, information, and analytics are critical to the success, and even survival in some situations, of companies and nations in today's new uncertain and volatile environment. Data is the currency of the supply chain and national security. Leading companies and organizations have begun to recognize their mission critical role in planning and in execution. The breakthrough thinking principles and guidelines we include here are relatively straightforward, but it is surprising that a large number of companies and governmental agencies do not address them adequately in their strategic agendas or road maps.

CORPORATE EXECUTIVES AND POLICY MAKERS

- Treat data as a corporate and organizational asset, assure security, and mandate against keeping private data.

- Focus on data: accuracy, integrity, process, ownership, accountability, ease of entry and maintenance, and, of course, the sharing of data across organizational boundaries. This is particularly true in larger companies and governments—a rather frightening state of affairs when one considers that national security depends on sharing data.
- Define analytics: they should be ecosystem wide, easy to use and understand at the different levels, business-driven, and result in tangible enterprise outcomes.
- Ask, "What is the next technology development and supply chain application after the next one?"
- Do not accept the religion of having data "real-time, all the time, ecosystem-wide" easily. Instead, ask:
  - What will we do with such data?
  - Can we afford it (looking at the real, complete costs)?
  - What are the benefits?
  - Is it essential for our company given our industry?
  - Are there alternatives?
  - Has anybody else done it effectively?
  - And, of course, what kind of data do we really need?
- Train, upskill, and reskill employees in data management, science, and analytics.
- Technology acquisition and implementation:
  - Insist on realistic ROIs with realistic assumptions—and don't accept the cost and benefit estimates of the people putting forward the proposal of the IT department.
  - Technologies acquisition must be tied to business strategies, goals, and outcomes, and, of course, affordability.
  - Have "proofs of concept" initiatives for new technologies targeted and specified carefully in terms of benefits and costs.
  - Monitor progress based on cost and benefit projections.
  - Provide incentives for achieving benefits, cost targets, and timelines.
  - Take action against the initiative and sponsors if projected benefits don't materialize, costs overrun, and timelines go beyond scheduled.

- Develop a vision and program for the digital supply chain, using a multifunctional, "best of the best" team to design it in phases, with an MVP (minimum viable product) plan, all-inclusive and end-to-end analyses of costs and benefits, and a rigorous examination of the assumptions used. Ensure that data accuracy, business continuity, progress reporting with go-no-go decisions, and developing strong relationships with supply chain partners are at the core of the effort.

- Assign accountabilities and resources, and execute.

- The Spatial Web: Design the future with the human in the center, using a multifunctional, multilevel, multiorganizational set of design sessions. Then lay out an MVP approach to quickly and efficiently find out if an initiative is viable without significant cost or risk to execute.

The vision and program for implementing the digital supply chain—from digitization to digital transformation—requires a comprehensive plan for the enterprise and its trading partners. As discussed in the preceding chapters, effective management and understanding of customers and the supply base, timely decision-making, and matching demand and supply are completely dependent on data and information. However, making these decisions to support strategic imperatives requires far more than functional knowledge (for example, how to run a warehouse). It demands a different knowledge base, perspective, and set of capabilities. The next chapter addresses this and discusses the elements and importance of business acumen, end-to-end costs, and supply chain financing.

CHAPTER 6

Knowledge

Business Acumen, Supply Chain Finance, and Costs

Science is the father of knowledge,
but opinion breeds ignorance.
—Hippocrates (460–370 BC)

Recently, at a workshop for developing and managing talent in what was labeled as the "new supply chain environment," a senior executive laid out his requirements for a "high-impact," high-value managerial education program for his global sourcing, purchasing, and planning function.

> I have plenty of people who know all about sourcing, purchasing, and planning—buying, negotiating, doing "should cost" analysis, managing purchase price variance, and doing sales and operations planning. What I really need are people who understand the following and bake it into their decisions and analyses—the impacts on company finances and shareholder value, our longer-term financial sustainability, cost levers and working capital, our risks, as well the impacts on other functions . . . and vice versa.

Traditionally, supply chain management education and training, mainly in business and, to a lesser degree, in engineering schools, has always been compartmentalized. These schools have tended to focus on either the technical mechanics and quantitative operations research analyses (some outdated and no longer used) for the various individual supply chain functions, or, recently, the very "soft behavioral" concepts (such as generic climate change, team composition, or diversity) that may or may not have relevance to supply chain success.

Given the high profile of the supply chain these days, we now have a plethora of books and college courses focusing on these topics. They may help in understanding functional but isolated pieces of the supply chain and various quantitative approaches (for example, Little's law, process quality, economic order quantity and its extensions, optimization modeling), or provide some perspective of the Western social agenda. However, they do little to help look at the strategic picture. They rarely take an end-to-end supply chain perspective, nor do they incorporate the new and critical elements of risk and national security. Equally important, they do not address the need for managing and making decisions from an enterprise perspective in today's international, highly linked, and complex networks. In many instances it is the old problem of "not being able to see the forest for the trees."

KNOWLEDGE

The key to sustained success in today's international and complex supply chain networks is having the knowledge needed to make decisions and trade-offs (optionality is increasingly becoming more important than optimality) that are in the best short-term and long-term interests of the company. Excellence in the supply chain is driven by knowledge. Effective and high-impact knowledge in the supply chain encompasses four categories, as illustrated in Figure 6.1. The Bibliography at the end of this book provides sources that have influenced the authors, books and articles that we recommend highly for all who want to develop an understanding of the emerging geopolitical landscape, the global supply chain, international trade, and the necessary skill sets.

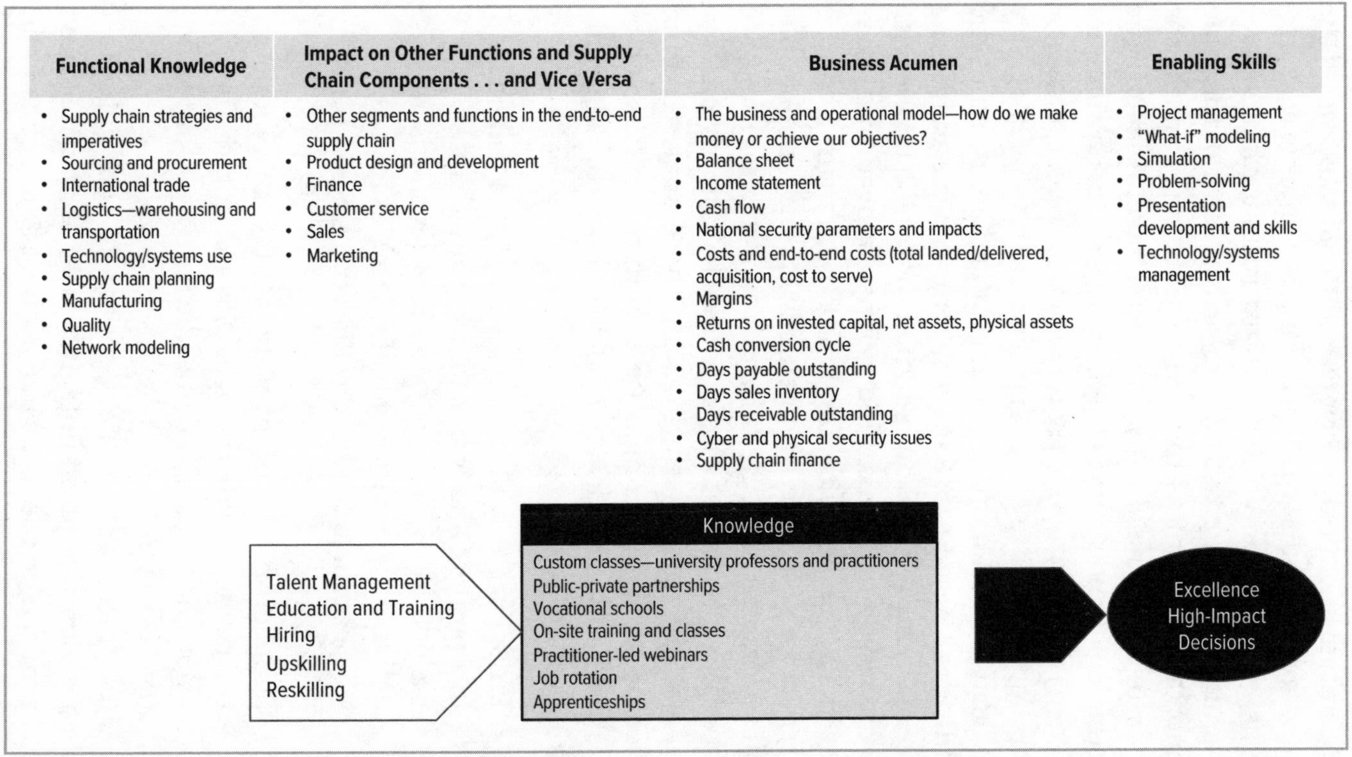

Functional Knowledge

- Supply chain strategies and imperatives
- Sourcing and procurement
- International trade
- Logistics—warehousing and transportation
- Technology/systems use
- Supply chain planning
- Manufacturing
- Quality
- Network modeling

Impact on Other Functions and Supply Chain Components . . . and Vice Versa

- Other segments and functions in the end-to-end supply chain
- Product design and development
- Finance
- Customer service
- Sales
- Marketing

Business Acumen

- The business and operational model—how do we make money or achieve our objectives?
- Balance sheet
- Income statement
- Cash flow
- National security parameters and impacts
- Costs and end-to-end costs (total landed/delivered, acquisition, cost to serve)
- Margins
- Returns on invested capital, net assets, physical assets
- Cash conversion cycle
- Days payable outstanding
- Days sales inventory
- Days receivable outstanding
- Cyber and physical security issues
- Supply chain finance

Enabling Skills

- Project management
- "What-if" modeling
- Simulation
- Problem-solving
- Presentation development and skills
- Technology/systems management

Excellence
High-Impact
Decisions

Knowledge

- Custom classes—university professors and practitioners
- Public-private partnerships
- Vocational schools
- On-site training and classes
- Practitioner-led webinars
- Job rotation
- Apprenticeships

Talent Management
Education and Training
Hiring
Upskilling
Reskilling

FIGURE 6.1 Knowledge: Excellence in the Supply Chain

The first and most obvious is *functional knowledge*—the functional skills and management techniques (e.g., sourcing, logistics, etc.). While many institutions offer courses in some of these areas, they rarely cover some of the more important elements—the end-to-end supply chain, the trade-offs that need to be made on several levels, the technologies and systems used, and the data and analytics needed. Furthermore, they tend to include concepts and techniques that are somewhat obsolete or only sparingly applicable. For example, the concept and approach to the traditional "should cost analysis" (an analysis addressing the question, What should an item or product or service cost based on materials, production, overhead, and activities?) is a *supply-oriented cost*, and often taught from the perspective of a time when supply chains were simple. Companies manufactured their own products from base materials and commodities or contracted for services that had just one service offering, and these analyses often relied on sometimes simplistic assumptions. These analyses don't address today's complex and networked supply chains where:

- Products are multidimensional—"data embedded in a product and wrapped in services." These include software, applications, order status and delivery information, and location, as well as services such as next-day delivery, tracking, and installation.
- Suppliers often design and manufacture products; the traditional methods do not account for the value chain costs of items like notebook computers, network equipment, toys, and apparel.
- Contract manufacturers, copackers, and suppliers provide assembled (integral parts) or manufactured products to the company or direct to the consumer.

- Service providers provide value-added services in addition to their primary services—for instance, major logistics providers also provide inventory, order management and fulfillment, tracking, and warehousing services.
- Companies are no longer vertically integrated, though some of the largest global players are considering a return to vertical integration (with variations including "captive" suppliers or "virtual" vertical integration) to gain control and reduce risk from their supply base (as discussed in Chapter 4).

Companies today adopt a "target" cost approach, utilizing a *market-oriented approach* and answering the question, What should the product cost in the marketplace—the supply costs, margins, elasticity of demand, total fulfilled costs, and competitor costs—where we can make the desired profit margin based on the competition and market price that customers are willing to pay for it? Instead of starting with materials and production costs and working upward, target costs start with the selling price, deduct the desired profit margin, and work backward. The challenge is to source in innovative ways so as to not exceed that target cost.

Functional knowledge is not enough—the role and impacts of individual functions must be considered from a perspective of the end-to-end supply chain, the enterprise, and the broader business environment. An ongoing danger for many companies is operations, strategy, and decision-making being conducted in organizational silos, with little regard for the impacts on other functions or supply chain stakeholders. Equally dangerous is a lack of awareness of the impact decisions made elsewhere in the organization, or in the interests of other stakeholders, have on operations. This can have serious consequences in areas such as product development and introduction, supplier sourcing and selection, and the total cost of the product. Equally important are the impacts on national security and the environment. One example of this attitude is that of a senior procurement officer for a large company who, when discussing the multiple issues involved in sourcing a component, stated, "I don't care where you get it from, as long as the cost is as good as the one from China."

Obviously, this executive had little understanding or regard for total costs of acquisition, transportation, sustained quality, schedule, lot and delivery control, supply and country risk, or national security issues. Only the minimum unit cost mattered.

Another situation occurred in a consumer products company, where the marketing department started offering next-day delivery to its online customers. Executives were surprised to learn that this involved increased inventory, expediting, and fulfillment costs. Meanwhile, the head of the supply chain was involved in implementing a lean, "just-in-time" system with low inventory, centralized distribution, and container-load shipping by ocean. The two sets of objectives did not align, and the results had significant adverse impacts on customer satisfaction, costs, and working capital. These situations are, unfortunately, by no means unique.

While these decision perspectives and impacts appear obvious as important knowledge areas, they are not enough to bridge the gap between end-to-end supply chain decision-making and business performance, impact, and sustained success. The missing link is *business acumen*—the knowledge and perspective to relate functional decisions to the critical business parameters and other functions, and to incorporate these into strategic, project, and everyday operations decision-making.

It starts with what is truly a set of fundamental questions, one that we've discovered many people in the organization cannot answer: "What are our business model and operational model, how do we make money, and what are our key supply chain imperatives to achieve this?"

Getting everybody in the organization to understand and internalize this is the responsibility of the senior staff and the chief operations officer. Failure to articulate and drive home this message leads to decisions being made at a granular functional level without relation to the real needs of the company.

One recent example was that of a CEO who announced that the company would set high sustainability goals in terms of greenhouse gas emissions and International Labour Organization (ILO) standards adherence. He then proceeded to communicate this in a series of briefings, setting the goals for the organization. However, managers in sourcing were still measured on material supply costs, and it turned out that fair trade and ILO-compliant suppliers cost a lot more than the company had paid in the past. As a result, only some sourcing managers attempted to use the new sustainability guidelines, while others maintained the same focus on minimizing the material costs and risk of disruption. Then came the Covid-19 pandemic, which led to a drop in margins. As a result, the company backed away from its aggressive sustainability goals, but the confusion and cynicism that this episode generated remains with the company employees.

The same company decided to move into e-commerce using a new product line as a spearhead. As in the earlier example, the key imperative was two-day delivery, which required inventory availability. The supply chain, however, focused on a lean supply chain paradigm targeting inventory reduction, and the conflicts regarding the different imperatives were not resolved. As a result, shortages led to poor delivery performance and margin-eating expedited shipping.

A critical aspect of business acumen is the solid understanding of the impacts of decisions on eight sets of parameters, namely:

- The balance sheet
- The income statement
- Shareholder value (driven by supply chain financial results)
- Other stakeholder values (stakeholders include employees, suppliers, channels, customers, communities, and the different governments)
- Other functions within the organization (for example, the impact of product design decisions on sourcing)
- National security
- Risk
- The local economy

However, attaining this understanding, analyzing the multiple inputs from all aspects of the environment and supply chain ecosystem, and making good decisions requires two sets of skills. One is strong analytical skills including critical thinking, which is the ability to objectively analyze and evaluate an issue and process complex information in making a decision. It includes the ability to combine functional knowledge, enterprise impacts, and strategic thinking. These skills rest on data and inputs that are free from opinions and political and social perspectives. The other critical skill set is the ability to work in cross-functional and cross-national teams in order to get multiple perspectives and disciplines involved in the analysis and decision-making processes.

Business acumen and these two skill sets require novel targeted interdisciplinary educational programs (operations, logistics, manufacturing, sales, finance, etc.) with additional focus on core data analysis, finance, risk, and national security considerations. Such programs are lacking today due to the rigidity of many academic institutions and a lack of incentives to promote interdisciplinary education and research that spans both fundamental research at early technology readiness levels (TRLs) and applied research at late TRLs. This research continuum is necessary in the new realities that corporations and governments face, and academia must rise to the occasion to emerge as an "honest broker" between the private and public sectors. This new paradigm is further highlighted in Figure 6.2.

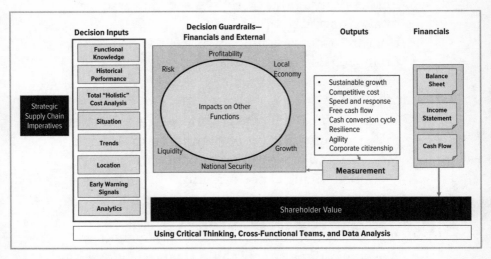

FIGURE 6.2 Business Acumen: The Decision Process

There are many inputs into a supply chain decision—whether it's strategic, project-related, or execution-related—and it's important that supply chain decisions are made using as many of these inputs as are available. However, decisions are driven by the supply chain imperatives and must stay within the decision guardrails.

DECISION GUARDRAILS

Decision guardrails encompass the parameters, limits, and imperatives driven by the supply chain strategic imperatives. They include the traditional imperatives of profitability, liquidity, and growth as well as the new imperatives of risk, local economy, and national security. The core components of these are as follows:

Profitability
- Major costs, including total costs of acquisition, total landed and delivered cost, and cost to serve
- Impact of functional activities and processes on total costs and margins
- How an income statement works
- Analyzing and improving processes
- ROI analysis across products, services, and initiatives
- Taxes, a critical but often overlooked aspect of the cost structure, driving everything from location decisions and offshoring to product investment
- Sustained financial performance

Liquidity
- How balance sheet and cash flow statements work
- Working capital, supply chain finance (the fuel that makes the engine operate)
- Cash conversion cycle and its components (payables, inventory, receivables)
- Fixed and "sticky" assets (Sticky assets are those that are believed to be variable but are not necessarily so. For example, in certain countries, it is difficult, owing to government regulations or union power, to reduce workforces to match decreasing demand.)

- Supply chain financing, including the various instruments, components of financing, trade-offs and analysis, and the financing deals with suppliers, financial institutions, and customers

Growth
- The customers' needs, wants, and priorities
- Profitable growth and cost to serve of various differentiated service offerings

Risk
- Managing inventory to ensure availability and hedge against disruption (safety stocks, emergency stocks, strategic stockpiles)
- Assessing the length and fragility of the supply chain
- Ensuring supply assurance
- Time to recovery and cost to recovery following a disruption, and what it takes to reduce them
- Sourcing—location in certain countries and regions, single sourcing, and lack of redundancy
- Guardrails for AI systems used in decision-making
- Risks of ESG-oriented disruption, particularly where these requirements (for example, greenhouse gas emissions, conflict minerals, ILO adherence, and deforestation are necessary, regulated, and mandated)
- The acquisition process and conflicts of interest
- Security processes, both physical and cyber, costs, and approaches to enhance security

Local Economy
- Impact on local jobs and small and medium-sized enterprises (SMEs)
- Social responsibility and contribution to community betterment

National Security
- Location in hostile or adversarial countries
- Sourcing with companies that are controlled by hostile foreign entities and/or state-owned enterprises (SOEs)
- Assurance of redundancy in the event of government action or disruption
- Bills of materials, sources, and "diamond" supply chains
- Sourcing in countries or with companies where intellectual property is at risk

Each of these could merit its own detailed discussion, but the scope of this book does not permit that. However, the issue of measurement and analytics is worth emphasizing. While straightforward functional performance metrics are invaluable in assessing and improving operations, leading companies take this to the next level by using *compound* (cross-functional, cross-organizational) and *holistic* (end-to-end supply chain) metrics. Business acumen includes being able to devise, read, and interpret these metrics, and then act on them.

THE MONEY SIDE: SUPPLY CHAIN COSTS, CASH, AND FINANCE

Supply chain finance, cash, and costs, as with most things in the supply chain, should be viewed from a "holistic" decision-making perspective. The supply chain is the cash and cost engine (or sinkhole!) of the company, and the costs must reflect this perspective.

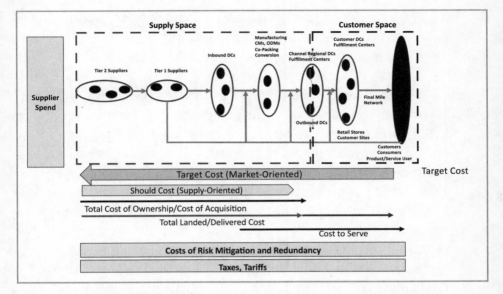

FIGURE 6.3 End-to-End Supply Chain Costs

Costs

There are eight sets of costs that span the supply chain, provide insights, and enable decision-making (further illustrated in Figure 6.3):

- Supplier spend (the money spent on supply and suppliers by component, product, commodity, and service)
- Target and "should" costs (The traditional "should" cost analysis is a supplier-focused cost; "target" cost—the cost that the company should aim for in the marketplace—is more relevant and customer-focused.)
- Total cost of acquisition/total cost of ownership
- Total landed cost/total delivered cost
- Cost to serve
- Time to value, realistic and comprehensive technology, and investment ROI analysis

- Costs of risk mitigation and redundancy, including cost to recovery following a disruption
- Taxes and tariffs across the supply chain

The hard analysis and ROI of information systems and technology (IT) are particularly important. As every executive knows, there are few IT investments that cost what the initial proposals said they would, came through in the planned time, delivered the results promised, or took any reasonable length of time to implement or integrate.

These costs include data types that have traditionally been maintained separately—financial, operational, customer, sustainability, risk, and national security—across "silos" and functional, organizational, and systems lines. This is the challenge and mandate for the IT department—obtaining the necessary data across these different data types (and probably systems) in a convenient, seamless, and timely way.

One good way for managers to think through this issue is to structure costs by three categories—customer-facing, supply-aware, and the "hidden" (or often ignored) costs. This focused approach allows decision-making by specific supply chain component while still maintaining a holistic perspective.

CUSTOMER-FACING	SUPPLY-AWARE	"HIDDEN" COSTS
• Product	• Supplier	• Overhead
• Customer	• Component	• Support (information technology, legal, finance, human resources, maintenance, etc.)
• Segment	• Location	
• Channel	• Geography	• Contractor costs
• Geography		• Part-time employee costs

Cash

There is one major set of end-to-end supply chain cash and efficiency metrics (aside from free cash flow from operations) that drives working capital management, operations efficiency, supply chain finance, and financing. This is the cash-to-cash conversion cycle (computed by the Days Sales Outstanding + Days Inventory Outstanding – Days Payable Outstanding, or DSO + DIO – DPO), one of the most important end-to-end supply chain metrics. Reducing the cash-to-cash cycle (and, hence, the needs for cash outlay and financing) requires an analysis of how to reduce its key components in a way that does not adversely impact the business.

Financing the Supply Chain

Financing the supply chain is one of the less-understood aspects of supply chain management. Historically, few alternatives existed to finance working capital and risk in the supply chain—factoring receivables, banks, and letters of credit. Today, however, advances in technology and visibility have made other, more innovative ways of financing the supply chain possible. Today's supply chain financing (which we first identified as a critical element in Chapter 4) is a series of practices and technologies that support the financial processes of an end-to-end supply chain and align the execution of trade finance instruments with the actual movement of goods and payments along the supply chain. The major methods are:

1. **Inventory financing,** which allows goods to be held in a warehouse for the buyer, usually by the seller, until needed.
2. **Reverse factoring,** which allows sellers to sell their receivables and/or drafts relating to a particular buyer to a bank at a discount as soon

    as they are approved by the buyer. (Factoring receivables is usually supplier initiated.)

3. **Invoice discounting,** where financing is made available to sellers by the buyers upon invoice approval, with full payment minus discount released upon acceptance of proposal.

4. **Purchase order–based financing,** which is made available to a seller based on a purchase order received from a buyer.

Companies are seeking to lower their costs of credit and increase the scope of their working capital using the credit ratings of their supply chain partners. Their supply chain partners are trading off days payable and receivable for margin points and other benefits, while banks are lending at better rates and terms owing to the powers of technology and transparency. The funding entities can include buyers, suppliers, banks of both buyers and suppliers, and third-party funding companies and agencies. Payments can be made at nearly any point in the order and delivery processes. Innovative thinking and analysis are key to providing the best "win-win-win" scenario for buyers, suppliers, insurance companies, and funding institutions. However, as recent cases have shown us, there is always the potential for cybercrime and fraud ("creative accounting"), whereby companies focus on the valuation of future cash flows rather than a valuation of past transactions.

THE KEYS TO INCORPORATING KNOWLEDGE AND BUSINESS ACUMEN IN THE SUPPLY CHAIN AND WIDER BUSINESS ORGANIZATION

Education in business acumen, strategy, and operations. This includes obtaining a clear picture of what's expected of the employee and the function, the strategic imperatives of the organization and how they relate to individual jobs and functions, and the benefits to employees and the corporation. Equally important is the direct line, and impacts, of major functional decisions to the business parameters, corporate financials, and key elements of the supply chain.

Education in supply chain functional knowledge, problem-solving, and strategic thinking skills. These are critical aspects of the knowledge portfolio and skill sets that are needed in today's uncertain and complex world.

Keeping an education focus on outcomes and capability. The goal is talent enhancement, upskilling, and reskilling for the benefits of the employees and the organization. These should include the "soft" skills of teamwork, motivation, analysis, and presentation skills, not just the "in vogue" classes pushing a social agenda.

Moving away from the short-term, financially driven, and share price—based compensation mindset of the past several years where we "engineered the balance sheet and income statement" to drive financial gains. This "short-termism" included decisions such as offshoring and outsourcing; sales of intellectual property (IP) and equity stakes to companies and investment houses from other (sometimes adversarial) countries; the search for the lowest unit cost (usually cost of labor); moving to low-tax countries; trading IP (and sometimes national security) for access to other markets; and implementing just-in-time supply chains with low system inventory while lengthening the supply chain. We must now move toward "engineering the supply chain" for sustained success.

Investing wisely in data and analytics from a business perspective: business-driven approaches to data and analytics, as well as assessing technology investments, return on investment, time to value, and specific outcomes.

Examining the allure of environmental, social, and governance (ESG) issues with a careful eye. ESG can become "preachy" rather than business oriented. We are, after all, here to make the company successful, have a satisfied and skilled workforce, and build a strong and resilient supply chain. We need to look at the business necessity, risks, regulation, and cost and revenue impacts of ESG initiatives.

Identification of and management to metrics. KPM stands for "key performance measures" (also called KPIs—key performance indicators) tied to outcomes, instead of "every metric we can think of." Furthermore, good business acumen dictates that single metrics are not enough and can often result in myopic and thus poor decisions. Decisions must be based on groups of complementary metrics, often with data and insights that cross organizational and sometimes even company boundaries. For example, the cash-to-cash cycle is an excellent metric—but it measures something at a specific point in time. It is far better to couple it with customer service levels/fill rates, shortages, customer retention, and supplier performance to get the bigger business picture. Inventory by itself just shows what's on the books at a given point in time; to provide effective insight, this metric must include trends, total inventory in the system, including committed inventory from suppliers, orders, in-transit pipeline inventory, at channels (with return policies), and customer demand. Similarly, revenue metrics must be combined with profitability and percentage of revenue from single customers. A critical part of this process is building these decision parameters into the performance management system—and this applies equally to senior executives who may make decisions based on their own personal preferences.

BREAKTHROUGH THINKING

The realization that knowledge—in terms of business acumen, an understanding of end-to-end costs and working capital, and supply chain finance—plays a critical role in supply chain decision-making has led to several novel and powerful approaches in today's leading supply chains. The breakthrough thinking that we have identified based on our work with leading companies, senior executives, and academic and governmental institutions is summarized in the following list.

CORPORATE EXECUTIVES AND POLICY MAKERS

- Integrate supply chain education into the core operations of the company.
- Tailor supply chain education in business acumen, end-to-end costs and levers, corporate priorities (a must), the

impacts of decisions on supply chain functions, and vice versa. Focus on the costs that matter to provide people with the "binoculars" to understand the impact of their decisions downstream and upstream in the supply chain. Some companies have centers of excellence that hire outside expertise or develop this in-house.

- Make this education and training an integral part of the skills/talent inventory part of the people development program.
- Disseminate relevant and interesting information, articles, and news on supply chain issues, trends, and international business to managers and executives.
- Implement programs for role and job rotation to increase experience and competence.
- Encourage universities to develop novel interdisciplinary, pragmatic educational modules as part of their undergraduate and graduate programs and for customized offerings to industry (eg., dual vocational programs).
- Eliminate or separate social training from the supply chain education and training curricula.

The old days of focusing on purely functional skills and specific cost elements are gone. The best management looks at the right costs, liquidity, risk, environment, and the customer. This is done holistically, and with compound metrics and analytics that allow for quick response and fast decisions aimed at sustained profitability and growth with minimum risk. The best workforce is one that is aligned with the strategic supply chain imperatives, with employees who are educated in their functions and with the necessary business acumen to make decisions in the best long-term interests of the company and its major stakeholders. Applying business acumen, supply chain finance, and an understanding of the end-to-end cost and working capital elements is a critical foundation to achieving effective and efficient supply chains. In the preceding two chapters on data, technology, and knowledge, we have examined the three most important enablers of the modern supply chain. However, in today's volatile and ambiguous environment, supply chains have to be more than "customer-centric, supply-aware, enabled by data and knowledge." They must be resilient and able to withstand an increasing number of risks, many with significant, if not catastrophic potential impacts, and must adhere to the mandates, expectations, and necessities of sustainability. The following chapter addresses the first, and probably the more critical of these two major issues—risk and resilience.

CHAPTER 7

Risk, Assurance, and Resilience

Allowance must be made for the intervention of the unexpected.
—**Winston Churchill**[1]

Supply chains have been at the nexus of globalization, exploiting the cross-border flows of goods, capital, and information. It is imperative that supply chain executives today be aware of geopolitical and macroeconomic issues—they must know the world they are sourcing from, selling into, and redesigning supply chains from end to end. Knowing about purely functional areas such as inventory management and logistics is no longer enough. Since the 1990s, and especially after the inclusion of China in the World Trade Organization (WTO) in 2001, many companies expanded their operations on an international basis. They globalized their sourcing, production, and sometimes even design to low-cost countries. Many of these companies further employed just-in-time manufacturing and supply techniques to reduce production costs and minimize inventory. China's entry into the WTO, made under Western countries' false assumptions (that were more like wish lists) and eagerness to access the potentially huge Chinese market, coupled with the Chinese national industrial policies, set the stage for mass offshoring to that country and the foundation for a large part of the supply chain risks companies and nations face today.

THE NEW SUPPLY CHAIN LANDSCAPE

While companies initially embraced offshoring as a way to reduce unit costs and, for some, to gain market access, they later took advantage of lower environmental and labor standards, lower taxes, foreign financing, and increased foreign government handouts. During this process, companies often displayed a lack of consideration for, or even deliberate ignorance of, national economic and security policies. As previously discussed, this trend was accelerated by the increasing adoption of stock price–based compensation for senior executives, a practice that sometimes encouraged short-term cost cutting, often at the expense of local jobs and communities. The integration of developed and emerging market economies into global supply chains was also supported by an array of technological (IT, logistics, containerization), institutional (lower tariffs and taxes), ideological (a belief in the neoliberal concept of free trade), financial, and structural reforms that allowed companies to invest easily in offshored factories. Consequently, global commerce increased from 39 percent of world GDP in 1990 to 58 percent in 2019, causing a boom in the international trade of intermediate goods. It should be noted, however, that in some cases offshoring has been encouraged by governments as a pillar of economic statecraft and to further increase national security. A prime example is the globalization of the semiconductors supply chains (starting in the late 1960s, first in Japan and later in South Korea, Taiwan, and Singapore) supported by the US government. Under this premise, US companies still dominate the most profitable links in the semiconductor supply chain (such as chips design and software tools for translating designs into actual chips), while the fabrication of semiconductors has mainly been outsourced in Asia where the majority of cutting-edge chips are produced by the Taiwan Semiconductor Manufacturing Co. (TSMC) and by South Korea's Samsung Electronics Co.

These trends resulted in efficient supply chains in an era when supply chains were rather simple in structure and the impacts of crises were mostly local. Today's global supply chains, however, are complex, lengthy, often concentrated, multitier, interconnected networks that are highly vulnerable to a wide range of risks and disruptions. The impacts of these disruptions can be significant. For example, the massive earthquake and tsunami in Japan in 2011 shut down a nuclear plant and had impacts beyond just Japan. The global automotive and fishing industries were the most affected. Owing to the importance of Japan in automotive manufacturing and automotive parts supply, this disruption caused supply chain shortages and delays around the world. The effects lasted several years, and, it must be remembered, Japan was a recognized leading nation in disaster preparedness.

Figure 7.1 illustrates some of the risks and challenges faced by the four major entities in the supply chain—the customer base, the supply base, the manufacturing base, and the environment these operate in. These risks across all four entities include extreme weather events, supplier disruptions, labor issues, customer buying pattern changes, cyberattacks, terrorist and activist attacks, public health emergencies, intellectual property theft, and a host of adversarial and geopolitical events.

The global financial crisis of 2007–2009 was an inflection point for supply chain executives of multinational corporations (MNCs) who began recognizing that their overextended and just-in-time supply chains located in far-away and potentially risky countries were too fragile. This, coupled with the new (at the time) needs for regionalization and faster response times to customer orders, led to a slowdown in global trade and a restructuring of the global supply chain, with a shrinkage of global trade from 61 percent in 2008 to 58 percent of global GDP in 2019, just before the Covid-19 pandemic.

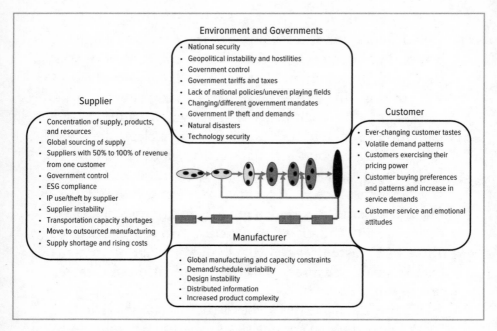

Environment and Governments
- National security
- Geopolitical instability and hostilities
- Government control
- Government tariffs and taxes
- Lack of national policies/uneven playing fields
- Changing/different government mandates
- Government IP theft and demands
- Natural disasters
- Technology security

Supplier
- Concentration of supply, products, and resources
- Global sourcing of supply
- Suppliers with 50% to 100% of revenue from one customer
- Government control
- ESG compliance
- IP use/theft by supplier
- Supplier instability
- Transportation capacity shortages
- Move to outsourced manufacturing
- Supply shortage and rising costs

Customer
- Ever-changing customer tastes
- Volatile demand patterns
- Customers exercising their pricing power
- Customer buying preferences and patterns and increase in service demands
- Customer service and emotional attitudes

Manufacturer
- Global manufacturing and capacity constraints
- Demand/schedule variability
- Design instability
- Distributed information
- Increased product complexity

FIGURE 7.1 The Complex Global Supply Chain Faces New and Increased Risks

However, many companies continued to ignore these risks given the prospects of low costs, inexpensive engineering talent, financing, and favorable regulations and market access (especially in China, where many MNCs are often "willing hostages" of the government). This was compounded by the "financialization" of the supply chain, driven by a focus on short-term financial results—operating margins, cash conversion, asset efficiency, and short-term share price increases tied to quarterly reports and executive compensation. It is not surprising then that the trend toward outsourcing and extensive offshoring to China and other Asian countries recovered and continued. This has led to the design of lean, offshored, and *fragile* global supply chains. In other words, companies often engineered the financials and the balance sheet and not the supply chain.

This became painfully evident during the Covid-19 crisis, which constituted another major inflection point for global supply chains. The global pandemic—the largest global disruption in recent history—has had a huge impact on supply chains around the world. Risk mitigation was not strong enough, and supply chains were not resilient enough, to withstand these massive disruptions and their cascading effects across all industries. Almost every industry, every nation, and every citizen were affected. Manufacturing, retail, household products, and healthcare were among the most impacted, resulting in issues such as shortages, delays, facility closings, and arbitrarily canceled contracts (which hurt mainly small companies across the globe). The supply chain lessons from the pandemic demand new structures, a move away from unfettered globalization and toward an increased emphasis on decentralization and local operations (facilitated by modular supply chain design and technologies such as 3D printing), and new practices for risk management and cost-competitive supply chain resilience well into the future.

Supply chains were brought to the forefront of the public view for the first time. They attracted the attention and scrutiny of national governments and policy makers, who often lacked an understanding of supply chains, their complexities and impacts, and their roles in national economies and security, and importantly, any "supply chain playbook." Though they are now realizing that their supply chains are important, many still do not understand completely what their supply chains are, what to do about them, or how they should engage with the private sector, which has spearheaded the development of these supply chains for the past four decades.

The Covid-19 pandemic, compounded by the war in Ukraine, the Russian weaponization of its vast energy stores and food supply chains, and Chinese belligerent actions in Asia, led to widespread customer uncertainty and drove dramatic increases in customer demand for some products, large decreases for others, and high volatility in e-commerce (with an initial huge surge followed by an expected contraction). This was accompanied by (and perhaps resulted in) consumer products demand that shifted temporally and spatially, including inflated orders leading to an increased "bullwhip" effect—where changes at the customer demand level lead to massive changes upstream to manufacturers and suppliers. Sales forecasts continued to project sales demand by regular customers and products as they did during normal times. Supply chains often lacked the flexibility to repurpose their manufacturing and supply to essential consumer products. This situation was compounded by severe disruptions in supply, loss of production capacity, and erosion of the supporting intermodal logistics networks (involving multiple modes of transport such as ocean, air, road, and rail, mainly under the auspices of fragmented local, state, and national governmental agencies). The latter manifested in clogged ports, long lines of container ships outside major ports, massive increases in the costs of ocean freight, and inefficient inland distribution hampered by a lack of trains, shortage of truck drivers, and limited warehousing space. These disruptive events, coupled with ineffective economic and energy policies, also triggered historically high inflation and drove changes in manufacturers' order patterns that further magnified the bullwhip effect. This over ordering, coupled with poor planning on the part of many companies, led to dramatic shortages of many products and commodities: a "perfect storm," one might say. The retail industry, which suffered major bankruptcies and significant damage to several prominent department store chains, was hit the hardest, as many of their products were made in China or Southeast Asia. The technology industry was impacted directly due to supply chain shortages of materials, components, and manufacturing capabilities, the last mainly from China.

During these shortages, the lack of coordinated efforts between government and industry became increasingly more pronounced, making rapid supply chain recovery and optimization difficult. These shortages also highlighted the lack of a national industrial policy, particularly in the West, that addressed national security and critical supply chains (for strategic sectors such as aerospace, microelectronics, medical devices and pharmaceuticals, rare earth minerals, and energy and agricultural resources).

BUILT TO BREAK

The title of this section, "Built to Break," is not just hyperbole. Many global supply chains have buckled and others have broken over the recent years under the new VUCA realities. The pre-2020 supply chains clearly lacked resilience, leading to shortages and rising prices of everything from medical supplies to food to consumables. However, a positive result has been that the supply chain is now part of the national discussion, with risk, resilience, and national interest forming integral parts of the corporate and national security agenda.

Supply chains and supply chain expertise have had tremendous and positive impacts on the world in terms of health, product availability, food security, industry, and the increase in the standard of living in emerging economies. However, the design of the processes and structure of these supply chains relied on nine structural pillars that supported the supply chains of the past few decades. These pillars were the construct of economists, academics, media pundits, and, yes, some executives and policy makers, who had little idea of international dynamics and how cross-border trade worked:

1. The neoliberal based premise of unfettered globalization and the seamless flow of goods and services across countries, regions, and continents.
2. A level industrial playing field, which has never existed.
3. Consistent standards across countries for labor, environment, and finance, which have never existed.
4. A belief that suppliers would remain trustworthy, stakeholders would be objective, and intellectual property (IP) was safe from suppliers, competitors, and other adversarial countries.
5. Capacity and resources decisions would be driven by economics rather than by short-term executive perspective or national interests.
6. Technology viewed as good for automating processes, not driving and changing the business.
7. Economic interdependence would prevent major conflicts. We previously heard this one in 1910, when Ralph Norman Angell's book *The Great Illusion* argued that the costs of wars had become so high as to outweigh any prospective gains. In 2006, Thomas Friedman, in his book *The World Is Flat*, argued that adversarial countries embedded in global supply chain networks would never go to war as they would then be excluded by the supply chains of leading MNCs, at a great cost to their economies.
8. Nations would not seek to weaponize the supply chain.
9. The belief that customers would not change in terms of their buying preferences, habits, emotions, and expectations.

The crumbling of these pillars, along with an avalanche of "black swan" events and geopolitical crises, has clearly revealed the flaws of these strategies and thinking. The new realities mandate a reset in the design and management of supply chain networks, accommodating a heightened interest in supply chain resilience and national security. While these disrupted or broken supply chains have affected consumers, they have also had a serious impact on national security capability.

HOW DID WE GET HERE?

There are very few men—and they are
the exception—who are able to think and
feel beyond the present moment.
—Carl von Clausewitz[2]

Von Clausewitz's observation is still relevant today and applies equally to supply chain executives and public sector leaders. However, some nations (with China as a prime example) take a "long view" in terms of industrial policy and security, a perspective that gives them an advantage in the global trade and supply chain environment. Three major sets of factors got us to this point.

The Confluence of Major Disruptive Events
The most important of these disruptive events that have exposed the "built to break" nature of global supply chain strategies include the Covid-19 pandemic, the war in Ukraine, the impacts of climate change and ESG (environmental, social, and governance) mandates, the tensions with China, and increased geopolitical instability. The new geopolitical landscape is increasingly shaped by tensions between democracies and autocracies (mainly

China and Russia), and economic tensions between allies and trading partners. While natural disasters are not new, it is estimated that pandemics will be more commonplace in the twenty-first century, and climate change has been identified as a leading cause for more frequent and severe hurricanes, tsunamis, floods, forest fires, and droughts. Over the course of the next decade, one estimate suggests that companies may face disruptions that would wipe out 30 to 50 percent of annual earnings before interest, taxes, and depreciation.

The Financialization of the Supply Chain

Financialization and "short-termism" ignored resilience and undermined national security, and to a large degree these resulted from the dogma of shareholder primacy. This perspective started its dominance in the 1980s and was amplified throughout the era of Jack Welch, the famed CEO of General Electric. It was further exacerbated by extensive deregulation, directed, at the time, at addressing the structural problems of often bloated public sectors while unleashing entrepreneurial innovation. All these drove the financialization of the supply chain, mergers and acquisitions, and monopolization of different industries. In the United States and Western Europe, stock prices were driven by earnings per share, profit margins, free cash flow from operations, and revenue growth.

This was followed by a period in the 1990s where we experienced several policies and trends that took short-termism, the financialization of the supply chain, and concentration of supply to new heights as:

- Stock options and grants became a dominant part of executive compensation.
- Globalization made cheap foreign labor, low taxes, and the potential of large foreign markets attractive.

- Governments bypassing and having minimal enforcement of antitrust regulation (e.g., the Sherman Antitrust Act in the United States).
- An increase in corporate taxes and national regulatory interventions that made doing business in many Western countries and regions unattractive.
- A lack of concerted national industrial security policies in the West, coupled with aggressive national industrial policies by other countries (especially China).

These practices resulted in supply chain strategies that drove toward lower unit costs, reducing inventory and increasing free cash flow from operations. This, in turn, led to just-in-time supply chains, minimum safety stocks, pressures on suppliers to hold inventory and increase days payables, and attempts to generate revenue by the offering of services to customers without considering the cost to serve. They also resulted in strategies to increase returns on net assets, leading to the outsourcing and offshoring of manufacturing, design, and operational capabilities. Pressures to reduce costs led to the search for low labor costs across the globe, which in turn gave rise to sourcing and manufacturing in low-cost countries regardless of risk, and sole/single sourcing dependencies with often devastating impacts on workers, communities, and national interests. Finally, industrial policies in many countries included low taxes and tariffs, which led to relocation to low-tax havens, while lack of such policies and increases in taxes by other countries, notably in the West, led to a flight of manufacturing industry eroding social cohesion.

In the process, companies gave major concessions in terms of intellectual property and supply contracts, while conforming to the offshored local government and political social agenda demands, in the hopes of market access (which rarely materialized). Companies conducted their supply chain planning without thinking much about supply chain visibility, risk, national security, impact on local economies, or environmental standards.

The consequences were enormous, leading to:

- Increased industry concentration through the acquisition of competing and startup firms, with little control by government. This has resulted in monopolistic control over platforms and distribution channels driving anticompetitive policies and raising barriers to entry.
- Foreign acquisition of critical US and EU firms and technology, with little oversight by their governments and sometimes even with their encouragement.
- "Big tech" shutting out conflicting opinions on trade and national media.
- Companies relinquishing intellectual property to foreign governments and going silent on social policies and human rights violations.
- Building up the capabilities of foreign countries, reducing the home country capability, and sending jobs to foreign countries.
- The globalization drumbeat by politicians and the media (often driven by ideology and financial gain for large multinational companies) led to consumers (with increasingly stagnating purchasing power) ignoring the source of products in favor of low cost.

Supply chain executives, supply chain stakeholders, governments, communities, and citizens are living with the effects of these consequences today.

Industrial Policies of Adversarial Nations

Adversarial nations have weaponized supply chains through mercantilism (which refers to policies of economic nationalism whose objective is to increase the prosperity and power of a nation through restrictive trade practices), through state-owned-enterprises (SOEs) dominating specific markets, and by ensuring and supporting the development of "diamond" supply chains. These manifest in diamond-shaped supply chains when at low levels in the product's bill of materials (BOM) there is a concentration of material supply. This results in the risk in one deep tier supplier threatening many intermediary suppliers and original equipment manufacturers. (A BOM is the hierarchical structure that outlines the products and other key parameters that go into making a finished product.) Effectively, these practices have led to the control of the global manufacturing and supply of certain (often critical) products and commodities, and they constitute a potent political and economic weapon. Additionally, certain countries exploited the lack of Western national industrial and security policies, the tech industry's focus on monetizing its intellectual property and conducting exit strategies to the highest bidder, and Wall Street's addiction to short-term growth to expand their global reach and capability to capture critical private, corporate, and national assets across the global supply chain. China, for example, is attempting to do this via its "debt trap" $1 trillion Belt and Road Initiative.

Much of the situation, however, is the West's own making—deliberately or through naivete. An example of government naivete and lack of forward thinking includes, as we will discuss in Chapter 8, mandates to ban gasoline-powered vehicles and promote the adoption of electric vehicles (EVs). As a result, companies are incentivized to build enormous factories to manufacture EV batteries. The huge quantities of minerals and materials (cobalt, lithium, nickel, and other rare earths) that are required will be run through global supply chains that are in danger of being controlled, by China—mainly through its own mines and refineries (with few environmental or safety standards), and in Africa, where China owns many of the mines, contracts, and distributors (another instance of a "diamond" supply chain). In short, EV sustainability policies are fast developing supply chains and a lifestyle that is poised to be disrupted in a way far greater than the pandemic. Better transparency over the environmental impact of building electric vehicles is absolutely necessary before supply chains are committed to long-term investments and structures.

Key Indicators of a Supply Chain That's Built to Break

Some of the key indicators of built-to-break supply chains are discussed in the paragraphs that follow.

The ignoring of risk and lack of risk planning and mitigation. This includes little formal risk monitoring, management, or mitigation; shortsighted sourcing policies that result in single sourcing and lack of redundancy; and reliance on a small number of suppliers controlled by a few (and some hostile) governments, often leading to "diamond" supply chains. This is amplified by a lack of adequate inventory to withstand temporary disruptions in the supply chain, brought on by the use of just-in-time systems and traditional methods of calculating and managing economic order quantities and safety stocks.

Overly complex and stretched supply chains. These supply chains, as a result of extensive offshoring and jobs being shipped overseas, have led to a reduction in manufacturing, supply chain, and R&D capability and a loss of visibility of the sources of materials and components at low levels in the product structure. Despite their increased complexity, supply chains are still perceived and managed as "deterministic" (an approach that assumes a supply chain always behaves the same and returns the same results if one uses the same equations and inputs—which is obviously unrealistic) and "functional," where the supply chain is managed as a series of "silo" functions, rather than as an end-to-end network.

Management practices with little oversight on labor and environmental issues, leading to potential erosion of brand equity and sales, an acute focus on social agenda rather than on the basics, and a focus on exerting power on governments to change laws or maintain the status quo.

In this environment, industry executives are often either unaware of or unconcerned about national interests and security considerations, while on the other side, governments do not recognize the true risks and are struggling to develop policy and supply chain playbooks. Policy makers, along with the media and the general public, are now realizing that supply chain resilience should be an "enduring national priority" and is a "burning platform" for the United States, the European Union, and several allied countries, and that many companies, usually unknowingly, work against the national interest because key parameters of national security are often absent from executive decision-making on sourcing, location, and financing.

What is less often realized is that major disruptions in certain products and materials can bring countries and economies to their knees. It must be realized that there is no "one size fits all" solution for supply chains, that global supply chains require lengthy time periods to transform, and, most importantly, that supply chains are not easily built or modified for resilience without a change in executive priorities and governmental policies. What's more, they often demand cooperation between the public and the private sector.

To summarize, global supply chains were designed well enough to provide huge benefits to the world economy, health, food supply, and standards of living in a period when supply chain risks did not raise their heads. However, driven by short-termism, several false expectations about globalization, and lack of supply chain playbooks by many Western governments, supply chains became fragile. As new frictions surfaced, it became evident that some supply chains were resilient enough to survive, others were designed well enough to thrive, but a number did buckle and break.

SUPPLY CHAIN RISK MANAGEMENT AND MITIGATION

Risk is one of the two most highly discussed issues in today's board, industry, government, and national security circles (the other being sustainability). Even before 2020, leading multinationals had recognized that managing supply chain risks is necessary for their sustained competitiveness. As firms incorporated global sourcing strategies, integrated contract manufacturing relationships, moved closer to the customer, and dealt with an increasing number of events that caused supply chain disruption, managing risk in the supply chain became a necessity and a critical competency. To this end, the focus of supply chain risk management (SCRM) has been on avoiding disruption or reducing its impact and shortening the recovery time and cost after a disruptive event—assuming that the disruptive event is not catastrophic.

As illustrated in Figure 7.2, the impacts of supply chain risks on a company's financial results can be mitigated and reduced through SCRM strategies and monitoring, and reduced even further if some risks are planned for and avoided. The impacts of a major supply disruption can linger for a long time until the point when the company or nation gets alternative sources of supply or substitute materials.

Risk mitigation demands appropriate levels of investment, asking, Can we minimize the spend and maximize our ability to avoid or recover from disruptive events? Investing in risk mitigation strategies must be done in a measured and structured fashion. Some of these investment areas can involve a significant set of costs, including the costs of redundancy in supply, suppliers, manufacturing capacity and plants, hedge inventory, and the need for close to 100 percent availability in areas such as defense and pharmaceuticals, along with diversifying supply sources away from high-risk countries. However, risk mitigation also includes additional costs that some companies fail to consider, such as costs related to redesigning a product to eliminate commodities from high-risk areas and countries, periodic and continuous risk monitoring, the costs of supply chain financing to develop tighter relationships with suppliers and assure supply, and forward buying capacity and resources when the probability of risk increases. Some companies are adopting "back to the basics" strategies: for example, structuring arrangements to share capacity with other companies, and looking at vertical integration or "virtual" vertical integration. After all, nothing comes free, and the trade-offs of the benefits of SCRM versus additional costs should be assessed carefully.

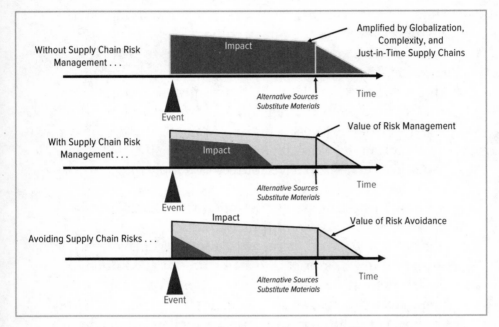

FIGURE 7.2 The Impact of Supply Chain Risk Management

The Different Types of Risk

Businesses face different types of supply chain risks on a global level. At a high level, there are seven types of risks faced by supply chains, each composed of several sub-risk elements: financial, regulatory, geopolitical, health and environmental crises, strategic, and operational risks. A detailed listing of many of these risk elements with examples is presented in Table 7.1.

TABLE 7.1 Examples of Supply Chain Risks

RISK ELEMENTS	EXAMPLES
Natural disasters	Earthquakes, floods, tsunamis, volcanoes
Health/environmental	Spills, leakages, toxic releases
Corporate social responsibility, regulations, and expectation	Conflict minerals, bribery and corruption, international labor standards, child and slave labor
Hostile countries	Conflicts, blockades, supply shutoffs and disruptions (e.g., for rare earths, grains, and other minerals)
Government regulations and policies	Antidumping, local content, taxes, tariffs, duties, market protection, environmental regulations
Loss of intellectual property	IP theft, lack of IP protection laws, government mandates
Security and cybercrime	Loss of data, loss of trade secrets, hacking, malware
Political changes	Changes in governments, political shifts, instability
Data center outage—IT	System shutdown—multiple reasons
Delivery/transportation problems	Shipping disruptions, local regulations, carrier issues, lead time increases, capacity shortages
Physical security	Cargo theft. Each logistics step—transportation, containers, and distribution centers—poses a risk of theft. This drives up the costs of insurance, risk premiums, and costs to make up for the thefts.
ERP—IT	ERP system breakdown, inaccurate data, loss of data
Currency	Currency fluctuations
Labor issues	Strikes, unrest, go-slows
Suppliers	Price increases, quality issues, bargaining power, loss of control, loss of flexibility of response, supplier financial and business issues, supplier nonconformance and lack of adherence

(continued)

TABLE 7.1 Examples of Supply Chain Risks (*continued*)

RISK ELEMENTS	EXAMPLES
Manufacturing	Quality, equipment failures, outsourcing, and loss of control and flexibility
Inventory—new products and product changes	Obsolete, rapid cost declines, shrinkage
Legal and customs compliance	Wrong or incomplete documentation and global trade compliance
Product liability claims	Product issues
Product integrity	Product content and quality, conflict minerals
Commodity situation and supply prices	Changes in prices; commodity shortages
Major customer loss	Major contract loss, market loss, customer demands for sustainability
Corporate citizenship	Jobs, value-added, local taxes, environment
Internal company risks	Engineering changes, poor planning

Strategic Sourcing and Risk Dimensions

Strategic sourcing is probably the supply chain function whose decisions deal with the greatest number of major risks. In the past, companies developed good strategic sourcing plans and were able to deal with chronically occurring risks to deliver results reliably. However, the type, scope, and severity of today's risks are far greater, and their impacts can be "make or break." Sourcing risk dimensions span various geographies and BOM echelons. In developing a sourcing strategy for a product or commodity, an effective approach should be to address these in a well-structured hierarchical fashion.

First: Geography or Country

This refers to the locations where we are considering using suppliers and contract manufacturers, or where the commodities come from. The major risk components of the geography or company analysis include:

- Political: regime, stability, consistency, predictability, social cohesion, customs and barriers, unions and strikes, human rights violations
- Legislation: new and revised laws, environmental directives and mandates (e.g., material composition rules such as RoHS, REACH), local permit laws
- Criminal: terrorism, vandalism, corruption, organized crime, theft and fraud, intellectual property theft
- Government-sponsored intellectual property theft and extortion as a price of doing business or getting market access
- Economic: currency and exchange rates, interest rates, inflation, taxes and tax relief, growth
- Resources: education and STEM skills, engineers, technicians, labor fluctuation (labor retention rate), unemployment rate
- Infrastructure: intermodal transportation (truck, train, air, ship, barge); logistics industry and reverse logistics; condition of infrastructure; consumables supply (energy, water, telecommunication); data transfer accuracy, reliability, security of systems
- Natural disasters: earthquakes, landslides, floods, tsunamis, droughts, hurricanes, wildfires, volcanic activities, diseases and pandemics

Second: Risks Associated with Raw Material, Components, and Commodities

The major components of assessing the risks associated with raw material, components, and commodities include:

- Country of origin: country risks
- Sourcing: single source; sole source (single supplier, particular country/region); customer-directed source
- Host government dominating control of supply and capability (the "diamond" supply chain), minerals, materials
- Supply constraints: demand, limited availability of resources, capacity constraints and flexibility, supply capability for end of production, and end of life
- Price volatility: commodity price, exchange rate
- Quality issues: reliability, purity
- Environmental and social issues: conflict minerals, worker exploitation, environmental degradation
- Limited availability of qualified, credible, and low-risk sources
- Technology: unique technology needs depending on specific material or manufacturing process

Finally: The Risks Associated with the Supplier Under Evaluation

The major components of assessing the risks associated with suppliers include the following:

- Organizational risks: structure, communication flows, interactions, subcontractor management, mergers and acquisitions or spin-offs
- Capability risks: adequate facilities, adequate equipment, qualified resources, after-sales service,

manufacturing flexibility, SCRM practices and playbooks
- Technology risks: ability to handle required technology, R&D capabilities, support and services available in surrounding area (universities, vocational educational programs, etc.)
- Degree of dependence on competitors
- Degree of control by adversarial governments
- Capacity constraints: manufacturing space, status of equipment
- Quality system: product quality, certified quality processes, other certifications
- Financial and credit ratings
- References: customers' and industries' reputation; well-known in the market, firsthand experiences
- Sustainability: compliance with social, environmental, and International Labor Organization (ILO) standards; audit performance; and first-tier and sub-tier ESG records

Not all of these components will be relevant or significant in assessing risk in every company or supply chain. But they are all important and must be considered and tracked as part of the supply analysis.

RISK ASSESSMENT MITIGATION AND MANAGEMENT: A STRUCTURED APPROACH

Companies must adopt a measured, structured, multifunctional, and multiorganizational approach to managing risk. Relying on media headlines, opinion pieces, or executives vested in the status quo is a good way to distort what is actually happening and what could actually happen. It is always worthwhile recalling von Clausewitz, on war and battle: "All action takes place, so to speak, in a kind of twilight, which, like fog or moonlight, often tends to make things seem grotesque and larger than they really are."

Too many companies use an "it won't happen again" or "let's hope for the best" approach, or worse, a knee-jerk response to something. An indicative structured approach—a Supply Chain Risk Assessment and Mitigation Framework that we, the authors, have used in our collective extensive engagement with industry—is shown in Figure 7.3. It encompasses five distinct stages.

Stage 1: Map the Supply Chain(s) from the Point of First Supply

Understanding and mapping the entire supply chain(s) in a company is a critical first step in identifying, managing, and mitigating risk. Many companies stop their mapping of their supply lines at Tier 1 suppliers. This is not because of the extra effort involved (which is indeed significant) so much as because many companies simply do not see the need to do so. At the national security level, this flaw can prove disastrous, because real dangers lie toward the bottom of the bills of materials for critical products (such as pharmaceuticals, semiconductor chips, weapons systems, and food). It is at this level that adversarial countries control the supply of everything from ascorbic acid to passive electronic components. The supply chain(s) mapping—plural because most companies have more than one supply chain—must include location, capacity, products made and stored, transportation modes, flows, times, and costs. The good news is that today there are several automated tools that can help in this process. Once completed, this mapping becomes a "living" document that changes with strategy and structure. Equally important,

Supply Chain Risk Assessment, Mitigation Strategy, and Plan

- Understand the risk environment.
- Identify risks and critical processes.
- Quantify likelihood and business impacts.
- Develop risk mitigation strategies and recover capability—structural, process, contracts, technology.
- Identify key risk indicators.
- Establish partners—internal, end-to-end supply chain, and ecosystem.
- Prioritize options.
- Develop and assess business cases for the risk mitigation options.
- Develop implementation road map based on priorities.

Map the Supply Chain(s) from the Points of First Supply

Risk Mitigation and Implementation

- Incorporate risk management into the organization's process, technology, and organization structure.
- Develop contingency plans.
- Assign responsibilities.
- Develop and implement communication and training programs.
- Implement phased plan with priorities:
  - Supply
  - Manufacturing
  - Logistics

Risk Monitoring and Control

- Identify third-party monitoring providers and arrange for risk monitoring and key risk indicator reports.
- Monitor actual performance (versus expected) of key risk indicators and trends:
  - Real-time
  - Periodic
- Develop control plans to handle emergency situations.
- Reevaluate risk probabilities, impacts, and sources.

Recalibrate—Revise or Maintain Status Quo

FIGURE 7.3 Supply Chain Risk Assessment and Mitigation Framework

189

it can visually provide insights into risks, flows, customer service improvement, and cost reduction opportunities.

Stage 2: Supply Chain Risk Assessment, Mitigation Strategy, and Plan

Supply chain risk assessment and developing and implementing the mitigation strategy and plan are the critical parts of the process—the hard thinking that goes into:

- identifying the potential risks across all dimensions,
- the range of likelihoods of occurrence, and
- the range of impacts on the business if they were to occur today.

Not all risks leading to supply chain disruptions are the same. Executives would be well served by viewing them in the following categories. The *known-known* include risks of which we are fully aware, have a good idea of their likelihood of occurrence, and can plan for in advance. For example, typhoons impact suppliers in Southeast Asia every summer, and hurricanes disrupt the oil and gas industry clustered in the US Gulf Coast every hurricane season. The *known-unknown* are those risks that we know exist but can't accurately quantify their potential impact: for example, earthquakes in Japan. Finally, the *unknown-unknown* include "black swan" events leading to disruptions (also known as "novel risks"); we do not know what can happen, when it might happen, and what the impact will be. The Covid-19 pandemic is a prime example of the unknown-unknown category.

Equally important in this process is defining the true source of the high-impact risks—the source being more than just a commodity or country. Sources can span countries, manufacturing sites, suppliers, supplier sites, supplier hubs, commodities, and materials. To address this, executives and planners need (1) the key risk indicators that will alert them when something is happening, the current situation has changed, and the risk probability is increasing (or decreasing); (2) the available options for mitigating these risks, their costs and impacts; and (3) an implementation road map, with timelines that can range from "urgent and immediate" to "phase in gradually" to "do nothing for now but monitor the situation."

One method, adopted in different variants by many companies to start developing risk mitigation strategies, is to categorize risks by likelihood (probability of occurrence) and impact, as illustrated in Figure 7.4.

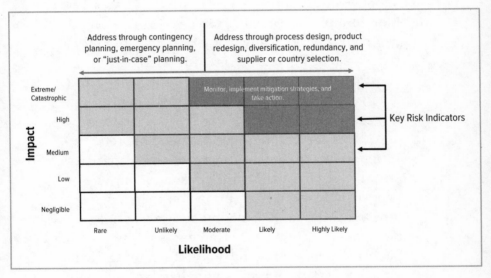

FIGURE 7.4 Mapping Risks

The risk mitigation strategies and options are intuitively sound The hard work comes in determining the scope, extent, and phasing of these strategies. For those we choose not to implement at the moment (for low-probability, low-impact risks), we must decide whether we have some just-in-case options and key risk indicators that trigger Plan B, and anticipate the costs associated with each strategy and option. These strategies and options cover five aspects of the supply chain and include:

- **Product design** to remove commodities and materials at risk.
- **Process design** to incorporate risk and national security issues into the acquisition, sourcing, financing, and inventory processes.
- **Sourcing strategies** that involve redundancies in terms of assets and capacity, reshored and "friend-shored" operations, and diversification in terms of suppliers and supplier countries.
- **Monitoring, and planning for, risks.** This would begin with periodically or continuously monitoring risks (depending on the risks involved), often using third-party services; developing contingency and emergency plans for certain low-probability, high-impact risks; and taking "just-in-case" actions (e.g., build certain in-house or friend-shored supplier capabilities, contract for surge capacity, etc.). Effective planning includes modeling the supply chain in a dynamic fashion to manage flows, capacity, and deployment. For example, deployment can include strategies such as a "China plus one" policy—having duplicate manufacturing outside of China—and "regionalization"—locating duplicate manufacturing facilities in different key geographical regions or countries. Such modeling, coupled with improved end-to-end supply chain planning and execution based on end-to-end visibility (which should, ideally, include visibility into second- and third-tier suppliers), can be

powerful in terms of developing and revising supply chain strategy.

- **The most basic of risk mitigation strategies— increase in hedge inventory** to guard against disruptions and slowdowns. Supply availability should be planned based on ranges of service levels and lead times of critical products and components that demand near-100 percent availability. It is again wise to remember that one size does not fit all.

Risk assessment and mitigation must be a multifunctional exercise across the enterprise. Equally important is the recognition of the fact that much of it is subjective, based on experience and knowledge of the end-to-end supply chain and the environment. For instance, here are some guidelines based on our experience. Risks are first identified by a combination of executives and outside experts and advisors—often through structured questionnaires and interviews. The results are then collated and aggregated, Delphi-style (a structured iterative process used to arrive at a group opinion or decision by surveying a panel of experts), up to the top-line brand level, to obtain the best estimates based on experience and expertise. Individual supplier risks, supplier site risks, and commodity risks, on the other hand, should be evaluated by a council of supply executives, country managers, and outside expert advisors based on an enterprise and/or a local view, depending on the risk being evaluated. The monitoring of these risks could be periodic or continuous, depending on the specific risk, using third-party service providers and in-house resources.

Stage 3: Risk Mitigation and Implementation

Much of risk mitigation and implementation is organizational and cultural, starting with incorporating the risk management method, approach, and critical value into the organization. As with all major initiatives that become part of the ongoing business process of the organization, responsibilities must be assigned, and a structured change management program built upon communication, training and feedback, and transparency must be developed and executed.

Stage 4: Risk Monitoring and Control
Risk monitoring and control is typically done using third-party risk assessment services and in-house experts, focusing on key risk indicators and subjective evaluations of the situation. Reporting is generally divided between a few specific indicators of risks and aggregate weighted average ratings based on key parameters of the risk. Equally important is the decision about which risks should be monitored periodically (and at what periodicity), and which should be monitored continuously. It is as much a consideration of information overload as it is of cost.

Stage 5: Recalibrate
Situations change, whether they are risks, supply, supplier, country, logistics, or customer- and government-induced scenarios; some situations can be in a constant state of flux. It is critical to monitor, recalibrate, reassess business impact and investment cases, and revise strategies if and when required.

WHAT IS SUPPLY CHAIN RESILIENCE?

We titled this chapter "Risks, Assurance, and Resilience." We have discussed risks, their assessment, and mitigation. Let us now address supply chain resilience.

Contrary to what is often reported, supply chain resilience is not something ambiguous. Rather, it refers to the adaptive capability of the supply chain to prepare for unexpected events and then quickly adjust to sudden disruptions that can negatively affect supply chain performance. This includes recovering quickly to its pre-disruption state, or even exploiting the situation to grow and increase customer service, market share, and financial performance.

There are a few other terms that often used, sometimes (and incorrectly) interchangeably, and can create additional degrees of confusion. *Stability* refers to the ability of the supply chain to return rapidly to a predisturbance state when limited-scope shocks cause disruptions to specific functions in the supply chain. *Robustness*, unlike resilience, is the ability of a system to withstand most disruptive events without any noticeable impact or adaptation. A robust system is more expensive to operate and does not possess the flexibility, agility, and adaptability of a resilient system.

The resilience life cycle includes the proactive planning of preparedness measures (e.g., diversified sourcing, risk mitigation inventories) and reactive measures (e.g., detection, response, and recovery), as shown in Figure 7.5. An important component of this is continual learning along three dimensions—the risks themselves and their impacts on the supply chain and financials, business impact and investment analysis, and the effectiveness of various mitigation strategies.

Achieving a degree of supply chain resilience requires several capabilities. The most important of these include the following:

- **Processes and structure (supply chain network) to enable agility and responsiveness.** Supply chains

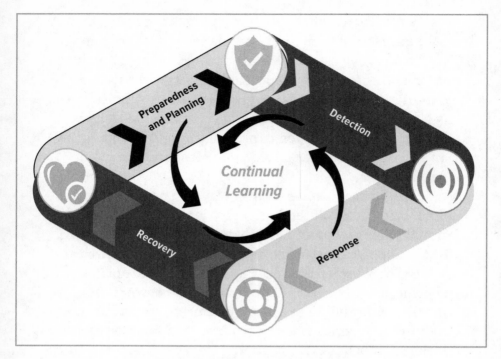

FIGURE 7.5 Resilience Life Cycle

must be able to respond rapidly to changed and changing conditions.

- **End-to-end supply chain integration, transparency, and visibility.** This enables executives to monitor the supply chain in as near real time as possible (or financially justifiable). The post-2020 crises resulted in some companies frantically conducting laborious supply chain mappings on paper to check relationships, products, commodities, and flow from "suppliers' suppliers to customers' customers" to identify vulnerabilities across the multiple tiers of the supply chain.
- **Redundancies,** which include emergency stockpiles, safety stocks, and inventory across the

supply chain (raw material, work-in-progress, and the final product) and diversified sourcing with nearshored, friend-shored, or reshored suppliers. This is critical when we look at national security considerations. The nearby and/or trusted suppliers will help ensure business continuity when there are disruptions of supply from offshore suppliers. Supply chain resilience is strengthened by increasing inventory levels, adding manufacturing and/or storage capacity to improve manufacturing surge capability, and increasing the number and ensuring the surge capability of suppliers of key materials or work-in-progress to mitigate potential supplier disruption.

- **Collaboration,** trust, and harmonization of private and public supply chain stakeholders often manifesting in the form of public-private partnerships.

- **Not forgetting about the small but critical stuff.** Companies and nations often tend to lose sight of low-volume or low-profile materials and components that become important only when they are unavailable in a shortage situation. For example, at a corporate level, this could mean not keeping track of semiconductor supply in high-end electronics, while at a national level, this could involve ignoring lower-end chips (memory or analog chips) in a national semiconductor policy.

- **Effective, data-driven integrated business process planning** with end-to-end supply chain visibility, and using technology and optimization for advanced planning. For instance, digital twins of the supply chain for war-gaming, stress-testing, and artificial intelligence for the conduct of "what-if" analyses.

Some of the most impactful key performance indicators (KPIs) for supply chain resilience are listed here.

- **Time to recovery (TTR):** The time for a supply chain node in the network to be restored to full functionality after a disruption. The TTR metric can include the critical resources involved in the supply chain—for example the time it takes inventory levels of the entire supply chain to return to normal, lost revenue and total supply chain costs.
- **Time to survive (TTS):** The maximum time that the supply chain can operate matching supply with demand after a disruption. Relevant measures include shortages, fill rates, and expediting costs.
- **We can use TTS and TTR in combination.** If TTS is greater than TTR, the supply chain is considered resilient. TTR and TTS can both be used to identify bottleneck suppliers. They were both introduced by David Simchi-Levi[3] for using supplier risk exposure while, very importantly, avoiding the need to estimate the likelihood of a disruption. Next, we add to the list by recommending two additional important KPIs to capture the costs to recovery.
- **Cost to recovery:** The total costs required for the supply chain or a node in the supply chain to be restored to full functionality after it has been disrupted. Example of costs include total supply costs and alternate supply and fulfillment costs.
- **Leverage for risk mitigation initiatives:** Defined as the following ratio:

$$\frac{\text{(Risk exposure before reduction} - \text{Risk exposure after reduction)}}{\text{Cost of Risk Reduction Initiative}}$$

Examples of costs of risk reduction include the investment in the initiative over a reasonable time period, the revenue impacted, along with the impacts on costs, working capital, and supply.

NEXT-GENERATION, DATA-DRIVEN COST-COMPETITIVE RESILIENCE

Risk mitigation strategies can be expensive. Competitive advantage will result if a firm's supply chain resilience and agility are identical to those of the competition, but at a lower cost. A new paradigm for estimating and assessing cost-competitive resilience is necessary now more than ever for companies to redesign their supply chains for the long term in light of today's VUCA environment. While traditional SCRM techniques worked well in the relatively stable environment of the past, supply chains should have the posture to bounce back as quickly as possible after "black swan" events (low-probability high-impact events).

A resilience portfolio is often based upon high levels of redundancies, resulting in higher costs and financing. As a result, executives have often resisted these redundancies. Despite all the hype about stakeholder capitalism (for example, the Business Roundtable's Statement of August 19, 2019, in which the most prominent CEOs advocated a shift from shareholder to stakeholder priorities), existing performance measurement systems and compensation schemes of senior executives have not changed, and this hinders the adoption of risk mitigation strategies.

Collaboration, alignment, and systems thinking—which avoids disconnects across the supply chain—are critical toward the new demands for cost-competitive resilience, speed, and agility. The Aristotelian reminder that "the whole is greater than the sum of its parts" should act as a guide to how we need to rethink developing resilient supply chains.

The strongest synergies from across the links of the supply chain result when the links work not only for their own best interest, but also for the best interest of the entire network. This requires developing a strong business case and selling the value proposition to supply chain partners in the ecosystem.

Here is an example of these synergies: Unilever has developed deep connections with its employees, communities, supply chain partners, and governments. Within days of the Covid-19 pandemic–induced lockdowns, Unilever was able to reconfigure its supply chains to source and ship medical equipment, and increasing the production of hand sanitizer by 14,000 times.

Data-Driven Supply Chains

Resilience can be further enhanced through reorienting the supply chain network by redesigning products for modular production, revising manufacturing processes, and relocating capacity and storage. Lean and just-in-time supply chains that focus on minimizing cost may be unable to effectively respond to and recover from unexpected and disruptive events. A dynamically resilient data-driven supply chain network can quickly detect such changes and respond to and recover from them by making the necessary adjustments in capacity, stocking location, expediting, substitution, and communications to customers. Rebalancing inventories in real time based on real-time data is now possible owing to transparency, process automation, and the use of advanced technologies such as artificial intelligence. Increasing the speed with which one can access real-time data and obtain managerial insights, either on the demand or the supply side, then becomes a key source of competitive advantage by enabling a company to be more responsive to a supply chain disruption. The promise of artificial intelligence/machine learning (AI/ML) systems is that they can further learn on their own to become more efficient, smarter, and faster in data collection and task performance through reinforcement learning algorithms. The next generation of such technology will fuse more advanced automation (AGI/ML and robotics) with tools that allow human-to-machine collaboration (cobots), thereby increasing resilience and speed of response even further.

A point to note: as real-time data and machine action take on a more prominent role in the control and management of supply chains, the importance of cybersecurity grows exponentially, as does the necessity of oversight into all aspects of information technology outsourcing. Resilience then refers also to the ability to guard and respond to cyber threats from the competition, nefarious agents and adversarial governments alike.

The Role of Supply Chain Mapping, Visibility, and Transparency

Resilience and rapid response to disruptive events hinges on end-to-end supply chain visibility. It is imperative to be able to view products, work in progress, components, and materials from a supplier's suppliers to customers and the end consumer. While visibility is important, real-time visibility is even more powerful. The Covid-19 pandemic emphasized the lack of visibility in critical supply chains to many executives and policy makers, as it prevented them from matching supply with demand. Recent developments in technology, such as control towers, 5G networks, and the Internet of Things, can enhance near real-time visibility on the factory floor and across the supply chain. Real-time visibility can then identify rapidly changing bottlenecks and break points across the supply chain;

provide accurate estimates of shipment and volumes, both of which are essential inputs in risk management planning and execution; and allow for expediting and real-time repositioning of inventory to avoid critical "hot spots" or to meet an emergency need.

Real-Time Visibility

The availability of technology to provide visibility raises the question, Why do many supply chains still lack near real-time visibility and transparency?

It all comes down to cost, capability, and trust.

First, such solutions are costly in terms of systems, integration, process design, and implementation, and in many instances, there may be no business case compelling enough to warrant such investments. Information system acquisition and implementation usually cost a lot more and take a lot longer to successfully implement than projected.

Real-time visibility may be nice, but in many cases, it is not necessary for all products and supply chains. Additionally, some companies lack the resources and the expertise to work with supply chain partners to synchronize their flows and address issues of interoperability. Logistics networks are often a major bottleneck; the bulk of intermodal logistics networks (where a shipment uses multiple modes of transport such as airfreight and trucking) still employ old "legacy" technology (ERP-driven), which is difficult to integrate with and can result in data errors. Furthermore, the rate of adoption of new standards in the industry, such as those employing application programming interface (API) from the Dutch-based Digital Container Shipping Association, is still very low. APIs, as opposed to the anachronistic EDI, supports real-time data exchange and has the potential to attain real-time visibility and unleash significant customer-centric innovations in the ocean freight industry.

Finally, many organizations are reluctant to exchange data, as they fear that data exchange will lead to security vulnerabilities and transparency while undermining their competitive advantage.

PUBLIC POLICY AND SUPPLY CHAIN RESILIENCE

There are a number of ways in which public policy issues are tied to supply chain resilience.

Shortening the Supply Chain

The dangers and risks of extended supply chains, and particularly those extended into adversarial countries, are now obvious. Over the last few years, there has been increased pressure and a movement toward diversifying and bringing supply chains of critical medical and high-added-value technological products back to the United States and Europe—a trend referred to as reshoring (transferring manufacturing back from other countries to the home country), nearshoring (transferring manufacturing back from other countries to close surrounding countries of the home country), and friend-shoring (transferring or locating manufacturing in allied or friendly countries). This push for reshoring is clearly demonstrated by the $280 billion CHIPS and Science Act in the US to develop domestic semiconductor manufacturing capacity, and the EU's plans to invest $43 billion in its own semiconductor industry. Another policy initiative toward reshoring involves the North America Free Trade Agreement and its update, the US-Mexico-Canada free trade agreement, which went into effect in 2020.

Given the variations in product complexity, labor content, and technology, 100 percent reshoring is clearly not the answer. The choice for companies and policy makers, however, is not an "either/or"—rather, it is a well-thought-out combination of home country, offshoring, insourcing, and outsourcing. The trade-off is risk versus competitiveness.

Impact on National Security

In Chapter 4, we discussed the weaponization of the supply chain and the resulting "diamond" industry supply chains. Products of critical importance to defense, security, health, and national competitiveness require national governments to take a special interest in their supply chains. Such products include rare earth metals, artificial intelligence, autonomous and "intelligent" vehicles, hypersonic weaponry, 5G technology, semiconductors, antibiotics and pharmaceuticals, synthetic biology, specialized medical equipment, food, and energy.

The Diamond Supply Chain— The Hidden Supply Risks

Diamond supply chains for critical industries, minerals, chemicals, and components pose significant threats to companies and nations. It becomes an issue of supply, assurance, and capacity and demands the following from companies and governments.

End-to-End Supply Chain Perspective

An end-to-end supply chain perspective on industrial policy that includes tier 1, 2, and 3 suppliers, at least. Discussions of reshoring, nearshoring, and friend-shoring of manufacturing often omit two major issues. The first is the question of supply: if essential materials, ingredients, components, or minerals must be sourced from non-allies, there is not much use in bringing manufacturing or final assembly nearby. Second, supply chain, engineering, technical, and manufacturing skills are critical to manage the supply chain. Without addressing the development of this talent, it does not make much sense to restore manufacturing locally.

Deciding on Critical Materials and Supply Chains

Deciding which materials and supply chains are to be deemed "critical" cannot be restricted to just overall end products or a few components. There must be a rigorous method to assessing this, determining vulnerability, sourcing, capacity, structuring, and the time to execute. The Center for a New American Security's project on Securing America's Critical Supply Chains (part of their US National Technology Strategy project) has developed a framework that helps determine these critical supply chains, with one of the key goals being the identification of the supply chains "where known vulnerabilities pose excessive risks to a country's well-being."[4] This is a landmark project but still appears to narrowly define "well-being" as defense-related, addressing strategic and critical materials, innovation, talent, cybersecurity, manufacturing technologies, and small businesses.

While necessary, this is not enough. The approach must be broadened to include the supply chains (including products, capabilities, and materials) that impact health (PPEs, antibiotics, active pharmaceutical ingredients), food, renewable energy products, aircraft, and automobiles, among others. Equally important, this analysis must go to the bottom of the bills of material for every critical product and system.

Location of Supply

Given that some allies are long-standing while others are temporary, and that the definition of a "trusted trading partner" can change dynamically over time, we are faced with the question as to how do we decide on whether to reshore, nearshore, or friend-shore, or to embrace some combination of the three. Scenario planning, simulation, and cost analyses by supply chain experts are excellent ways to address this issue.

Understanding the True Impact of Diamond Supply Chain Disruptions

Critical supply chain disruption causes a cascading effect of industry disruptions. For instance, the semiconductor supply shortage that started in 2020 impacted industries from automobiles to communications. A stoppage of semiconductor supply (a major disruption) would have far worse effects. For a start, the primary industries affected would include automobiles, heavy trucks, aircraft, computers, consumer electronics, weapons systems, networking, guidance and navigation, construction equipment, and industrial machinery. These would, in turn, impact the secondary and tertiary industries such as freight, maintenance and services, tourism, retail, construction, manufacturing, petroleum products, media, toys, food, and the operations of infrastructure (traffic lights, signals, air traffic control, etc.). Quantifying this impact on the economy is a mind-numbing exercise, with one conclusion being that a semiconductor supply disruption (e.g., due to a blockade of Taiwan by China, disrupting the supply by the Taiwan Semiconductor Manufacturing Co., which in 2023 accounted for roughly 90 percent of the world's super-advanced computer chips) could bring the economy and part of the national security capability to a standstill.

Similar scenarios could be built for food, pharmaceuticals, medical equipment, and supplies. For example, carbon dioxide (CO_2), a potent greenhouse gas, is also a necessary component of food production and is widely used in the food and beverage industry. A recent shortage of CO_2 seriously affected multiple aspects of food production and supply, from meat suppliers to pizza makers to beer. Major producers in the United States and the United Kingdom had to search for supplies to prevent shortages. This carbon dioxide shortage, as simple as it sounds, has the potential to be amplified across industries and the food supply. Additionally, China now controls most of the production of the world's antibiotics—posing a serious threat to all countries should this supply be cut off for political or quality reasons.

Key Factors in Determining Critical Supply Chains

The competitiveness, resilience, and security of critical supply chains, along with the cultivation of a national manufacturing ecosystem of small to medium enterprises, is key to national security and social cohesion. Achieving this requires a comprehensive understanding of four key elements in the industrial landscape.

Industry analysis: A given industry's "clock speed," which refers to the speed at which it introduces new products and processes.

Supply chain analysis: An analysis of which supply chains would pose a high risk to national security should they be controlled by hostile foreign governments. This includes mapping bills of material to identify "low-level" risky components and materials. Equally important, it involves ascertaining and documenting the real source of products coming in from friendly and neighboring countries. For example, foreign companies are investing in warehouses and companies located in Mexico to avoid scrutiny of the origin of their products. This includes the full impact of companies' products, technologies, and capabilities on the critical national supply chain networks, with cascading industry impacts.

Foreign government influence and ownership: An analysis of the impacts should the critical supply chains be controlled by hostile foreign governments or foreign government–controlled or state-owned enterprises (and this does not necessarily refer only to large firms). An inherently risky cost-cutting strategy, and one often overlooked, is the outsourcing of information technology systems and operations to foreign IT service providers. While this can be very effective if done selectively with appropriate controls, to friendly countries, it can potentially expose and make vulnerable the critical data of government, suppliers, contractors, and those companies embedded in critical supply chains. Furthermore, the negative impact of outsourcing (and offshoring) IT systems, development, and operation to foreign IT companies is significant in terms of lost local skills and jobs.

Financial and infrastructure needs of supply chains located in Western countries: This is closely aligned with the location of key manufacturing and supply facilities and centers. Bearing in mind that capital is mobile and will follow the path that makes the best business sense for the company, the issues of corporate tax reduction and increase in working capital financing must be considered as part of a national security and resilience policy.

Private and public sectors must work together and implement policies and strategies for trade and supply chain design and management. They must focus on supply assurance, competitiveness, capability building, national security, risk, and resilience.

Our discussions with industry and services executives have revealed a deep vein of support for government action around a national industry policy and suggestions for increasing resilience, capability, and national security. Some of the suggested initiatives, and ones that are often overlooked in favor of more high-profile policies, are well known to supply chain executives and some academics, and include:

- Investing to improve national logistics infrastructure, including its "hard" (ports, roads, rail networks) and "soft" infrastructure (the service industries that underpin logistics).
- Providing potent incentives for business, such as tax breaks and financing for research and development and working capital financing to small and medium-sized businesses at discounted rates.
- Establishing "one-stop shop" agencies for harmonizing relevant regulatory interventions and procurement policies toward the development of new strategies for competitive and resilient national supply chains. This includes a focus on improved customs performance, streamlined regulations and service quality, and the development of consistent regulations, based on both economic and environmental considerations.
- Assuring the supply of critical products and supplies through government ownership or investment through public-private partnerships and employing public procurement and preferred buying rules to create stable demand for their supply chains.

- Incentivizing "smart reshoring" portfolios by offering financial incentives for developing resilient supply chains, while mandating certain national security parameters for critical supply chains. As Napoleon pointed out so succinctly, "Men are moved by two levers only: fear and self-interest," and we must pull both levers.
- A dedicated, well-funded, national, and coordinated effort on cybersecurity.
- Addressing the skills shortages in terms of science, technology, engineering, and mathematics, with supply chain capabilities—a combination often called STEMX.
- Adopting leading practices in supply chain management, talent management and development, and back-office processes from private companies. A point to note: leading practices go both ways. It seems to be an accepted truism that all leading practices are resident in the private sector. Transfer of leading practices should not just be limited from the private to the public sector. Commercial supply chains have a lot to learn from the capabilities of military logistics (as demonstrated during the Covid-19 pandemic).

Public-Private Partnerships for Data Exchanges

A good example of a public-private partnership for data exchange is the United States' Freight Logistics Optimization Works (FLOW) initiative to increase visibility for emergency response and critical supply chains. This is an initiative indicative of the novel public-private partnerships that are needed, benefiting both individual businesses and national security. As such, we feel it deserves some explanation.

We have argued that supply chain visibility is a critical element in supply chain response and quick decision-making. This takes on increasing importance in terms of emergency response and the critical product, capability, and component supply chains. In response to the need for total supply chain and logistics system visibility for crisis management, the FLOW initiative was announced in 2022. Led by the US Department of Transportation, FLOW is a voluntary data-sharing program directed toward the secure national exchange of freight information, available to all its participants. Some of the initial participants include port authorities, ocean carriers, terminal operators, cargo owners, small and medium-size businesses, agricultural producers, chassis leasing companies, and heavy and light asset logistics and integrated service companies. It is envisioned that FLOW could eventually lead into speeding up delivery times, reducing consumer costs by improving communication across US supply chain stakeholders, and improving supply chain agility and resilience.

While the FLOW initiative is a positive first step forward, it should further encompass participants from yet unrepresented US supply chain stakeholder segments (e.g., rail, truckload, pipeline, cargo airlines, passenger airlines that carry cargo) and logistics software providers (who have much better technological capabilities than any governmental agency). It should be augmented by additional insights into policies surrounding crisis planning and decision-making (e.g., lines of authority, responsibility, and objectives) that will be better informed by better data. The government must work together with industry to ensure that no technical intellectual property data, personal data (protected under GDPR, the General Data Protection Regulation rules), or personnel data are mandated. This can be a costly initiative for individual companies, and we believe that such data-sharing initiatives should be supported financially by means of national industrial policies.

Comprehensive public-private partnerships could further raise a nation's ranking in supply chain performance, global logistics connectivity, and competitiveness. One example of a national competitiveness score is the World Bank's Logistics Performance Index (LPI) report, which polls a large number of freight forwarders to reach its findings. While the LPI report does not cover the end-to-end supply chain, it addresses the critical physical logistics issues, including infrastructure, effectiveness, domestic logistics base, and ease of arranging shipments and assesses the national logistics system to embed a nation more effectively into globalized supply chains and attract additional investment. Such long-overdue investments unfortunately were not made in the globalization-driven economic rush of the past few decades (until 2016), when policy makers failed to embrace long-term thinking.

It was pointed out to us that, over the past few years, several countries have stepped in with infrastructure support to provide redundancy and support the shortening of global supply chains, and shift or preserve regionalized capabilities closer to the end markets. To this effect, some European countries have developed policies to protect domestic firms from foreign takeovers, while others have allocated significant sums to help their manufacturers move out of hostile countries and reshore production. For personal protective equipment and generic drugs, multiple countries and trading blocs have placed export restrictions on global manufacturers. This includes supporting or mandating local supply chain capability and manufacturing content to meet local needs and critical industries. Today's and tomorrow's trade-offs are among *free trade*, *national economies*, and *sovereignty*.

BREAKTHROUGH THINKING

The following list highlights some of the relevant breakthrough thinking that we know will add value to corporate executives and public policy makers as they develop their supply chain playbooks.

CORPORATE EXECUTIVES

- Redundancy strategies: capacity, supply, and moving away from risky and hostile countries.
- Hedge inventory.
- Risk management (including national security) part of the strategy, with continuous and periodic risk monitoring.
- End-to-end supply chain perspective for costs and cash.
- Modular strategies.
- Supply chain finance.
- End-to-end supply chain visibility, illuminations, and supply mapping to suppliers' suppliers.
- Data-driven and "intelligent" demand-supply planning, scenario planning, stress-testing, war-gaming, and simulation.
- Stop optimizing the "perfect" supply chain and instead develop flexible and resilient supply chain networks. A quick-moving "sense and respond" system is far better than a rigid system that seeks to anticipate everything in detail. As von Clausewitz said, "The enemy of a good plan is the dream of a perfect plan."

POLICY MAKERS

- Government action and rationalization for transparent, consistent, and streamlined regulatory management and one-stop shopping.
- Analysis and impact of companies' products, technologies, and capabilities on the critical national supply chain networks.
- Redundancy strategies: capacity, supply, and moving away from risky and hostile countries, reducing concentration, and increasing supplier diversification.

- Develop the programs to identify risks and actions for risk mitigation.
- Develop and provide incentives for cost-competitive resilience for critical supply chains.
- Develop novel public-private partnerships to harmonize the needs of the public sector with those of the private sector.
- End-to-end supply chain visibility and illuminations and supply mapping to tier 1, 2, and 3 suppliers to also highlight "diamond" supply chains.
- Talent management, hiring, retention, reskilling, and upskilling at the national level for STEMX disciplines; incentives and programs for generating and developing talent.
- Development of rigorous methods to evaluate critical industries and materials, reshoring versus friend-shoring versus nearshoring, and combinations. This includes the real and comprehensive impacts of disruptions across all industries.
- Evaluation of the supply and acquisition process to manage conflicts of interest and revolving-door policies, supply chain planning in order to take into consideration risks, surge, supersurge, and "black swan" events.
- Critical industry and supply chain financing for in-country production and supply, with vigilance and oversight on M&A, hiring and visa activities, outsourcing and offshoring; starting the decoupling of supply chains from adversarial countries.
- Investments in logistics infrastructure, ensuring transportation and shipping capacity.
- Cyber- and data security in the critical supply chains.
- Financial incentives and competitive tax policies and incentives for working capital, local sourcing and operations, and training.
- Public-private partnerships to share technology and for data exchanges to ensure critical supply chain visibility.
- Government action scrutinizing transactions that allow adversaries to control critical supply chains and technologies.

- Oversight of outsourcing government and critical supply chain information technology systems and operations to foreign companies.

Supply chains are at a crucial inflection point. Under the "new normal" they will be required to operate in an uncertain and variable economic and geopolitical environment with current risks and new risks surfacing—all of which have potentially high impacts. As a result, supply chains will have to explore new trade-offs between cost-competitiveness and resilience in meeting their financial, strategic, and customer objectives, while managing both corporate risk and national security considerations. However, supply chain resilience is one of the two critical and high-impact strategic imperatives of today's supply chains (and the most important)—the other being sustainability. We address this important area in the next chapter.

CHAPTER 8

Sustainability

*The New Imperative:
Environmental, Social, and
Corporate Governance (ESG) Issues*

There's no such thing as a free lunch.
—Milton Friedman[1]

The UN secretary-general's August 2021 statement on the much-anticipated Intergovernmental Panel on Climate Change (IPCC) report:

> Today's IPCC Working Group 1 Report is a code red for humanity. The alarm bells are deafening, and the evidence is irrefutable: greenhouse gas emissions from fossil fuel burning and deforestation are choking our planet and putting billions of people at immediate risk. Global heating is affecting every region on Earth, with many of the changes becoming irreversible.[2]

It is very difficult to discuss sustainability and environmental, social, and governance (ESG) issues in the global supply chain at any length without coming over as preachy, financially driven, or occasionally cynical. Over the past three decades, supply chains have focused on margins, costs, cash, returns on investment, and customer service. It is only recently that supply chain risk and sustainability have surfaced as major discussions in corporate boardrooms, national government, and security policy forums.

To start with, let's define the terms. We will use the term *sustainability* as a thematic umbrella for all the many and relevant terms encompassing:

- Corporate social responsibility (CSR)
- Environmental, social, and governance (ESG)
- "Circular economy"

CSR is an older term, focused more on corporate engagement and based on the idea of the social contract, namely, that companies function and exist because of public consent, and therefore they have an obligation to contribute to the needs of society and all relevant stakeholders. It has essentially been replaced in the narrative by the term *ESG—environmental, social, and governance.*

The "circular economy," a relatively new term, represents an expansion of the total life cycle approach to sustainability, from raw material extraction to recycling, refurbishing, and reuse, with little left over for disposal. In 2022, more than 90 percent of S&P 500 companies and 70 percent of Russell 1000 companies had published some sort of ESG report, and aspects of ESG reporting are increasingly becoming mandatory in certain countries. The definition of ESG becomes clearer if we look at its various elements, illustrated in Figure 8.1.

ENVIRONMENT AND SUSTAINABILITY	SOCIAL	GOVERNANCE
• Deforestation	• ILO standards adherence	• Corruption and bribery
• Greenhouse gas emission	• Worker exploitation	• Executive and employee income inequality
• Carbon emission	• Slavery and forced labor	
• Resource depletion	• Working conditions	• Political activism
• Water shortages	• Conflict minerals	• Lobbying
• Pollution	• Health and safety	• Taxes
• Waste	• Living wages	• Dumping
• Disposal and landfills	• Good citizenship	
• Climate change	• Local jobs and investment	
• Endangered species	• Restricted substances and product Integrity	

FIGURE 8.1 ESG: The Definition

ESG covers everything from the environment to social issues to political issues. Environmental issues deal with the impact on the environment and climate change. Social issues address the societal impacts of supply chain decisions. Governance is a category that extends "ES" and incorporates corruption, lobbying and political activism into the mix (something that many large companies have begun to include in their messaging and advertising to curry favor with activist groups and appear progressive to customers). We will not deal with the "G" part of ESG in this book, as it is more policy-driven and mired in politics.

While sustainability started off as a "nice to have," it is fast becoming a business and supply chain imperative, driven by government mandates, NGOs, pressures by stakeholders (e.g., banks' financing demands) and shareholders, and environmental activism. These pressures have resulted in many businesses committing to improve their ESG performance—from reducing their greenhouse gas (GHG) emissions and water use, to utilizing renewable energy sources, to eliminating modern slave labor and conflict minerals. Investors and other stakeholders increasingly expect full disclosure of companies' sustainability performance.

There are some public perceptions that ESG initiatives can result in significant financial benefits. One, for example, is process cost reductions; however, total cost analyses of returns do not always support this. Another perception is that products made with environmental and socially friendly materials and methods bring increased margins; however, surveys and experience have shown that this is marginal, at best. Finally, there is the perception that ESG products and services can be business opportunities; while the "products" aspect is debatable, the "services" aspect is definitely true, given the number of ESG consultants and certification bodies.

An example includes the admirable initiative by one of the largest medical manufacturing companies in the world to address ESG issues head-on but without going into the details of costs and benefits. The corporation has committed to using 100 percent recyclable, reusable, or compostable plastic, paper, and packing within a few years in all its products at hospitals, clinics, and doctors' offices, direct to consumer, and to final equipment manufacturers around the world.

Senior supply chain executives are now increasingly being held responsible for the environmental and social impact of their end-to-end supply chains. For example, a recent McKinsey study shows that "a typical consumer products industry supply chain creates far greater environmental costs than in-house operations; for instance, it is responsible for more than 80 percent of greenhouse-gas emissions and more than 90 percent of the impact on air, land, water, biodiversity, and geological resources."[3]

The issues that are driving sustainable supply chains are arriving from every conceivable direction. The impacts of some of these are real and substantial, others are marginal, and still others constitute nothing but wishful thinking. Some of the more significant include trends in climate change and the resultant extreme climate conditions that threaten consumer buying, transportation, manufacturing, and distribution infrastructure. An increase in "socially responsible investors" has provided a financing marketplace for companies that adopt sustainable practices, and, very important, the integration of ESG into corporate strategy and financial analysis is driving the institutionalization of ESG into supply chain decision-making.

For example, in 2021, Schneider Electric, a leader in energy management and automation, was ranked the most sustainable company in the world by the Corporate Knights Global 100 Index. According to Gartner, "Its STRIVE (2021–2023) program seeks to have 70 net-zero carbon plants and distribution centers by 2025, and the company continues to look for other efficiencies across its remaining manufacturing and warehousing facilities."[4]

There are changing expectations among consumers and the public, and preferences for ESG and green products and companies. Government programs and subsidies are increasingly incentivizing the building of manufacturing capacity for renewables. These are having some major impacts on the global capacity for solar panels and electric car batteries.

For example, Chinese solar companies have dominated the solar panel industry through subsidized investments, built huge solar panel production capacity, and then decimated global competition through a dumping strategy. As a result, both Germany and the United States lost most of their manufacturing capacity. US tariffs and significant tax credits and other incentives for renewable-power projects that use American-made equipment (under the Inflation Reduction Act of 2022) are leading to a rebound, and now First Solar (the last remaining major manufacturer in the United States) is investing in large facilities and capacity in the United States, while Swiss, Norwegian, and South Korean manufacturers also aim to build US solar supply chains. As a result of such governmental interventions, the solar supply chain can now emerge more distributed and local, rather than being controlled by one country.

Similarly, electric vehicle (EV) manufacturers are striving to shift sourcing and production into North America to qualify for the EV tax credits under the Inflation Reduction Act. This has resulted in some of the major automobile and battery manufacturers investing billions of dollars on large battery production and mining facilities in North America, and specifically the United States. As with the solar chain, this will result in battery supply becoming more distributed and local, leading to a reduction in the "diamond" supply chain concentration. These are prime examples where policy-making can positively influence sustainability, supply chain resilience, and national interests alike (policy makers and executives should make note that, in general and contrary to popular belief, a sustainable supply chain does have to be resilient and vice versa).

Some additional trends and factors influencing the advancement of ESG adoption and compliance in supply chains include:

- The increased sophistication and activism of nongovernmental organization (NGO) campaigns and partnerships.
- Impacts on employees and new talent recruitment—the perception being that employees will want to join environmentally friendly companies over others.
- The changing executive and board of directors views and perceptions regarding ESG's importance and business impacts.
- New global and country legislation and reporting requirements.
- New green, social, and eco-minded suppliers entering the market, albeit at a slow pace.
- The increasing realization that ESG impacts the full life cycle of products and services.
- The development of new technologies, such as hydrogen fuel cells to power vehicles. For example, both Amazon and Walmart use fuel cells to power their forklift trucks as part of both companies' targets of becoming carbon neutral.[5]

SUSTAINABILITY IS NOT A SIMPLE DECISION

Supply chain sustainability is not as simple as it may appear and is being tested by several key business issues. Both sustainability and resilience investments, if not conducted thoughtfully and realistically, can increase operating costs, use investment capital that could be used for other purposes, and erode profits. While many consultants and analysts maintain that companies that embrace sustainability often display improved overall financial performance and resilience, this is mainly an indirect relationship and may not always be the case. Additionally, during a major disruption to the supply chain, nonsustainable supply chain solutions might need to be deployed to reduce the supply chain's time and cost to recovery.

Sustainability has not been embraced across the board, despite the many advocates for "social license" justification. While there are a few (mainly Western) companies that have incorporated sustainability into their mission statements and have launched sustainability initiatives, the majority of organizations have not done so.

There are several reasons for this. First, there does not seem to be any real, proven, and documented direct link between ESG expenditures (capital or operating) and financial returns and performance. There are no standards for performance, and ESG is very difficult to measure. Furthermore, ESG represents a grab bag of environmental and social issues; the links between worker exploitation and greenhouse gas emissions are tenuous, at best. Many countries do not mandate sustainability in their companies, thereby tilting the playing field in their favor. Another key issue of concern is that companies in countries such as China, India, and Russia and on the continent of Africa have not yet joined in—neither contributing to standards development nor committing to their own greenhouse gas emissions reductions (although, hopefully, this will change). Finally, we have a situation where national policies are often driven by ideology, naivete, or ignorance. Indicatively, studies from some leading car manufacturers have suggested that the emissions from the energy used to yield and process battery minerals will make an EV's carbon footprint larger than that of a gasoline car until it has been driven for at least 50,000 miles.

In order to meet mandates from governments planning to implement bans on gasoline-powered vehicles, companies in the European Union and the United States are frantically building dozens of gigafactories (a term coined by Elon Musk for the huge EV battery plants). Each of these $2 billion monsters will procure around $20 billion worth of battery materials and minerals over the course of a decade! The core question of these supply chain issues is: Can we mine enough materials for our electric vehicle planned investments? Hundreds of new mines will need to be built for several minerals (nickel, cobalt, lithium, and rare earths), each requiring a decade or two to develop, which will lead to environmental degradation and huge increases in mineral prices. Interestingly, China dominates the global supply chains of these materials—both with Chinese domestic production and through investments and contracts in Africa. There are also several environmental complications. For one, the European Union is considering labeling lithium as a toxic mineral, and the major global source of cobalt is the Democratic Republic of Congo, a major source of conflict minerals. Adding to this is the fact that Indonesia is the major provider of nickel for batteries, and much of its production is powered by coal.

The major crises of the past few years (following the 2020 pandemic) have pushed sustainability to a lower priority in the corporate agenda, some national priorities, and the public mind. Add to this the looming global food shortage (much of it caused by the impacts of climate change) to feed an expanding population, the energy crisis (owing to the war in Ukraine and the weaponization of energy flows by Russia) and the increasing need to power industrialization, air conditioning, and electric vehicles, and sustainability falls even farther down in the priority list.

Finally, ESG is as much a political as it is a social and environmental issue. As such, there are many stakeholders, and aligning and satisfying all of them is nearly impossible. As many of these stakeholders have little interest in the performance of the company, its shareholders, employees, or the immediate community, it becomes very difficult to prioritize initiatives and resources and harmonize the efforts of the public and private sectors.

The generalization is that all these issues can improve over time and companies should embark on these initiatives because of the trust they generate among the public and society. However, for supply chain executives, this is a stretch, given their tenure and performance measurement. The examples typically advertised in the press are either those of very big companies (e.g., Walmart and Unilever) with huge power over their supply chains, or of niche companies with little impact on the environment. Most companies fall in between these two ends, and for them, ESG initiatives are cumbersome, complex, and costly.

Consequently, the relevant supply chain landscape is increasingly shaped by the "people, planet, profit" triad as defined by activist investors and nonelected international bodies, in conjunction with impacts on costs, competitive position, investment decisions, and returns on investment.

The supply chain is a major driver in the national and global ESG agenda, encompassing all the issues illustrated in Figure 8.1. One can add to this the ambitious goal of attaining not just "net zero," but rather "net positive" footprints (e.g., Unilever).

Most of the ESG issues and relevant actions lie in the supply chain and can pose severe business risks. To this effect, company executives need to ask a range of relevant questions:

- Are customers willing to pay more and cover the costs? *Indications are that they are probably not.*
- Are suppliers willing to bear the burden of the costs? *Not unless they are forced to by a very big customer.*
- Are shareholders willing to take the reduced returns? *Very few are.*
- Are employees willing to accept job reductions? *Certainly not.*
- Do the relevant investments carry any financial or strategic returns? *The jury is still out.*
- In terms of investment analysis, how do we compare the costs and returns of alternative technologies—such as battery-powered electric vehicles and hydrogen fuel cell–powered vehicles? *It depends on the assumptions made in the analysis.*
- Is there harmony and consistency with national interests? *Perhaps, but there are major contradictions.*
- Will our competitors incur similar costs and investments? *Only if they are in the same country.*
- What will the impacts be, both positive and negative, on demand, risks, and costs? *There will be impacts, and they must be assessed realistically.*
- Is being socially responsible tied to leaders' ideological or social agendas? *In some instances, yes.*
- Can we articulate the impact of ESG interventions into the executive suite language of stock price, returns on investment, sales, and free cash flow? *That's a tough sell but one we should try for.*
- Is ESG good for business, good for image, necessary for compliance, or a major cost item? *Perhaps it's good for image if marketed well, and it's certainly good for compliance, but not necessarily for the rest.*

The answers to these questions have often led to a backlash from companies. The return on investment (ROI) can be vague or downright optimistic in terms of business benefits, and unrealistic in terms of true costs. In addition to these, there are concerns from companies about governments "weaponizing" ESG regulations, corruption in ESG reporting by competitors, and concerns from the public about "greenwashing" and false marketing. Supply chain executives need to understand that while ESG covers a wide spectrum of issues, these can have a potentially significant impact on revenue, brand equity, cost, and working capital.

The consequences of not complying with government mandates, and not taking action to mitigate the issues of climate, resource depletion, and labor unrest, can range from inconvenient to disastrous. These can include issues with supply, including supply disruptions, through the banning of certain materials, increased labor unrest and reduction in certain types of mining and farming practices, loss of control of sources of supply, and issues with product quality, owing to the mandated use of alternate materials. The consequences on noncompliance also include government fines and penalties, and the potential loss of ability and permission to do business in certain countries. And, while companies must deal with increased costs due to investments, increased costs of materials, labor, and the use of different, more expensive materials, a much more significant threat is the erosion of brand equity (and the resultant loss of sales and market share), mainly through the work of social activists, or due to disasters such as the 2013 Rana Plaza collapse in Bangladesh.

A relevant example: In July 2020, a UK online fashion retailer lost over $1.5 billion in market value over two days after revelations of poor working conditions at one of its contracted garment manufacturers in England came to light. Companies can no longer disassociate themselves from the workings of their supply chains nor feign ignorance of what goes on with their suppliers.

It is clear that the old excuse of "I had no idea; the supplier did this!" does not work anymore. Add to this the new concept being put forward of extended producer responsibility (EPR) making manufacturers responsible for the entire life cycle of the product through the supply chain, and it is clear that the era of corporate accountability is near.

Finally, there is the very real case of unintended consequences. Take, for example, the US governmental push for electric vehicles. While EVs do have lower emissions, their supply chains have a very unfavorable sustainability footprint through the mining of lithium and cobalt, with issues of scarce water contamination and depletion, with adverse impacts on the environment, and embroiled in issues surrounding conflict minerals. Fossil fuels powering most of the manufacturing and disposal of the batteries is another challenging environmental issue. Looking at the environmental consequences from an end-to-end supply chain perspective, it could be argued that, all things being considered, they are as bad as the alternative. In a similar vein, shifting to renewable energy for supply chain use must contend with the issue that solar installations and wind farms result in significant ecological damage. There are no easy answers.

SOME CRITICAL ISSUES

ESG compliance has a number of issues that have come to the fore and are likely to stay there in various forms. We will discuss some of these in the following sections.

Are Customers Willing to Pay for Sustainably-Produced Products?

Many companies will pay a premium for green products and services only if they can charge customers more down the line, according to an October 2012 McKinsey survey of 500 executives.[6] On the other side, upward of 70 percent of consumers surveyed about purchases across several big industries stated they would pay an additional 5 percent for a "green" product if it met the same performance standards as a non-green alternative. However, as the premium increases, the willingness to pay melts away. For all but one category (packaging), less than 10 percent of consumers said they would choose green products if the premium rose to 25 percent. The question that companies must ask themselves is: Will this trend continue, and will consumers and governments expect companies to absorb the costs and investment?

Decarbonization/Net-Zero Requirements

Decarbonization has emerged as a key issue in the ESG agenda. Global supply chains account for about 80 percent of the world's total carbon emissions, while eight industry supply chains are responsible for more than 50 percent of global emissions.[7] These include food, construction, fashion, fast-moving consumer goods (FMCG), automotive, electronics, other freight (shipping, rail, aviation), and professional services. The implications are huge: it is estimated that a $100 trillion investment would be necessary to decarbonize global supply chains by 2050.

Even though the global regulatory landscape is still uncertain and fragmented, total carbon emissions have been recognized as critical enablers of climate action, and there is a growing interest in carbon markets. The percentage of global emissions covered by some form of carbon pricing has gradually increased over the years, but the jury is still out as to whether there will be a global action on this—a price on carbon in the form of an emissions trading system (ETS), a carbon tax, or Carbon Border Adjustment Mechanism (CBAM); and whether the price will be consistent globally or vary from region to region.

ETSs function under a "cap and trade" principle, where regulators set the cap (total number of allowed emissions) and then auction them to the companies of the sector targeted in the scheme. Companies can then trade the emission allowances amongst them, shaping up a price on carbon dioxide. Some ETSs are limited to a sector (for example, transport, energy, buildings, etc.), while others such as California's are more comprehensive.

However, ETSs have not been effective. For ETSs to work effectively, governments and policy makers must be willing to set caps that are low enough to lead to relatively high carbon prices. These would provide incentives for companies to go green. However, this is a significant challenge for policy makers as increased carbon prices will lead to higher consumer prices and can create a political backlash. This led, for example, to the European Commission's decision to sell an additional 200 million permits in 2022 as a response to pressures from member states to reduce energy prices.

The European Union boasts the second-largest ETS in the world and has been a global leader in making ETSs more sustainable after it cut out excessive permits in 2019. It further plans to implement a CBAM that will have importers to the European Union pay the difference between their corresponding foreign carbon price and that of the bloc. This would further provide incentives for countries that want to export to the bloc to bring their carbon prices close to the European Union's. On the other hand, it could lead to a decline in trade and a drop in fossil fuels use that is now exhibiting itself in widespread and severe energy shortages. China's ETS is the largest in the world, but its meager price of $9 per ton is clearly ineffective. Out of the 64 ETSs that exist today, only a fraction of them price the carbon above $40 a ton, a price that is regarded as the minimum social cost of carbon.

Inconsistencies among ETSs and their fragmentation can give some countries and companies an unfair competitive advantage. To this effect, at the 2021 COP26 climate summit at Glasgow, the European Commission pushed for a consistent global price on carbon. Additionally, it is hoped that by linking ETSs to bigger and more liquid markets, such harmonization will eventually provide more meaningful prices.

It is clear that in this environment, companies need to be proactive in keeping track of the various developments. For example, having a consistent global price on carbon would have huge implications for their supply chains.

The United Nations' Race to Zero initiative requires companies to make public commitments to ongoing GHG emission reductions. The Greenhouse Gas Protocol, a global framework for measuring and managing GHG emissions, stratifies emissions into three categories:

1. Scope 1, which includes direct emissions from owned facilities and vehicles.
2. Scope 2, which captures indirect emissions from the use of purchased energy.
3. Scope 3, which includes value chain–related emissions (upstream and downstream in the supply chain, during the life cycle of a product, and for its disposal) and is the largest and most complex category. Scope 3 emissions are often responsible for far more than half of a company's total carbon footprint.

The difficulty hinges on the ability to measure, track, and monitor emissions, particularly in scope 3, in today's supply chains. Companies outsource to a complex network of suppliers, and for many of these, greenhouse gas emissions are a very low priority, if they are a priority at all. Decarbonizing supply chains is hard and would require costly measures; often, it involves the use of technologies that are not yet mature and thus are very expensive.

For example, UPS's air transportation scope 1 air emissions increased nearly 5 percent in 2021, as alternatives to conventional jet fuel remain limited around the globe.[8] The carrier aims to cut its carbon intensity in half from 2020 levels by 2035, the same year it wants 30 percent of its aviation fuel to be from sustainable sources. That goal remains elusive, however, as supply remains limited and it has not reached economies of scale, making it cost prohibitive for wide adoption.

In addition, many companies have limited transparency in their upstream supply chain emissions. Many of the upstream suppliers are small and medium-sized businesses and lack the resources and the know-how to independently put in place decarbonization initiatives. This further raises the issue of who should pay for any relevant solutions.

For example, scope 3 encompasses emissions up and down the value chain, from materials to the supply chain and so on to the consumer's final use of a product. It is, by far, the largest share of retail's footprint. Indirect scope 3 emissions account for 90 percent, and sometimes up to 98 percent, of retailers' greenhouse gas emissions, according to the National Retail Federation.[9] And because of their vast scope 3 footprints, retailers are responsible for roughly 25 percent of global emissions, according to an April 2022 report from Boston Consulting Group and Ascental's World Retail Congress.[10] This is a challenge when profits are under pressure and survival is the main consideration.

Conflict Minerals

Conflict minerals are those mined in a "conflict zone"—typically controlled by warlords and local governments (mainly associated with the country of Congo). These minerals are mined in inhumane conditions while exploiting the labor of adults and children, and are often sold to buy arms, prolonging the conflict. As of today, the conflict minerals that are covered by regulations in the United States and the European Union are commonly called 3TG—tin, tantalum, tungsten, and gold. "Blood" diamonds are often included in this mix. However, there is pressure to include more minerals as part of these regulations. The current regulations include those from the European Union, the United States, and a nonmandatory guide from the OECD.[11] This last one covers all minerals, requiring that companies source minerals from responsible sources and report the usage of any conflict minerals in their supply chains.

An additional challenge arises when material cannot be traced from source. Some countries have set up distribution companies in conflict zones to mask the purchase and eventual destination of these minerals. As much of the reporting involves self-reporting, the veracity of many of the supply chain positions is doubtful. Technologies such as blockchain can be used to track certain discrete products, but this is expensive and requires collaboration and trust among supply chain stakeholders and a lot of resources.

Social Implications and Risks

Social impacts and risks have become increasingly prominent over the past decade and represent another source of a growing chronic supply chain risk. Public attention has been drawn to the many horrific disasters in Bangladesh and to the reports that several Chinese factories had forcibly relocated Uyghur Muslims working in slavelike conditions. As a result, multinational corporations are increasingly realizing that working conditions, broadly defined to include forced labor, child labor, human trafficking, and a wide range of conditions tied to domestic labor law and international labor standards, are a critical component of their supplier risk analysis.

For example, one of the largest ice-cream manufacturers has started working with a major supplier to end modern slavery and child labor in the chocolate industry, according to a joint statement issued recently by the two companies. This will include adhering to sourcing to improve working conditions for farmers, moving to traceability of cocoa beans while paying an additional premium to producers for their cocoa beans to provide them with a living income.

Ensuring that supplier factories are in compliance with both national labor law and international labor standards is one of the leading risk and sustainability challenges that companies face when designing and managing their global supply chains. The responses to increasing concerns about working conditions across countries has been widespread, and differences in policies across countries pose additional challenges to international companies.

Amazon, for instance, regularly evaluates its suppliers to identify concerning practices and works to address them through remediation efforts.[12]

Recognition of the Impact on Resilience

A critical aspect of sustainability, often ignored in the discussion, is its impact on risk and resilience. The impacts of climate change, labor unrest, and strident social activism pose a threat to the operations—product design and content, sourcing, manufacturing, packaging, and distribution—of many companies. The increased frequency and impact of unseasonal and overly fierce weather such as floods, droughts, and hurricanes on supply chains is apparent and well documented. Companies and the government must start, and in some cases accelerate planning for the mitigation of these risks.

A Plethora of Rules and Regulations

Governments, business, unions, and nongovernmental organizations (NGOs) often promote very different perspectives about the rights and responsibilities of different supply chain stakeholders. To help reconcile conflicting views, the United Nations Ruggie Principles (2008) outline a "protect, respect, and remedy" doctrine to illustrate how governments, corporations, and civil society can all play a role in reducing the "adverse human rights consequences" of supply chains.[13]

In 2011, the United Nations Guiding Principles on Human Rights called for explicit steps to ensure that human rights would be protected in global value chains,[14] while the Organization for Economic Co-operation and Development (OECD, 2011) offered specific suggestions, including a focus on due diligence standards and responsible supply chain management.[15]

In 2014, the European Union released a directive that eventually became binding legislation in 27 member states that required reporting on human rights conditions within supply chains.[16] The European Union's response has focused primarily on a "due diligence" regulatory approach, following nearly two decades of debate over the best way to resolve the tension between lower standards in production countries and higher standards in retail market countries.

The push for regulations in Europe continues to gain strength. The French Duty of Vigilance Law for international companies operating in France requires them to develop and implement plans to prevent serious violations or mitigate potential risks of violations under the penalty of civil court damages.[17] Similarly, Germany's Supply Chain Act (Lieferkettengesetz, 2021) makes it mandatory for every company exceeding a size of 3,000 employees in 2023 and 1,000 in 2024 to have full transparency and control along its entire end-to-end supply chain.[18] The act aims to further eliminate child labor and guarantee quality products from known sources. As Germany is the economic engine of the bloc, the act has the potential to be adopted across all EU member countries. Even more daunting are the proposals, perhaps soon to become law, mandating near-total traceability and compliance across the supply chain as a condition of doing business in the European Union. If executed, this will force companies to conform or, in some cases, leave the market. It will certainly add huge costs and change the competitive playing field.

The United Kingdom's 2015 Modern Slavery Act requires that international companies either implement policies to ensure that slavery and human trafficking are absent from their supply chain or declare the absence of policies to detect slavery and human trafficking in their supply chains.[19] Several other countries, most notably Australia, have passed similar legislation.

In the United States, California's Transparency in Supply Chains Act (2011/2015) requires companies to report their verification, audit, certification, internal accountability, and training activities to mitigate and redress human trafficking and forced labor.[20] Since 2016, the US Customs and Border Patrol (CBP) has taken aggressive steps toward stopping imports that it deems to have been made with slave labor, imposing penalties for certain forced labor offenses and following with criminal investigation.

Rising concerns about labor conditions in China have led the CBP to restrict imports from China that have been linked to forced labor. The Uyghur Forced Labor Prevention Act, enacted June 22, 2022, has the potential to impact procurement and supply chain operations across many industries.[21] It assumes that any work performed in China's Xinjiang region is forced. To avoid disruptions, importers will need to prove to the CBP that forced labor was not used for any products coming from that territory.

In addition to government legislation and administrative enforcement, other global stakeholders (including activists and interested parties) are pushing for more responsibility on the part of multinational corporations and their supply chains. We have listed a number of international and national regulatory frameworks (by no means a comprehensive list) that dictate compliance and, most importantly, show the wide, diverse, and sometimes inconsistent range of regulations that executives are required to consider:

- The ISO 14000 Series, a family of standards related to environmental management, dealing with the prevention of pollution, continual improvement, compliance with all statutory and regulatory requirements, setting performance objectives and targets, and an audit program.[22]
- The United Nations' Global Compact focusing on human rights, labor standards, the environment, and anticorruption.
- The International Labor Organization's (ILO) Declaration targeting freedom of association and

the right to collective bargaining; the elimination of all forms of forced labor; the abolition of child labor; and the elimination of discrimination in employment.

- The Electronics Industry Code of Conduct (EICC) focusing on issues related to labor, the environment, ethics, health, and safety.[23]
- The Restriction of Hazardous Substances Directive (RoHS).[24]
- The Registration, Evaluation, Authorization and Restriction of Chemicals (REACH) Act.[25]
- Greenhouse gases regulations of the US Environmental Protection Agency (EPA).
- The 2010 Dodd-Frank Wall Street Reform and Consumer Protection Act, Section 1502, Conflict Minerals.[26]
- The Foreign Corrupt Practices Act of 1977 (FCPA).[27]
- The European Union's Waste Electrical and Electronic Equipment (WEEE) directive, imposing collection, recycling, and recovery targets.[28]
- The Securities and Exchange Commission (SEC) of the United States is considering new rules in 2023 that would demand comprehensive reporting of climate-related risks and GHG emissions.

It is important to note that, despite all these mandates and efforts to manage social risk across different countries, doing so is still a near-impossible task. This owes to the different levels of economic need, social customs, and expectations, and significant differences between developed countries and others. In discussions we have had with several non-Western business executives, there is a resentment of Western countries trying to force their social agenda on other countries. For example, in many of these countries, adhering to the EU standards and regulations has become part of a "paper-filing, false-compliance" set of activities. It is important that Western countries do not impose their social agendas on other countries; instead, they should yield, adapt, and conform, taking into account the non-Western countries' own customs, constraints, and expectations for effective supply chain performance.

Add to these the ideologically inspired rules being proposed, and companies are increasingly faced with both a slanted playing field and an increase in costs. With this dizzying array of rules and regulations from various governments and unelected international bodies, it is no wonder that many companies respond only when they must.

ASSESSING ESG INITIATIVES

Supply chain executives need to confront some major decisions in their ESG strategies. These range from "do what's mandated and comply with guidelines and regulations" to "do what's right." There is no one right answer, and all of these decisions have cost implications. Executives, therefore, need to navigate the ESG dilemma by asking the following important questions:

- Is our responsibility to the shareholders, employees, financial performance of the business, and mitigation of business risk?
- Alternatively, is our responsibility to "people, planet, and profit" simultaneously, and to all the stakeholders involved? If so, what are the priorities?
- Do we simply comply, or do we go beyond compliance toward "doing what's right"?

Companies are faced with operating and strategizing along a spectrum of ESG options, from a strict compliance with regulations and laws in the countries they operate in, to complying with the nonmandated guidelines set for them by special interest social activists, NGOs, and some governments, and to doing (altruistically) "what's right for the planet." This last option, while admirable, is often driven by CEOs of very large companies who sell the idea to their employees and shareholders that such bold initiatives will bring large business benefits. Much of this tends to fall on their suppliers, who, of course, must comply. Figure 8.2 illustrates the total costs versus total benefits of compliance that come into play along this range of options.

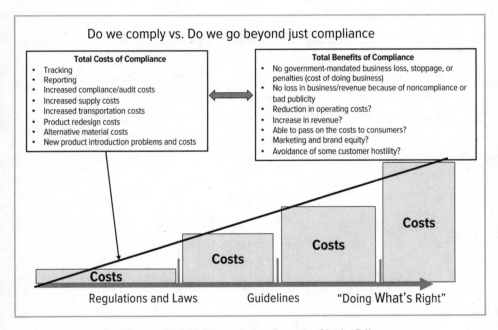

FIGURE 8.2 ESG/CSR and the Supply Chain Dilemma

In order to assess sustainability and ESG initiatives, their ROI analyses have to be realistic and holistic, over a reasonable time period and with reasonable assumptions.

Supply chain executives must tie their strategies and objectives to corporate strategy and model, and push back if they see that the company is in danger of falling into the "sustainability trap"—the zone where companies expect their "commodity" products to command premium pricing.

HOW WE CAN INCREASE SUPPLY CHAIN SUSTAINABILITY

*Thinking is easy, acting is difficult, and
to put one's thought into action is the
most difficult thing in the world.*
—Johann Wolfgang von Goethe

Companies can take action on sustainability across their supply chain from product concept and design to end of life and end of service life. The key approaches and actions for the development and execution of an effective sustainable supply chain strategy are discussed next.

Make Sustainability Part of the Risk Mitigation Strategy

The risks posed by sustainability are a very real part of the company's risk profile. These include impacts of climate change, labor unrest because of poor labor conditions, and noncompliance with government mandates and standards, to name a few. Companies need to identify these risks and their impacts and build this into the risk management, mitigation, and monitoring processes. Many of the strategies were discussed in Chapter 7 and will sound similar—diversification and redundancy, to name a few—but there are a whole lot of other actions that companies can and should take if they are financially feasible. Several of these are outlined in the sections that follow. However, a key aspect is the financial analysis that underlies these strategies and actions. While it is a good practice to show the costs and impacts of historical disruptions, it always begs the question of relevance. We have seen a corporate analysis that references the 2011 tsunami in Japan and the floods in Thailand, even though the company has no operations there, while another company presented an analysis that showed the costs over a 10-year horizon in an effort to minimize the annual cost for their analysis. Analyses of catastrophic events must be linked with probabilities and costs of risk mitigation strategies and must be realistic. If not, they are likely to be treated as just another example of somebody's social activism.

Focus on Strategic Sourcing, Supply, and Procurement Management

These control a huge part of the company's sustainability profile. The challenge for strategic sourcing is to determine how to incorporate ESG principles into the decision-making process. Paramount to accomplishing this is understanding the trade-offs between sustainability and optimal supply chain efficiency (and increased resilience). In particular, sourcing executives must understand that sustainability mandates, regulations, and customer expectations pose major risks. ESG must be embedded in the entire strategic sourcing process, from developing the key imperatives based on overall supply chain strategy, to developing the category profile, to supplier selection and negotiation. Equally important are the postsourcing activities of supplier relationship management and auditing for quality and ESG compliance. These include developing value chain emissions baselines and data exchanges with suppliers, setting clear goals for scope 1–3 reductions, instituting emissions metrics, and tracking performance.

Collaborate with Suppliers and Providers

Most executives generally recognize that genuine collaboration across the supply chain has a greater impact than the sum of each stakeholder's individual efforts. Companies should work with their suppliers to ensure compliance and meet sustainability targets, and to assist those suppliers that fall short. Sustainable material selection and supplier manufacturing processes need to be incorporated in supplier selection criteria, as well as reduced emissions by exploiting the appropriate transportation modes and inventory lot sizes.

Additionally, companies must embark on concerted efforts jointly with suppliers (at least with their most important, "type A" suppliers) along three fronts. The easiest is to reduce process waste, scrap, rework, and energy consumption, while adopting a "circular economy" mindset by increasing the share of recycled materials across the enterprise. Rather more complex is working with suppliers to utilize sustainable materials in their products and processes and, finally, to help suppliers to employ operations for maximum sustainability and responsibility. Large companies should further proactively engage with their suppliers and educate them on different decarbonization drivers. These should be based on an end-to-end approach and include strategies and actions to procure renewable power and green raw materials; implement energy, material, and process efficiency practices; and develop long-term renewable energy power purchase agreements in order to stabilize electricity supplies and prices. An even more complex approach, and one that requires investment, is to adopt technology solutions such as CCUS (carbon capture, usage, and storage) and fuel switching to offset and remove carbon from the ongoing operations and the supply chain.

Employ Sustainable Product Quality Standards

Companies should employ business sustainability standards in material selection, manufacturing processes, and product packaging. Examples include raw materials that have a favorable environmental footprint and recyclable packaging materials.

Increase Efficiency in the Use of Operational Resources

Companies can explore a variety of activities to increase efficiency. These range from maximizing energy efficiency and reducing water consumption to reducing waste and inventory scrap and obsolescence. Increasing efficiency also includes maximizing the reuse of by-products and investing in the more difficult initiatives to redesign processes, install waste-to-energy capabilities, and retrofit plants to incorporate the most efficient production technologies.

Make Transportation and Delivery "Green"

Making transportation and delivery green involves the utilization of "greener" modes and carriers. For example, these can include rail or barge transportation (extensively used in Europe but also in the United States) instead of heavy-duty trucks. Other strategies can include using alternative-fuel vehicles and carriers who are moving away from carbon-based fuels. For example, Cargo Owners for Zero Emission Vessels noted that several major global companies such as Amazon, Ikea, Inditex, Brooks Running, Frog Bikes, Michelin, Patagonia, Tchibo, and Unilever will progressively switch all of their ocean freight to vessels powered by zero-carbon fuels by 2040.[29] This is a prime example of maritime freight customers motivating the rest of the maritime value chain (a legacy business) to invest in zero-carbon shipping.

However, a great deal of the responsibility rests with customers and their need for immediacy and speed of delivery, and the shippers themselves who want rapid delivery from their suppliers. Shippers must set expectations with their customers regarding service levels and delivery. Recently, we have had discussions with companies about incorporating the delivery trade-offs into the choices they give customers. For example, they would offer delivery in 15–20 days at lower costs with low greenhouse gas emissions, versus delivery in 2 days at higher costs with high greenhouse gas emissions.

Embed Sustainability in Product Design

A critical and basic sustainability strategy is for companies to stop using eco-unfriendly materials in their products. This involves moving away from a management and design mindset that dictates the use of the lowest-cost material. If they want to be really serious about sustainability, companies must embed sustainability into their product design and portfolio in three ways: (1) by designing for landfill/disposal, (2) by using materials whose extraction and disposal do not damage the environment, and (3) by selecting suppliers that conform to ILO guidelines for worker management and safety.

Adopt Circular Economy Models

The adoption of circular economy models involves the development of reverse logistics networks and closed-loop supply chains to turn waste to value wherever possible. Incentives for recycling, reuse, and refurbishing are critical, as are initiatives to convert waste to energy (sometimes in collaboration with other companies and organizations). Such models can also substantially reduce the need for primary and secondary packaging. As with all strategies, they need to have both customer and supplier collaboration (while not neglecting value recovery from the returned product) for maximum effect. As illustrated in Figure 8.3, several of these strategies can form part of a sustainability portfolio and a set of integrated activities within the end-to-end supply chain.

Focus on Change Management— the Organizational Change and Mindset

The success of ESG strategy and execution revolves around organizational commitment, process, and change. These criteria for success include three distinct change management areas of focus. The first, and most important, is an executive leadership engaged with sustainable supply chain goals, and sustainable supply chain management aligned with corporate goals. The next area of focus involves embedding sustainability into the strategic sourcing mindset, aligning sourcing strategies and business goals with ESG objectives and targets, having well-defined and monitored supplier performance metrics across the total life cycle, and ensuring that sustainability is defined as a fundamental part of the total acquisition cost analysis and ROI analysis. Finally, a key element to extending ESG across the global enterprise and ecosystem is collaboration with the relevant supply chain stakeholders to align goals, educate on the value proposition, and set joint initiatives.

Pay Attention to the Law of Unintended Consequences

Companies should take special care to follow ESG policies as mandated by various governments before jumping into product development or supply chain structures— mandates tend to have unintended consequences. From a supply chain perspective, these consequences can impact

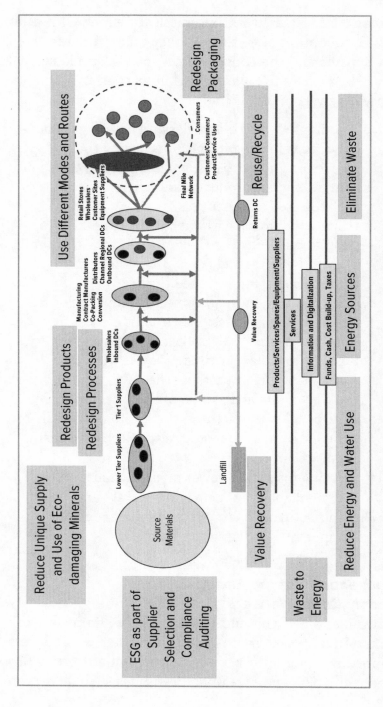

FIGURE 8.3 Making the End-to-End Supply Chain More Sustainable

demand, lead times, working capital, and supply. This owes to a combination of factors—policy is often made without considering the consequences, based on ideological grounds, a desire to favor certain industries, or just ignorance. A few examples include:

- Pushing for electric vehicles and banning gasoline-powered vehicles without considering the energy sources and costs to charge them, which can reduce demand for the product and increase use of fossil-fuel-powered electricity.
- Using wind farms without considering the bird populations killed, or the damage in the disposal of wind turbines and parts, all of which can increase costs and initiate litigation.
- "Slow steaming" ocean container ships to reduce greenhouse gas emissions without considering the impacts on time to delivery and costs to delivery.
- Pushing for solar farms and power without considering the impacts on the environment, worker welfare and safety, or the fact that many solar panel manufacturers are located in hostile or strategic competitor countries, thereby increasing supply chain risk.
- Banning fossil fuel power plants, while commendable, can increase corporate and manufacturing energy costs as there are few cheaper alternatives that can scale.

Optimization of the End-to-End Supply Chain Network

Optimization of the end-to-end supply chain network should involve new multi-objective models that address important trade-offs between supply chain efficiency (and resilience) and sustainability issues such as carbon footprint and negative environmental effects of logistics across the supply chain. It is all a series of trade-offs (where optionality becomes more important than optimality). Table 8.1 illustrates the trade-offs that a US company faced when considering sourcing from Europe versus sourcing from China.

TABLE 8.1 An Example of the Role of Optionality

	SOURCING FROM EUROPE	SOURCING FROM CHINA
Production	More advanced technology Greener energy alternatives Less labor intensive	Less advanced technology More carbon-intensive energy sources More labor intensive ILO standards noncompliance Conflict minerals issues
Transportation	Shorter transport distance Heavy reliance on unimodal road transport	Longer transport distance Sea freight is more CO_2 efficient, but we need to consider other emissions Airfreight is extremely carbon intensive
Inventory	Less inventory needed to cover transport lead time Smaller risk	More inventory needed to cover transport lead time Larger risk

This potential "friend-shoring" from Europe with an improved environmental footprint needs to be assessed and weighted against the other perks that sourcing from China offers. Such perks include lower labor costs, access to engineering talent, fewer labor unrest risks and increased cooperation, fewer government regulations, and faster response in factories to demand and schedule changes.

Another example of trade-offs that must be made manifests is found in the transportation industry, where the multiple and often conflicting regulations and pressures involving sustainability often clash with customer pressures. The pressures on shipping companies range from mandating the use of different fuels, centralizing distribution systems and optimizing the number of nodes, the use of newer, more efficient vehicles that use less fossil fuel, and shipping by the most eco-friendly (ocean) instead of the least (air). These mandates must be traded off against additional operating costs, the relevant capital costs, and, of course, the delivery speed and its variability, and response times to customer orders.

Just as there is no one-size-fits-all strategy for the diverse range of supply chains, there is no single sustainability strategy that is applicable to all supply chains. Companies that shift from passive compliance to proactively and cost-competitively embedding ESG into their strategic portfolios as an integral part of the corporate value proposition have the potential to drive long-term positive impact on society, along with revenue growth, margin increase, and competitive advantage.

However, it is important to caution that ESG is just not economically feasible for many companies today for a variety of reasons. These reasons include high investments, poor competitive position against noncompliant competitors or countries, poor returns on investment (when they employ true and realistic ROIs with a comprehensive end-to-end supply chain approach), customers unwilling to pay premiums for green products, and multiple rules and regulations.

As consumer behavior cannot be relied upon to drive systemic change, governments will have to intervene with incentives (i.e., tax breaks) and funding of sustainability initiatives, while taking into account national interests and aspects of national security. The "tragedy of the commons" is a term by Garrett Hardin that refers to "a situation in which individuals with access to a shared resource (also called a commons) act in their own interest and, in doing so, ultimately deplete the resource."[30] This cannot be solved through the efforts of individual companies, or even individual nations. Policy makers, ESG rating agencies, financial institutions, and regulatory bodies must engage the private sector and ensure that rules and regulations are consistent globally and are applied equally to all countries and companies. This will allow for investment flows, long-term planning, and innovation by the private sector, as well as for fighting deliberate misreporting and corruption in ESG reporting. In summary, incorporation of sustainability into the supply chain is determined by a few major factors: executive resolve and willingness to include sustainability in strategy and financial analysis, innovation in process and product design, sophisticated sourcing, smart use and reuse of material, and an eye on competitive advantage.

BREAKTHROUGH THINKING

Sustainability in supply chains is a fairly new phenomenon. The following lists highlight some of the relevant breakthrough thinking that would help corporate executives and public policy makers as they navigate this increasingly complex and challenging issue, while developing their supply chain strategies.

CORPORATE EXECUTIVES

- Identify the climate change risks that the company could face and integrate them into the risk mitigation and monitoring process at a company, regional, and site level.

- Ask the questions: Is ESG good for business, good for image, necessary for compliance, or a major cost item?

- Don't lead the pack unless it gives you some advantage; be a follower, not an innovator.

- Do your ROIs thoroughly while considering all aspects (including documentation and compliance).

- Evaluate the longer-term cost, demand, and working capital consequences before jumping into developing new products or supply chain design in response to government ESG policies.

- Develop fiscally astute ESG strategies.

- Develop a value proposition that shows the impacts to the business, employee jobs, and benefits to other stakeholders.

- Start small with recycle, reuse, value recovery, etc., before moving up to refurbish, remanufacture, redesign, re-source, etc.

- Use all progress as a marketing tool, inside and outside the company, to attract funding and for recruitment of new talent.

POLICY MAKERS

- Provide streamlined, steady, and transparent regulatory management, with clear and consistent disclosure schema across industry sectors.

- Do not impose the Western social agenda on other countries; rather, yield, adapt, and conform.
- Do not impose onerous conditions on domestic companies that will put them at a competitive disadvantage globally.
- Improve the policing of net-zero commitments and other regulations with both national and international companies doing business in the country.
- Pay attention and assess the unintended consequences of ESG policy.
- Implement tighter and more realistic carbon prices.
- Embed national interests and security in the regulatory agenda.

Achieving some degree of a sustainable supply chain can be slow and complex. This requires breakthrough thinking and requires realistic analysis and trade-offs in terms of risks, revenue, brand, costs, working capital, and compliance. Equally important, it requires measurement that is tied to outcomes and is able to track progress. The next chapter on measures and metrics provides a framework and meaningful metrics to help direct and manage this challenge.

CHAPTER 9

Measures That Matter

*Selecting the Right Key
Performance Measures (KPMs)
for the New Supply Chains*

*It is given to us to calculate, to weigh, to measure,
to observe, this is natural philosophy;
almost all the rest is chimera.*
—Voltaire

Measurement, data, and analytics are critical elements of effective and resilient supply chain strategy, management, and overall business success. For years, management theorists and practitioners have talked about measurement, with topics ranging from process measurements to key performance indicators (KPIs) and balanced scorecards. Yet, many companies and organizations fail to utilize measurement effectively to run their global supply chains.

CAUSES OF INEFFECTIVE MEASUREMENT

Effective measurement is something that many companies, government institutions, and nonprofit organizations still do not do well. Over the years, we have observed several reasons for this:

- Some departments don't want their performance and capability to be measured.
- Some organizations measure without any process or mandate to act on the results.
- Many define their measures without tying them to the objectives and imperatives of the organization.
- Many organizations define measures without tying them to necessary outcomes.
- Managers and executives believe that measurements are used as a "means to punish

the guilty" and provide inaccurate, and sometimes made-up, data.

- Some believe "the more the merrier"—one organization had no less than 300 KPIs. It is, obviously, next to impossible for executive management to manage a global supply chain with so much noise.
- In many supply chain organizations, executives and managers don't believe the data—either because the data is wrong or because they do not understand the origin or generation of the data— and therefore ignore the indicators.
- Many supply chain executives have measurement systems that are inward-looking, not imperative- or outcome-based.
- Most measures are historic, viewed at discrete points in time, so management is always looking backward at what happened.

While these are typical reasons for poor measurement systems, they also provide insight into what effective measurement systems must possess and do to drive supply chain success—today and in the future.

WHAT MATTERS IN GLOBAL SUPPLY CHAIN MEASUREMENT

There are several critical elements that must be considered when designing and implementing a high-impact, high-success supply chain measurement system. Figure 9.1 illustrates the building blocks of such a system. There are several different approaches to developing supply chain measurement systems. However, we have found that many companies and organizations lack a structured approach.

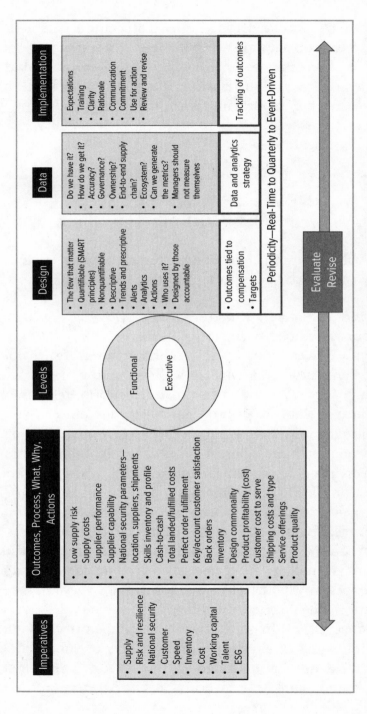

FIGURE 9.1 High-Impact Global Supply Chain Measurement Structure

As we have discussed, the series of disrupting events of the past few years have forced senior management to focus on things other than revenue, cost, market share, and short-term share price—metrics that appeared to work well in the past, when profitability was the sole end goal without any concerns whatsoever about risks, sustainability, local communities, and geopolitics.

DEVELOPING EFFECTIVE MEASUREMENTS

We will discuss the major characteristics of such a structured approach to designing effective measurements.

Metrics Driven by the Objectives and Imperatives of the Supply Chain

The objectives and imperatives state the overall "what do we measure" and "why," as well as the direction of the organization. Getting to this requires effort—few senior executives want to go into their colleagues' offices to ask these questions. In one instance, an executive with whom we were in a meeting greeted his subordinate's presentation on inventory replenishment and deployment with the question, "What is the strategic objective of the design?" The lack of a crisp response was met with the comment, "You mean you don't know?" It turned out the executive didn't know, either. Far too many organizations focus on the technology and presentation of metrics without a hard look at what they are measuring, why they are measuring it, the business outcomes to be measured, and the major supply chain imperatives. These imperatives should address the key supply chain objectives of supply, risk and resilience, national interests and security, customer, speed and agility, cost, working capital, people, and the environment. While these may vary in scope and emphasis, they are always present in today's global business and, in the end, nonnegotiable.

Executives and their measurement systems must answer the following questions:

- What are the necessary outcomes that need to be measured?
- What impacts are the supply chain(s) having on the corporate financials and stakeholder value?
- What do executives and managers need to monitor and manage to ensure the health of the business?
- What decisions will they support across the end-to-end supply chain?
- What insights will they provide into major trends that will impact the business?
- How are these tied to compensation systems?
- Who needs to receive and act on these measurements?
- What is the periodicity demanded of these measures?

These questions must be addressed. Once we know what we should be measuring, then developing detailed metrics for each function is as easy as going to the internet. The challenge is getting the timely and accurate data.

Measures Tied to Outcomes and Key Process Performance

It stands to reason that measurements must be tied to what we want to happen in the supply chain and the key processes that make them happen. These outcomes and key process indicators are derived directly from the supply chain imperatives and the state of the environment. This is a process that requires hard thinking, business acumen, an understanding of the end-to-end supply chain (being able to see the forest without being trapped into departmental silos), the impacts on the customer, national security, resilience, the environment, and, of course, cost and liquidity. The process must address all of the relevant aspects of the supply chain. In the past, we measured sales and costs; once we got past cost of goods sold, we quickly dived into specific functional costs in purchasing, quality, and production. The new VUCA environment demands much more for success; it demands that we measure outcomes and trends. In order to ensure common and concerted effort toward achieving these outcomes, the outcomes must be tied to the compensation system at all levels.

There are 10 key dimensions that must be measured:

1. We need to start with the customer: this includes nonquantifiable measures, such as net promoter score, customer satisfaction indices, customer emotion measures, and ease of doing business. Of course, this set of measures should also include quantifiable metrics such as perfect order fulfillment, share of wallet, customer repurchases, and customer profitability.

2. Supply has taken on far greater importance since in the post-2020 crises. It includes risk, location, concentration, supplier evaluation and performance, and supplier capability.

3. National security and national interests are increasingly important. Though in the past they were usually ignored, they now are coming into the limelight as a high-profile issue. This should include supply concentration, sourcing of materials, foreign government control, and risk of disruption.

4. Cash and working capital are the critical grease of the supply chain, including days payable

outstanding, days inventory outstanding, and cash-to-cash cycles.

5. Cost: at an executive level, this includes end-to-end costs such as total landed/fulfilled costs, cost to serve, and total costs of acquisition.
6. Product and quality include basic product quality measures by product and by supplier.
7. Inventory is always a basic issue in terms of location, deployment, quantity, excess and obsolescence, matching with demand, and value. Measuring inventory movement and position can provide valuable insights into the effectiveness of sourcing and demand planning.
8. Talent and people: more than ever, the effective international supply chain depends on its people and their capabilities, skills, adaptability, upskilling and reskilling, hiring, and retention.
9. Risk and resilience: while there are some indicators of resilience (time and cost to recovery and survival—discussed in Chapter 7), much of this is unstructured and includes scenario planning, third-party risk indices, country business assessments, and commodity analysis.
10. Environmental, social, and governance (ESG) if mandated by the government, necessary for the business, or needed for reporting. As there are no global standards for reporting on ESG metrics (with inaccuracy, corruption, and inconsistency rife in ESG reporting—discussed in Chapter 8), the measurement, reporting, and verifying of carbon footprint, greenhouse gas emissions, and sustainability progress is a challenge across different geographies.

It is at this point, after we define the key dimensions that must be measured, that periodicity becomes critical.

Periodicity can range from real-time to hourly, daily to monthly, and can even be event-driven. Today's technology allows real-time key performance measures (KPMs), enabling us to see what is actually happening now more than what did happen previously. Real-time data is invaluable to some measures, but it's also expensive to get and generate, demanding resources and management time. The key to evaluate periodicity is to assess the frequency of change and the importance of the changes. For example, while it may be critical to know order status in real time, it may not be so important to track logistics costs on the same basis. Defining measurements is one of the most important thinking processes and decisions a company or organization can make.

Metrics must always be geared to the appropriate organizational level—from the executive suite to the senior functional executives to managers and the employees at the front line. But they always must be derived from, and support, the higher-level metrics, imperatives, and outcomes that drive the organization. To this effect, the question that needs to be asked is: Who receives and acts on the measurement? The answer may be senior executives, functional executives and managers, or workers on the front lines.

Metrics must be designed with several key principles in mind. First, less is more; we should work toward and focus on the critical few metrics that can be used for decisions and insights.

Next, it should be recognized that not all measurements are financial or quantitative—some can be subjective or nonquantitative. Trying to put numbers on everything may give the illusion of precision. For those that are quantifiable, a good set of guidelines is the SMART approach: specific, measurable, achievable, realistic, and timely. Metrics fall into two categories: descriptive—what's going on today or what went on yesterday; and trend—indicators as to what will happen in certain critical areas. Finally, metrics should be designed by looking at the next step forward. The analytics we can derive from these metrics—typically cross-organizational, cross-functional, and across the supply chain—must provide us with managerial insights and direction for future actions or changes. We must always ask:

- What is being measured?
- What outcomes and actions result from this?
- How are these measures tied to compensation across the organization?
- What level of detail and what periodicity do we need?
- And the scope question: along what dimensions should we measure the business?

Everything rests on the data. The design, generation, and update of measurements must be driven by the organization's *data strategy*. There is no effective measurement if the underlying data is not accurate or if everybody in the organization is not confident in the data. Data has come to be recognized as a corporate asset, the currency of business and warfare, and a critical element in the supply chain, which is why we devoted Chapter 5 to this topic. For measures to be truly effective, the data must be accurate, timely, across the end-to-end supply chain, and across functions, the network, and providers.

Implementation is a function of people and change management; everybody in the organization (or those who use the measures) must be crystal clear on what the measures mean, how they are derived, and where the data comes from. An important aspect of this is communication, which must include the rationale for the metrics, how they will be used, what actions can be taken as a result of them, and ideas on how to suggest improvements. Addressing these will set the expectations for planning, execution, and measurement. Equally important is the setting of targets for the metrics, as without targets, one cannot ascertain progress or deterioration in performance. These targets should be set by the functional owners and the executive suite. Given these targets and the tying of outcomes to compensation, the outcomes must then be tracked, reported, and communicated.

DISPLAYING METRICS

Part of the strategy and execution of high-impact metrics is their display and presentation to decision makers, regardless of their level in the organization. The days of manual reports are gone. Also on the way out is the practice of manually entering measurements on PowerPoint slides for display. Today, there are four formats in which metrics are displayed to users:

- **Scorecards** are a performance management system that inform senior executives about how the end-to-end supply chain and the company are doing using a few well-selected metrics.
- **Dashboards** are a performance monitoring system; they are descriptive, informing executives and managers about the up-to-date state of their supply chain using interactive metrics with drill-down capabilities.
- **Alerts** proactively let supply chain managers know when a metric or leading indicator is moving out of the acceptable range, and that it is time for corrective action—alerts tie metrics to decisions that must be made in a forward-looking fashion.

- **Supply chain control towers** provide a complete picture of the end-to-end supply chain over critical dimensions, and permit users to monitor performance and status and make decisions on the spot, through up-to-date enterprise and supply chain ecosystem data, structured and unstructured data, while further providing visibility into unforeseen events and conditions. A further development that extends the concept of control towers is that of "nerve centers," using advanced technology such as artificial intelligence, automated processes, and a multidisciplinary approach to managing global supply chains.

Technology today has generated mobile management—metrics can be displayed on tablets, wearables, and smartphones, with decisions made and executed on the move.

MEASURES THAT DRIVE WRONG DECISIONS AND BEHAVIOR

Poor measurement systems—those that are not well thought out and well structured, that are developed with incomplete knowledge of the end-to-end supply chain and the imperatives, and that ignore outcomes—can be dangerous. One prominent example is the McNamara fallacy. The McNamara fallacy originated in the Vietnam War, in which enemy body counts were taken to be a precise and objective measure of success. War was reduced to a mathematical model: by increasing estimated enemy deaths and minimizing one's own, victory was assured. As a result, people in the field supplied false numbers, which had disastrous results. The measures were bad, and so the execution was even worse. Other examples of poor measurement systems include supply measures that focus on price and purchase price variance (PPV), sales measures that drive the "hockey stick" and unprofitable products, and production and manufacturing measures that focus mainly on capacity utilization, resulting in poor scheduling decisions, high inventory levels, and stockouts.

MAJOR AND CRITICAL MISTAKES IN MEASUREMENT

Metrics and measurements are a critical component of supply chain management and success. They must be descriptive, trend-based, and prescriptive; encompass the end-to-end supply chain and key external factors; and be in alignment with the strategic supply chain direction and objectives. Yet many companies keep on making the same set of mistakes in thinking through and designing metrics. These mistakes generally fall into five categories.

Measuring the Past

To use an old business cliché, "looking in the rearview mirror" doesn't do much to help the business; it is important to have an idea of what is coming ahead and what we're driving through. Traditional KPIs are "lagging indicators," meaning they may come too late to make a necessary pivot in operations. Many companies ignore the use of leading indicators in order to sense trends in risk factors, customer behavior, and employee attitudes. On the other side, pulse surveys, for example, are highly creative metrics that provide timely and actionable information.

Focusing on Internal Performance and Measures

Executive-level metrics, in order to be effective, need to reflect not only internal performance but the performance of the entire supply chain network. The danger lies in the belief that internal metrics reflect the real business imperatives. (Classic examples are "customer order date" versus "customer request dates" and "date shipped" versus "when the customer actually receives the order.") A point to make here is that while, ideally, all the trading partners should be aligned in terms of working toward common objectives of speed, working capital, cost management, and service to the customer, this aspect is very difficult given the conflicting business objectives of the different supply chain network players.

Not Aligning Metrics with Corporate and Strategic Supply Chain Goals

We have emphasized this repeatedly in the chapter. This often comes from a lack of understanding (and, often, inadequate executive communication) of the real mission and objectives of the organization and the supply chain, and a lack of discipline in thinking through the outcomes and imperatives that need to be measured. Metrics must be based on outcomes that matter, and a lack of this discipline results in measuring the wrong things and results in the additional lack of executive focus, attention, and consequence management.

Casual and Unstructured Approach to Designing Metrics and Measurement Systems

Designing measurement systems demands a degree of discipline in thinking through the process. Failure to do so results in familiar situations such as a reliance on classic financial indicators like revenue and profit trends that do not tell us much of anything that is actionable;

the assumption that one set of metrics measures all in a diverse product, customer, and supplier environment; and trying to measure everything, with too many metrics. This lack of discipline in design manifests itself in using metrics developed at "100,000 feet" by people who are unfamiliar with the business or the data availability and accuracy.

Lack of Organizational Alignment and Change Management

A common reason for the failure of metrics systems, no matter how well designed, is the lack of organizational alignment and change management. Implementation must include getting people in the organization to understand the metrics, their importance to the business and the supply chain, their rationale and use, the data, the outcomes, and how to interpret the results.

BREAKTHROUGH THINKING

Measurement systems and metrics have progressed in significant ways over the past few years. The focus has shifted from "How do we measure efficiency?" to "How do we succeed in this VUCA environment over the short and long terms?" and encompasses a series of basic approaches. There are several breakthrough concepts that enable effective measurement to drive strategy and results for both executives and policy makers.

CORPORATE EXECUTIVES

- Start with "What do we measure and why?"
- Tie metrics to business and supply chain goals, imperatives, and outcomes.
- Have a few critical measures at every level.

- Begin the journey with the basics—don't listen to vendors and consultants who want you to have a control tower immediately. Do the critical ones first: display metrics online (no PowerPoint decks compiled by subordinates) and in as near real time as possible, in scorecards and dashboards. Control towers and "nerve centers" can come later.

- Focus on the data, availability, accuracy, and end-to-end supply chain scope.

- Measures can be both quantified and nonquantified and reflect both descriptive and trend metrics.

- Measures must be understood by everyone and be actionable. The issue of people adopting, understanding, and using them is a key factor in their implementation.

- Periodicity, display, and visualization are essential and require trade-offs in terms of costs, time, and sometimes outcomes.

- Metrics must reflect end-to-end supply chain performance—for example, total landed and delivered costs, total costs of acquisition, and cost to serve.

- Plan on a system of real-time measures or leading indicators that proactively alert executives of the need for action.

POLICY MAKERS

Exactly as with corporate requirements, with some customization as described here:

- Recognize that some metrics are absolute (100 percent service levels could be mandatory for defense and pharmaceuticals), while others are target- or progress-based. For example, munitions must always be available, while clothing supplies can be managed using service levels.

- Not all metrics are transferable from the corporate world—for example, cash-to-cash, days inventory outstanding, etc.

- Determining the levels and periodicity is crucial, particularly for critical missions.

Key performance measures and targeted metrics have become the driver of the modern global supply chain. Their effective design, data, and implementation are core capabilities in today's uncertain and competitive environment. Supply chains contribute to, and often drive, business strategy. Key performance measures must clearly link with the strategic goals and imperatives of the business and its supply chains. The next and final chapter, "The Way Forward," brings this argument, and those we've made in the preceding chapters, together in a comprehensive set of guidelines for companies and nations to navigate and thrive in this uncertain environment. The Appendix that follows provides a compilation of the breakthrough thinking practices and concepts that we have identified throughout this book.

PART THREE

The Way Forward

CHAPTER 10

The Way Forward

I cannot teach anyone anything . . .
I can only make them think.
—Socrates

This book was written not to tell people what to do, but to lead executives and policy makers through a thought process that would help them develop and implement a successful road map for supply chain strategy and management. In the process, we have strived to provide leaders, interested academics, and informed citizens who have an interest in the supply chain and today's headlines with an understanding of the development and evolution of the supply chain, how it works, its beneficial and adverse impacts, and where it's likely to be going in the future. The landscape has been shaped by geopolitical tensions, technological advancements, major global crises, customers' changing demands, sustainability pressures, and national policies, and has changed dramatically. Many supply chains, however, still operate with "traditional" (legacy) approaches to supply, assets, priorities, and demand. While many of the basics of supply chain management still hold true and remain relevant, today's environment dictates new and breakthrough thinking to succeed in an increasingly uncertain world.

Supply chains have moved from an early buyer-seller-transport relationship to a lengthy chain, to a network, and finally to an ecosystem. The pace of change has increased exponentially over the past several years as global sourcing of products and suppliers has multiplied, technology has advanced, governments have increased their control and often "weaponized" the supply chain, and customers have demanded a comprehensive customer experience with higher levels of service, increased convenience, lower costs, and faster delivery. In short, we have unforeseen and unprecedented levels of complexity, digitization, uncertainty, and risk.

A key question we have posed and addressed in our book is, how can companies and nations survive and thrive in this VUCA (volatile, uncertain, complex, and ambiguous) environment? Different ways of thinking—"something old, something new, something borrowed"—are required, along with new strategies and focused and relentless execution.

While we can outline the new environment relatively clearly, we cannot predict the rate of future change, the pace of transformation, or the specific nature of the disruptions that will occur. We can, however, expect that changes will be happening increasingly quickly, and supply chains must be designed and positioned to adapt. A critical aspect of this is how, and whether, executives and public policy makers can sustain their commitment to supply chain cost-competitive resilience, sustainability, national security, long-term thinking, and constant change.

In this final chapter we will summarize the major trends that supply chains will face and identify the key breakthrough thinking that corporate and government leaders must adopt to thrive in this environment. In the Appendix, we have compiled a synopsis of the breakthrough thinking that we have outlined throughout the previous chapters of the book. Finally, we will pose some critical strategic questions for executives, policy makers, and other readers to ask of themselves, their organizations, and their communities—and, when appropriate, to act upon.

THE MAJOR TRENDS AND ISSUES FACING ORGANIZATIONS

Through the course of this book we have discussed the evolution of supply chains, from the simple structures of the previous decades to the complex networks of today. We have outlined the various management and government approaches (and, sometimes, lack of them) through globalization, "engineering the financials," and concentration phases that have provided major benefits to economies and people. However, the inevitable market imperfections, "frictions," and disruptions that occurred rendered supply chains fragile and brought about significant adverse social and environmental impacts. Supply chains were "built to break," and under stress, many did and still do just that—resulting in product delays and shortages, high costs of financing, rising product costs, and the undermining of national security, social cohesion and public health.

We have also laid out the major trends and the new environment that supply chains must navigate. The next several years will undoubtedly bring new challenges, complexities, developments, tools, and requirements that will both test and enable supply chains while unveiling new opportunities. These are the seven major trends we see ahead:

- First, *the growth of e-commerce* will continue and extend globally. The volumes of shopping and buying online will expand throughout the world, as will the growth of personalization, individual delivery, returns, and customer expectations of service.
- Second, there will be continued disruptions caused by *climate change and limitations of land, resources, and valuable and rare materials.* The "tragedy of the commons," as discussed in Chapter 8, includes both shared resources and the expanding human population, and needs to be part of our thinking and management strategies. These disruptions cannot be predicted precisely, but they can be expected and planned for. Supply chains should be designed to have the posture to deal with these disruptions effectively.

- We expect increased *geopolitical risks* owing to national interests, global conflicts and tensions, increasing "diamond" supply chains, concentration and the increased "weaponization" of the supply chain, and thefts of intellectual property and technology. Countries (and their allies) will compete with their supply chains more intensely than ever.
- The pace of *technology development*—automation, artificial intelligence, machine learning and "intelligent" systems, digitalization, virtual and augmented reality, additive manufacturing, and robotics—will continue to increase at an exponential rate. This will drive major changes to the end-to-end supply chain and the network from the point of first supply to the end consumer, and back.
- The increasing importance (and competitive necessity) for *companies and policy makers to think integratively and creatively* will lead to development of the Spatial Web—the intelligent, learning, resilient, data-driven, optimized working capital and cost-competitive supply chain of tomorrow. This vision is shaped by risk and competitive imperatives and is at the nexus of the human, physical, digital, and business environment (often involving the public sector) and eliminates the barriers among them. The applications for supply chains, infrastructure, resilience, and agility are nearly endless and are bound only by the imagination. While this vision may be somewhat futuristic, the journey must begin today. The pieces are already there, are being further developed, and creativity must follow.
- The *increasing demands of more than eight billion customers* on the planet will drive continued change. While these demands will depend on local conditions, they will continue to grow and

challenge supply chains in profound ways. More importantly, one size does not fit all, and there will be several different supply chains and stratified approaches for different countries, industries, products, and consumer types.

- *Talent will be at a premium.* This includes supply chain and business acumen, as well as STEM and interdisciplinary education and training. Success in hiring, retention, reskilling, and upskilling will provide an increasingly competitive advantage.

While today's supply chains already demand cost and working capital efficiency, customer centricity, supply assurance, and process efficiencies, the new environment will require these at even higher levels. Supply chains of the future must become even more flexible, resilient, and agile. They will have to move from being technology-enabled to "intelligent" supply chains, and from shareholder-driven to stakeholder-driven. They will be increasingly influenced by government mandates, nongovernmental organizations and activists, and consumer pressures, all enabled by ubiquitous communication. Management and policy makers will have to respond in a financially viable manner that also serves national interests including healthcare, local jobs, wealth creation, social cohesion, and security.

BREAKTHROUGH THINKING FOR TODAY AND TOMORROW: THE FOUR PRINCIPLES

Throughout this book we have identified the breakthrough thinking that we believe is necessary for supply chains to succeed today and tomorrow. We are aware that not every recommendation is applicable to every organization or public policy domain, as each has different priorities, products, structures, and competitive imperatives.

Throughout, we have defined breakthrough thinking as encompassing:

- Innovative thinking and constructs
- Structures and concepts that many have been aware of, but very few have tried and operationalized
- "The basics"—concepts that form the foundation of supply chain management and, unfortunately, have largely been ignored by many executives and academics over the past few decades

However, while each action or recommendation is important and needs to be understood and addressed, we will summarize some of the more important concepts and direction. These provide some of the key guidelines for thinking through the development of strategies for the supply chains of the future and executing them effectively.

Supply chain executives, shareholders, public policy makers, and the general public must realize that the supply chains and the trade environment of today are not, and have never been, "global" but rather "international" and "cross-border." Furthermore, supply chains are all different from one another; one size does not fit all in terms of capability, priorities, products, costs, speed, and, of course, risk. When supply chains are unpacked and analyzed, we find that companies in the same industry and even individual companies with different product lines and channels have different supply chains. Governments also have different supply chains (involving the private sector to various degrees) and priorities (and some have none at all), and they also often play a critical role in commercial supply chains.

Traditional design methods that assume a stable, reasonably predictable environment of continued growth have become outdated. However, there are several concepts and practices that apply to all (or most) supply chains. New methods and techniques, using both quantitative and qualitative factors, will drive the new supply chain network designs emphasizing agility, flexibility, and cost-competitive resilience rather than the rigid physical structures of the past. Given this, we have outlined four critical principles and guidelines to breakthrough thinking.

Design End-to-End Supply Chains from the Customer Back and from Suppliers Forward

End-to-end supply chains should:

- Emphasize a hybrid push-pull system that provides supply scale, customization, and response for the best long-term results.
- Recognize that national interests and security are essential (for critical supply chains), and supply chains must structure and operate within guardrails, even if these are not explicitly stated.
- Understand the customers, their wants, needs, and emotional quotient of today and tomorrow, and focus on using the supply chain to enhance the customer experience life cycle.
- Pay attention to supply chain finance in terms of supplier financing/working capital needs.
- Evaluate suppliers carefully in terms of foreign ownership and relations. Equally important, insist on knowing and documenting the source of the material at the lowest bill of materials level.
- Use a variety of tools, including optimization, simulation, and scenario planning, to develop and evaluate different strategies and trade-offs. Careful attention must be paid to where existing structure and suppliers can drive strategy.

- Design in multiple supply chain constructs and differentiated services for different markets, segments, and fulfillment models.
- For policy makers: Work in developing public-private partnerships to engage industry and academia, invest effectively in intermodal logistics infrastructure, implement preferred buying and supply chain financing, and focus on data and cybersecurity to support the nation's critical supply chains and ensure business continuity.

Treat Data as a Corporate Asset, and Develop a Data, Knowledge, and Technology Strategy That Encompasses the End-to-End Supply Chain and Network

The data, knowledge, and technology strategy should:

- Focus on data accuracy, timeliness, governance, and ownership.
- Provide true end-to-end visibility and transparency with the periodicity (real-time to quarterly) that is financially viable and necessary for operations.
- Enable automatic adjustments where possible.
- Support an analytics and measurement system with descriptive and prescriptive analytics that are both cross-functional and cross-organizational.
- Design in Web 3.0 spatial structures (to eventually eliminate the boundary between digital content and physical objects) that can place a company or nation way ahead of the competition or adversaries.

Collaborate Across Functions and Supply Chain Partners

- Adopt a stakeholder perspective toward sustainability initiatives, while addressing the

risks from a measured business perspective, with realistic and complete return on investment analyses.
- Adapt redundancy and hedging strategies and develop a diversified portfolio of reshoring, nearshoring, and friend-shoring as applicable to the product, manufacturing complexity and automation, talent, and material source.
- Reduce, through redesign and alternative sources of supply, the exposure of materials that are concentrated in strategic competitors and/or adversarial nations.

Manage Talent and Knowledge in the Organization

- Treat talent as an asset by crafting value propositions for hiring and retention, developing novel innovative programs for upskilling and reskilling current employees (by engaging willing and capable academic institutions).
- Make it a priority to place employees in positions and projects that are interesting and challenging to them.
- Educate employees on how the company operates and makes money, including total costs, risks, working capital, and the impacts of their decisions on other functions and corporate imperatives upstream and downstream in the supply chain.

These guidelines will change over the next several years to account for new realities and changes in technology, government actions, geopolitical tensions, and strategic imperatives and will be driven by competitive and societal pressures, national interests, and priorities.

QUESTIONS TO TAKE AWAY

We opened this chapter on a quote from Socrates: "I cannot teach anyone anything . . . I can only make them think." There are few methods more effective in enabling the thinking process than asking questions of the companies, organizations, and government institutions. We have provided a few in Boxes 10.1 and 10.2; we have found these to be very effective in developing strategy, obtaining consensus, drawing out priorities, and exposing some false assumptions. While the list is by no means comprehensive, it does provide an indication of the types of questions that must be asked and answered in both today's and the emerging business environment.

BOX 10.1

Questions for Corporate Executives and Managers

- Does your weekly management meeting cover the most important and urgent issues in terms of demand and supply status, costs, supplier performance, quality, customer order, and delivery performance?
- Do you have end-to-end supply chain visibility in terms of customer orders, supply status, inventory locations, transit status, bottlenecks, hold-ups, capacities, and expected arrivals?
- What is your performance in terms of perfect order fulfillment, time to delivery, and differentiated service costs? For major customers and for all customers?
- What is the delivery, shipment, quality, and cost performance of your key suppliers?

- Are any of your suppliers located in risky or adversarial countries?

- Is your supply base for critical commodities and manufacturing diversified? How soon can you switch supply from one provider to the other?

- Do you have a formal risk management process? Have you identified key risks, and are you monitoring them? Periodically, continuously?

- Is your inventory position good enough that you can withstand a one-week, two-week, three-week, one-month, or one-quarter disruption in supply? How quickly can your supply chain bounce back following a disruption?

- How soon can you return to full supply mode when the commodity or supply is disrupted?

- Is your acquisition process free of conflicts of interest?

- Do you have a senior executive as the sponsor and key decision maker for the global supply chain planning process?

- Do you use "what-if" and scenario planning and stress-testing for your international supply chain planning process?

- Is your international supply chain planning linked to execution in real time?

- Do you assess the benefits and costs of various initiatives and programs throughout the end-to-end supply chain?

- Do you succumb to the "customer obsession" and "overdeliver" trap when "no unnecessary excellence" should be the watchword?

- Are your key back-office processes automated?

- What are your source-to-settle/procure-to-pay times and costs?
- What are your order-to-delivery times?
- Do you measure your cost to serve by major customer or customer group?
- How would you rate your collaboration with suppliers, channels, and service partners?
- Do you maintain an inventory of talent?
- Do you have and track a talent development program? In terms of business acumen, functional knowledge, problem-solving, analytics, data management? Do you use outside resources for talent development?

While public policy makers must also deal with the above issues, they have an additional set that involves national interests, national security, and ESG regulations. Public policy makers must consider the questions in Box 10.2.

BOX 10.2

Questions for Public Policy Makers

- Do you have programs to reduce taxes, provide incentives for investment, and finance working capital to encourage companies to reshore or to friend-shore?
- Do you have consistent, accurate data across multiple organizations, and do you utilize end-to-end cross-organizational analytics for decision-making?

- Are regulations and ESG laws too onerous? Have you consulted in good faith with business groups instead of simply issuing mandates?

- Do you have preferred buying programs for the major programs and the defense industrial base?

- Have you identified critical supply chains, risks, and programs for reducing risk and assuring supply?

- Do you have incentives and investments for cost-competitive resilience for critical supply chains as part of your national industrial policies?

- Do you have programs to encourage STEM, supply chain, and manufacturing education and training? Are you developing novel programs in partnership with industry and academia?

- Do you have programs to encourage pragmatic, interdisciplinary research across the research continuum (basic to applied) to address the new challenges in supply chain design and management, while engaging industry?

- Have you identified critical products and supply chains, and developed the programs to identify risks and actions for risk mitigation?

- Do you have incentives for cost-competitive resilience for critical supply chains as part of the national policy?

- Have you developed novel public-private partnerships to harmonize the needs of the public sector with those of the public sector?

- Do you have ideas, designs, and plans for the future intelligent learning and resilient supply chains—perhaps the Spatial Web?

CONCLUSION

Based on our extensive work with a wide spectrum of leading organizations in the commercial, nonprofit, academic, and government sectors, we have described supply chains, their evolution, the nature of the emerging environment and its risks, and the breakthrough thinking concepts that companies and nations can use. Few organizations use all of these, and not all are applicable to every situation, but most of these are relevant to the complex and uncertain environment of today and of tomorrow. In the spirit of a picture being worth many words, we have summarized our thoughts in Figures 10.1 and 10.2, "Where We Want to Be" and "How We Get There."

It is important to reflect on the benefits and successes supply chains have delivered to business and society over the past few decades. It is also evident that market and shareholder demands, geopolitical tensions, neoliberal and "weaponization" government policies, environmental disasters and pandemics, coupled with the push toward unfettered globalization, have created fragile and vulnerable supply chains. We believe that the breakthrough thinking concepts and their application will unleash potent innovations and improvements in how supply chains are managed and reinvented, and help companies, nations, and relevant societal stakeholders thrive and prosper in this uncertain world.

Best wishes on the journey.

STAGES OF PERFORMANCE

KEY ATTRIBUTE	STAGE 1	STAGE 2	STAGE 2
High Resilience	Time and cost to recovery	No impact	Competitive advantage
Secure	Physical	IP	Cyber, data, transaction
Supply Assured	Variability hedging	Supply investing	Vertical (or virtual vertical) integration
Risk and Social Sourcing	Multiple/distributed, options ordering	Nearshoring	Friend-shoring, reshoring
Working Capital Optimized	Cash conversion—inventory, payables, receivables	Lead time reduction/velocity	Supply chain finance
Data and Analytics Driven	Governance and maintenance	Data accuracy and accessibility	Bottom-up analytics/"intelligent" analytics
Digitally Transformed	Process automation/visibility, transparency	Digital transformation	AI/"intelligent" operations, multiorganizational interoperability
Inventory Optimized	Safety stock—variability	Continuous review—all variables	Multi-echelon/risk-based
Effective Deployment	Risk pooling	Omnichannel	Point of use via all available channels and modes
Cost-Effective	Total landed/acquisition cost	Total fulfilled/ownership cost	ABC/cost to serve
National Security and Mandates	Bottom-top BOM analysis/IP mandates/re-source away from risky foreign sources	Friendly country suppliers/home manufacturing investment	Critical material/capability at home, including the organic industrial base
Designed for Business	DFx—manufacturing, packaging, logistics	DF E2E supply chain and ESG	DF national security
People	Online, low-cost, high-quality supply chain training, digital talent acquisition	Business acumen and analytics training, retention	Supply chain, digital analytics, and business acumen talent development, acquisition, and retention
Risk Management	Formal process—assessment, monitoring, risk mitigation strategies	Part of a data-driven, financially oriented decision process	Part of the senior management process with risk executive oversight

FIGURE 10.1 Where We Want to Be

Public Policy Makers

- Assure supply of critical products and supplies.
- Develop national industry security policy parameters.
- Implement preferred buying rules.
- Minimize risks and critical supply chain vulnerabilities through:
  - Focus on the organic industrial base
  - Tax breaks, subsidies
  - Working capital financing
  - Investment
  - Funding supply chain management, data, and technology education
  - Local source mandates
  - Transparency and reporting
  - Holding outsourcing companies liable for quality issues and critical IP loss/handover to unfriendly countries

Supply Chain Companies

- Engineer the supply chain, not the balance sheet, around the customer experience.
- Assure supply of critical materials, capabilities, drugs, and supplies.
- Source and finance around national security guardrails.
- Use new constructs and arrangements for supply chain financing.
- View the supply chain as an end-to-end network.
- Go digital—transformation, AI/"intelligent" operations, visibility, transparency.
- Minimize risks and increase resilience:
  - Formal risk management process
  - Through diversifying sourcing, reshoring, nearshoring, and distributed operations
  - Reducing dependence on potentially hostile foreign governments
  - Shortening the supply chain
  - Options ordering
  - Investing in local capabilities and operations
- Increase quality assurance, especially for foreign manufacturers.
- Ensure cybersecurity, data security, and IP protection.
- Back to the basics—manage, replenish, and deploy to point of use, focus on the customer experience and innovate new delivery constructs.
- Manage supply chain, analytics, and digital talent acquisition, retention, and development.

FIGURE 10.2 How We Get There

Breakthrough Thinking

The Process

Breakthrough thinking encompasses three major categories:

- Innovative thinking and constructs
- Structures and concepts that many have been aware of, but very few have tried and operationalized
- "The basics"—concepts that form the foundation of supply chain management and, unfortunately, have largely been ignored by many executives and academics over the past few decades

However, effectively adopting, customizing, and implementing breakthrough thinking requires a systematic and structured process that demands cross-functional and sometimes cross-organizational collaboration, a good understanding of the current situation, and analyses based on facts, trends, and data. Analyses must consider the current and future business success of the company, the *critical* stakeholders (not just anyone with an interest in the company and its operations), and national security. Strategies and plans must avoid "trying to boil the ocean at a single time" and focus on a time-phased approach based on resources, realities, and capabilities. Finally, they must include processes for measurement and monitoring of risks and progress, as well as decision points that allow for the discontinuation of projects and initiatives when necessary. Figure A.1 provides such a process.

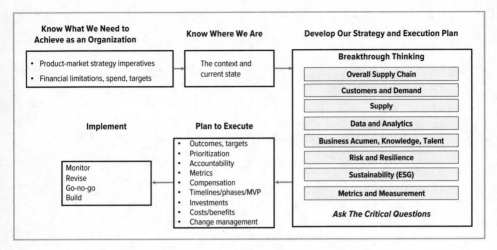

FIGURE A.1 The Breakthrough Thinking Process

We have compiled the breakthrough thinking developed and shown through the book in a single section here for ease of reference, discussion, and adoption.

CHAPTER 2: *How Supply Chains Have Enabled an Evolving World*

CORPORATE EXECUTIVES AND POLICY MAKERS

- View, structure, and manage the supply chain as an end-to-end network from the point of first supply to the end consumer and back (returns and reverse logistics), in terms of product, spares, materials, data, costs, and cash.

- Adopt a balanced time perspective, avoid "short-termism" and make risk an integral part of the management process.

- Globalization is, and always has been, a myth. International trade has always been about international supply chains, cross-border trading, and national interests.

- Nothing will go as planned; always plan and manage for risk—supply, demand, national and company security, infrastructure and logistics, environmental.

- National security must be an integral part of the supply chain—novel public-private partnerships and a "whole of country" approach should be adopted. Guidelines and guardrails for industry, government organizations, and NGOs must be developed at the senior policy level.
- In designing the supply chain, start with reality: focus on specific conditions, "gateway" elements, sources, and capabilities, and then develop supply chain strategies and designs that fit the company.

CHAPTER 3: *The Customer*

CORPORATE EXECUTIVES AND POLICY MAKERS

- Focus the supply chain on the customer experience life cycle and measure what the customer wants; understand the customer's tangible supply chain needs. Invest in technologies to understand the customer.
- Use ordering policies based on risks, lead times, and service levels—not just on trading off costs of holding inventory with ordering costs.
- Adopt and institutionalize an integrated, multifunctional sales and operations execution process with a member of the executive staff as the sponsor.
- Focus on the information needed for real-time and quick reaction to changing demand and conditions.
- Don't just identify demand—shape it to maximize margins and exploit product and component availability and shortages.
- Use "what-if" analysis and scenario planning, stated in terms of revenues, costs, and working capital, to analyze risks, changes in demand and supply, and disruptions.
- Invite key suppliers and channels/customers to be part of the process.
- Focus on the customer, but also on cost to serve (all customers may be equal, but some are more equal than others) and supply assurance. Segment customers to

determine cost- and revenue-effective services and strategies.

- Design the supply chain from the customer back and supply forward.

- Ensure that the customer's emotional state and attitude toward the company are considered, and take action to maintain a high level of satisfaction.

- While forecasting is important, focus on speed of customer response and product availability.

- The customer is both the entity or person ordering a product or service as well as the consumer.

- Address the concentration issues in the various industries that adversely affect customers' price and choice, and undermine the business continuity critical for communities and the government.

- Assign top people in a multifunctional effort to enhance the customer experience.

CHAPTER 4: *Managing Supply*

CORPORATE EXECUTIVES

- Partner with suppliers for demand-supply matching, technical developments.

- Shorten supply chains and/or make them much more robust through a diversified portfolio of onshoring, nearshoring, or friend-shoring.

- Focus on hiring the right talent with business acumen and supply chain knowledge.

- Diversify suppliers, nurture the supplier ecosystem, and build redundancy into the supply base.

- Know and develop personal relationships with key suppliers.

- Abide by national security guardrails—for example, source only noncritical components or manufacturing from adversarial countries; be wary of accepting financing from companies that are based in or controlled by hostile nations; carefully vet critical technical hires from such countries.

- Focus on the "back-office" processes—source to settle, procure-to-pay.
- Examine bills of material for supply sources.
- Strive for real-time information and status—as much as is necessary and financially feasible.
- Plan for hedge stock and capacity with suppliers to cover potential risks and system variability.
- Build risk identification, monitoring, and mitigation into the sourcing and acquisition process.
- Use options-based flexible supply ordering and planning.
- Use simulation for scenario planning and "what-if" analysis.

POLICY MAKERS

- Monitor the acquisitions process to incorporate strict national security parameters and conflict of interest rules.
- Evaluate demand-supply management to include major risk, disruption, and "black swan" type of events.
- Identify nationally critical products, materials, and supply chains; design and implement risk-mitigating strategies.

CHAPTER 5: *Information, Data, Governance, and Analytics*

CORPORATE EXECUTIVES AND POLICY MAKERS

- Treat data as a corporate and organizational asset, assure security, and mandate against keeping private data.
- Focus on data: accuracy, integrity, process, ownership, accountability, ease of entry and maintenance, and, of course, the sharing of data across organizational boundaries. This is particularly true in larger companies and governments—a rather frightening state of affairs when one considers that national security depends on sharing data.
- Define analytics: they should be ecosystem wide, easy to use and understand at the different levels, business-driven, and result in tangible enterprise outcomes.

- Ask, "What is the next technology development and supply chain application after the next one?"
- Do not accept the religion of having data "real-time, all the time, ecosystem-wide" easily. Instead, ask:
  - What will we do with such data?
  - Can we afford it (looking at the real, complete costs)?
  - What are the benefits?
  - Is it essential for our company given our industry?
  - Are there alternatives?
  - Has anybody else done it effectively?
  - And, of course, what kind of data do we really need?
- Train, upskill, and reskill employees in data management, science, and analytics.
- Technology acquisition and implementation:
  - Insist on realistic ROIs with realistic assumptions—and don't accept the cost and benefit estimates of the people putting forward the proposal of the IT department.
  - Technologies acquisition must be tied to business strategies, goals, and outcomes, and, of course, affordability.
  - Have "proofs of concept" initiatives for new technologies targeted and specified carefully in terms of benefits and costs.
  - Monitor progress based on cost and benefit projections.
  - Provide incentives for achieving benefits, cost targets, and timelines.
  - Take action against the initiative and sponsors if projected benefits don't materialize, costs overrun, and timelines go beyond scheduled.
- Develop a vision and program for the digital supply chain, using a multifunctional, "best of the best" team to design it in phases, with an MVP (minimum viable product) plan, all-inclusive and end-to-end analyses of costs and benefits, and a rigorous examination of the assumptions used. Ensure that data accuracy, business continuity, progress reporting with go-no-go decisions, and developing strong relationships with supply chain partners are at the core of the effort.

- Assign accountabilities and resources, and execute.
- The Spatial Web: Design the future with the human in the center, using a multifunctional, multilevel, multiorganizational set of design sessions. Then lay out an MVP approach to quickly and efficiently find out if an initiative is viable without significant cost or risk to execute.

CHAPTER 6: *Knowledge*

CORPORATE EXECUTIVES AND POLICY MAKERS

- Integrate supply chain education into the core operations of the company.
- Tailor supply chain education in business acumen, end-to-end costs and levers, corporate priorities (a must), the impacts of decisions on supply chain functions, and vice versa. Focus on the costs that matter to provide people with the "binoculars" to understand the impact of their decisions downstream and upstream in the supply chain. Some companies have centers of excellence that hire outside expertise or develop this in-house.
- Make this education and training an integral part of the skills/talent inventory part of the people development program.
- Disseminate relevant and interesting information, articles, and news on supply chain issues, trends, and international business to managers and executives.
- Implement programs for role and job rotation to increase experience and competence.
- Encourage universities to develop novel interdisciplinary, pragmatic educational modules as part of their undergraduate and graduate programs and for customized offerings to industry (eg., dual vocational programs).
- Eliminate or separate social training from the supply chain education and training curricula.

CHAPTER 7: *Risk, Assurance, and Resilience*

CORPORATE EXECUTIVES

- Redundancy strategies: capacity, supply, and moving away from risky and hostile countries.
- Hedge inventory.
- Risk management (including national security) part of the strategy, with continuous and periodic risk monitoring.
- End-to-end supply chain perspective for costs and cash.
- Modular strategies.
- Supply chain finance.
- End-to-end supply chain visibility, illuminations, and supply mapping to suppliers' suppliers.
- Data-driven and "intelligent" demand-supply planning, scenario planning, stress-testing, war-gaming, and simulation.
- Stop optimizing the "perfect" supply chain and instead develop flexible and resilient supply chain networks. A quick-moving "sense and respond" system is far better than a rigid system that seeks to anticipate everything in detail. As von Clausewitz said, "The enemy of a good plan is the dream of a perfect plan."

POLICY MAKERS

- Government action and rationalization for transparent, consistent, and streamlined regulatory management and one-stop shopping.
- Analysis and impact of companies' products, technologies, and capabilities on the critical national supply chain networks.
- Redundancy strategies: capacity, supply, and moving away from risky and hostile countries, reducing concentration, and increasing supplier diversification.
- Develop the programs to identify risks and actions for risk mitigation.
- Develop and provide incentives for cost-competitive resilience for critical supply chains.
- Develop novel public-private partnerships to harmonize the needs of the public sector with those of the private sector.

- End-to-end supply chain visibility and illuminations and supply mapping to tier 1, 2, and 3 suppliers to also highlight "diamond" supply chains.

- Talent management, hiring, retention, reskilling, and upskilling at the national level for STEMX disciplines; incentives and programs for generating and developing talent.

- Development of rigorous methods to evaluate critical industries and materials, reshoring versus friend-shoring versus nearshoring, and combinations. This includes the real and comprehensive impacts of disruptions across all industries.

- Evaluation of the supply and acquisition process to manage conflicts of interest and revolving-door policies; supply chain planning in order to take into consideration risks, surge, supersurge, and "black swan" events.

- Critical industry and supply chain financing for in-country production and supply, with vigilance and oversight on M&A, hiring and visa activities, outsourcing, and offshoring; starting the decoupling of supply chains from adversarial countries.

- Investments in logistics infrastructure, ensuring transportation and shipping capacity.

- Cyber and data security in the critical supply chains.

- Financial incentives and competitive tax policies and incentives for working capital, local sourcing and operations, and training.

- Public-private partnerships to share technology and for data exchanges to ensure critical supply chain visibility.

- Government action scrutinizing transactions that allow adversaries to control critical supply chains and technologies.

- Oversight of outsourcing government and critical supply chain information technology systems and operations to foreign companies.

CHAPTER 8: *Sustainability*

CORPORATE EXECUTIVES

- Identify the climate change risks that the company could face and integrate them into the risk mitigation and monitoring process at a company, regional, and site level.

- Ask the question: Is ESG good for business, good for image, necessary for compliance, or a major cost item?

- Don't lead the pack unless it gives you some advantage; be a follower, not an innovator.

- Do your ROIs thoroughly while considering all aspects (including documentation and compliance).

- Evaluate the longer-term cost, demand, and working capital consequences before jumping into developing new products or supply chain design in response to government ESG policies.

- Develop fiscally astute ESG strategies.

- Develop a value proposition that shows the impacts to the business, employee jobs, and benefits to other stakeholders.

- Start small with recycle, reuse, value recovery, etc., before moving up to refurbish, remanufacture, redesign, re-source, etc.

- Use all progress as a marketing tool, inside and outside the company, to attract funding and for recruitment of new talent.

POLICY MAKERS

- Provide streamlined, steady, and transparent regulatory management, with clear and consistent disclosure schema across industry sectors.

- Do not impose the Western social agenda on other countries; rather, yield, adapt, and conform.

- Do not impose onerous conditions on domestic companies that will put them at a competitive disadvantage globally.

- Improve the policing of net-zero commitments and other regulations with both national and international companies doing business in the country.

- Pay attention and assess the unintended consequences of ESG policy.
- Implement tighter and more realistic carbon prices.
- Embed national interests and security in the regulatory agenda.

CHAPTER 9: *Measures That Matter*

CORPORATE EXECUTIVES

- Start with "What do we measure and why?"
- Tie metrics to business and supply chain goals, imperatives, and outcomes.
- Have a few critical measures at every level.
- Begin the journey with the basics—don't listen to vendors and consultants who want you to have a control tower immediately. Do the critical ones first: display metrics online (no PowerPoint decks compiled by subordinates) and in as near real time as possible, in scorecards and dashboards. Control towers and "nerve centers" can come later.
- Focus on the data, availability, accuracy, and end-to-end supply chain scope.
- Measures can be both quantified and nonquantified and reflect both descriptive and trend metrics.
- Measures must be understood by everyone and be actionable. The issue of people adopting, understanding, and using them is a key factor in their implementation.
- Periodicity, display, and visualization are essential and require trade-offs in terms of costs, time, and sometimes outcomes.
- Metrics must reflect end-to-end supply chain performance—for example, total landed and delivered costs, total costs of acquisition, and cost to serve.
- Plan on a system of real-time measures or leading indicators that proactively alert executives of the need for action.

POLICY MAKERS

Exactly as with corporate requirements, with some customization as described here:

- Recognize that some metrics are absolute (100 percent service levels could be mandatory for defense and pharmaceuticals), while others are target- or progress-based. For example, munitions must always be available, while clothing supplies can be managed using service levels.

- Not all metrics are transferable from the corporate world— for example, cash-to-cash, days inventory outstanding, etc.

- Determining the levels and periodicity is crucial, particularly for critical missions.

BIBLIOGRAPHY

All In on AI: How Smart Companies Win Big with Artificial Intelligence. Thomas H. Davenport and Nitin Mittal. Harvard Business Review Press, 2023.

Bricks Matter: The Role of Supply Chains in Building Market-Driven Differentiation. Lora M. Cecere and Charles W. Chase Jr. John Wiley & Sons, 2013.

Bulletproof Problem Solving: The One Skill That Changes Everything. Charles Conn and Robert McLean. John Wiley & Sons, 2018.

Chip War: The Fight for the World's Most Critical Technology. Chris Miller. Scribner, 2022.

Competing on Analytics: The New Science of Winning. Thomas H. Davenport and Jeanne Harris. Harvard Business School Publishing Corporation, 2017.

The Crisis of Democratic Capitalism. Martin Wolf. Penguin Press, 2023.

Flow: How the Best Supply Chains Thrive. Rob Handfield and Tom Linton. Rotman-UTP Publishing, 2022.

From Source to Sold: Stories of Leadership in Supply Chain. Radu Palamariu and Knut Alicke. Grammar Factory Publishing, 2022

Homecoming: The Path to Prosperity in a Post-Global World. Rana Foroohar. Crown, 2022.

Insightful Leadership: Surfing the Waves to Organizational Excellence. Jim Tompkins and Michael Hughes. BrightRay Publishing, 2022.

Introduction to Supply Chain Resilience: Management, Modelling, Technology. Dmitry Ivanov. Springer, 2021.

Liberty from All Masters: The New American Autocracy vs. the Will of the People. Barry C. Lynn. St. Martin's Press, 2020.

Makers and Takers: How Wall Street Destroyed Main Street. Rana Foroohar. Currency, 2016.

Managing the Supply Chain: The Definitive Guide for the Business Professional. David Simchi-Levi, Philip Kaminsky and Edith Simchi-Levi. McGraw Hill, 2004.

Mission Economy: A Moonshot Guide to Changing Capitalism. Mariana Mazzucato. Harper Business, 2021.

Net Positive: How Courageous Companies Thrive by Giving More Than They Take. Paul Polman and Andrew Winston. Harvard Business Review Press, 2021.

Radical Uncertainty: Decision-Making Beyond the Numbers. John Kay and Mervyn King, Norton, 2020.

The Rise and Fall of the Neoliberal Order: America and the World in the Free Market Era. Gary Gerstle. Oxford, 2022.

Supercharging Supply Chains: New Ways to Increase Value Through Global Operational Excellence. Gene Tyndall, Christopher Gopal, Wolfgang Partsch, and John Kamauff. Wiley, 1998.

Supply Chain Management for Sustainable Food Networks. Eleftherios Iakovou, Dionysis Bochtis, Dimitrios Vlachos, and Dimitrios Aidonis (editors). Wiley, 2016.

The 5-STAR Business Network: And the CEOs Who Are Building the Next Generation of Super-Corporations with It. Vivek Sood. Jardine Thompson, Australia, 2013.

The End of the World Is Just the Beginning: Mapping the Collapse of Globalization. Peter Zeihan. Harper Business, 2022.

The Long Game: China's Grand Strategy to Displace American Order. Rush Doshi. Oxford University Press, 2021.

The Power of Resilience: How the Best Companies Manage the Unexpected. Yossi Sheffi. MIT Press, 2017.

The Resilient Society. Markus K. Brunnermeier. Endeavor Literary Press, 2021.

The World Turned Upside Down: America, China, and the Struggle for Global Leadership. Clyde Prestowitz. Yale University Press, 2021.

Unchain Your Corporation: From Supply Chains to B2B Networks. Vivek Sood. Global Supply Chain Group, Australia, 2015.

War by Other Means: Geoeconomics and Statecraft. Robert D. Blackwill and Jennifer M. Harris. The Belknap Press of Harvard University Press, 2016.

When More Is Not Better: Overcoming America's Obsession with Economic Efficiency. Roger L. Martin. Harvard Business Review Press, 2020.

NOTES

CHAPTER 1

1. Winston Churchill, prime minister of Great Britain, *Post-War Councils on World Problems: A Four Year Plan for England*, broadcast from London over BBC, March 21, 1943.
2. Carl von Clausewitz, *Vom Kriege* ("On War"), 1832 (published posthumously by his wife, Marie von Brühl).

CHAPTER 2

1. Voltaire, "Letter to Mme. d'Épinal, Ferney (December 26, 1760)" from *Oeuvres Complètes de Voltaire: Correspondance* (Garnier frères, Paris, 1881), vol. IX, letter # 4390 (p. 124).

CHAPTER 3

1. George Orwell, *Animal Farm* (London: Secker and Warburg, 1945).
2. Peter Dorrington, *Anthrolytics,* interview by the author, June 2021.

CHAPTER 4

1. Carl von Clausewitz, *Vom Kriege* ("On War"), 1832 (published posthumously by his wife, Marie von Brühl).
2. von Clausewitz, *Vom Kriege.*
3. Y. Chang, E. Iakovou, and W. Shi, "Blockchain in Global Supply Chains and Cross Border Trade: A Critical Synthesis of the State-of-the-Art, Challenges and Opportunities," *International Journal of Production Research* 58, no. 7 (2020): 2082–99.

4. C. Gopal, quoted in C. Meyer, "What Does It Take to Redesign an Industry?," *Harvard Business Review*, March 2013.

CHAPTER 5

1. Thomas Hobbes, *Leviathan*, 1651.
2. Tadhg Nagle, Thomas C. Redman, and David Sammon, "Only 3% of Companies' Data Meets Base Quality Standards," *Harvard Business Review*, September 11, 2017.
3. Mariana Lenharo, "The Science Behind Grouping Package Deliveries: How Customer Order and Network Density OptimizeR (CONDOR) Has Led to Improved Delivery Routes," *Amazon Science*, August 24, 2022, https://www.amazon.science /latest-news/the-science-behind-Grouping-amazon-package -deliveries.
4. Carl von Clausewitz, *Vom Kriege* ("On War"), 1832 (published posthumously by his wife, Marie von Brühl).
5. Pepe Rodriguez, Stefan Gstettner, Ashish Pathak, Ram Krishnan, and Michael Spaeth, "Why AI-Managed Supply Chains Have Fallen Short and How to Fix Them," Boston Consulting Group, September 1, 2022, https://meet.aeratechnology.com/hubfs /benefits-of-ai-driven-supply-chain.pdf.

CHAPTER 7

1. Winston Churchill, *Churchill by Himself*, ed. Richard Langworth (Public Affairs, 2008), 495.
2. Carl von Clausewitz, *Vom Kriege* ("On War"), 1832 (published posthumously by his wife, Marie von Brühl).
3. David Simchi-Levy, "Find the Weak Link in Your Supply Chain," *Harvard Business Review*, June 9, 2015.
4. Martijn Rasser, "Pandemic Problem: America's Supply Chains Are Dangerously Brittle," *The National Interest*, March 17, 2020.

CHAPTER 8

1. Milton Friedman, *There's No Such Thing as a Free Lunch* (Open Court Publishing Company, 1977).

2. "United Nations Secretary-General's Statement on the IPCC Working Group 1 Report on the Physical Science Basis of the Sixth Assessment," United Nations, August 9, 2021.

3. McKinsey & Company, "How to Prepare for a Sustainable Future Along the Value Chain," January 20, 2022.

4. *Supply Chain Management Review*, 2022.

5. Larry Rulison, "Plug Power Plays a Huge Role Helping Amazon and Walmart Supply America During Covid-19 Crisis," *Albany Times Union*, May 7, 2020.

6. Mehdi Miremadi, Christopher Russo, and Ulrich Weihe, "How Much Will Consumers Pay to Go Green?," *McKinsey Quarterly*, October 1, 2020.

7. Boston Consulting Group and World Economic Forum, *Net-Zero Challenge: The Supply Chain Opportunity*, January 21, 2021.

8. Max Garland, "With Limited Fuel Alternatives, UPS Air Cargo Emissions Continue to Rise," *Supply Chain Dive*, August 11, 2022.

9. Scot Case, "Retailers Set Science-Based Targets to Address Climate Change," National Retail Federation, November 8, 2021.

10. Boston Consulting Group and the World Retail Congress, "Sustainability in Retail Is Possible, but There's Work to Be Done," April 2022.

11. OECD, "The Due Diligence Guidance for Responsible Supply Chains of Minerals from Conflict-Affected and High-Risk Areas," 2016.

12. Amazon, "Sustainability," https://sustainability.aboutamazon .com/.

13. John Ruggie, "Promotion and Protection of All Human Rights, Civil, Political, Economic, Social and Cultural Rights, Including the Right to Development: Protect, Respect and Remedy: a Framework for Business and Human Rights: Report of the Special Representative of the Secretary-General on the Issue of Human Rights and Transnational Corporations and Other Business Enterprises," Human Rights Council, April 7, 2008, https://media.business-humanrights.org/media/documents /files/reports-and-materials/Ruggie-report-7-Apr-2008.pdf.

14. "UN Guiding Principles on Business and Human Rights," United Nations, June 1, 2011.

15. "OECD: 2011 Update of the OECD Guidelines for Multinational Enterprises," OECD, May 25, 2011.
16. EU Directive 2014/95/EU.
17. European Coalition for Corporate Justice, "Strategic Framework 2017–2020."
18. "Lieferkettengesetz," 2021 (German Supply Chain Act).
19. Modern Slavery Act 2015, Legislation.gov.uk.
20. The California Transparency in Supply Chains Act, 2015.
21. US Customs and Border Patrol Act, Uyghur Forced Labor Prevention Act (UFLPA), December 23, 2021.
22. International Organization for Standardization (ISO) 14000 Family Environmental Management.
23. Electronic Industry Citizenship Coalition Code of Conduct (EICC) Version 4.0 (2012).
24. Restriction of Hazardous Substances (RoHS), EU Directive 2002/95/EC.
25. Registration, Evaluation, Authorisation and Restriction of Chemicals (REACH), EU, European Chemicals Agency, June 1, 2007.
26. 2010 Dodd-Frank Wall Street Reform and Consumer Protection Act, Section 1502 Conflict Minerals (3TG: Tin, Tantalum, Tungsten, Gold).
27. The Foreign Corrupt Practices Act of 1977 (FCPA).
28. European Union Waste Electrical and Electronic Equipment (WEEE) directive, European Commission, August 2012.
29. Cargo Owners for Zero Emissions Vehicles (coZEV), 2021.
30. Garrett Hardin, "The Tragedy of the Commons," *Science*, New Series, vol. 162, no. 3859 (December 13, 1968): 1243–48.

INDEX

ABOUT THE AUTHORS

Christopher Gopal

 Christopher Gopal has over 40 years of industry and consulting experience in global supply chain, operations, and technology management, and is recognized internationally as an innovator, using a systems-thinking and multidisciplinary approach to global supply chains. He has held senior positions at several leading companies, including Dell Computer, Unisys, Overland Storage, and SAIC, and was partner and director of Global Supply Chain and Operations at Ernst & Young Consulting. His consulting clients have included prominent global and regional companies across a range of industries.

Dr. Gopal serves as a member of the Defense Business Board (DBB) in Washington and is a member of the Supply Chain Advisory Board at the Global Fund based in Geneva.

He has been an invited speaker and panelist at several international forums and is the coauthor of three books. He currently consults with companies, serves as a strategic advisor, and teaches at the University of California, San Diego, and at the University of Southern California. Chris holds a PhD from the University of Southern California and an MBA from the Cranfield School of Management, UK.

Gene Tyndall

 Gene Tyndall is a globally recognized authority on supply chain management with over four decades of experience as a management consultant and a president of a leading logistics service provider. His career includes service as a US Navy Officer and as a member of the Office of the Secretary of US Transportation.

Gene was a senior consulting senior partner in supply chain management at Ernst & Young, president of Global Supply Chain Solutions at Ryder Corporation, and an EVP for Strategy and Solutions at Tompkins International. He is currently a cofounder and senior partner with eMATE Consulting and the Supply Chain Strategy consulting leader with Tompkins Ventures.

He has coauthored four books, delivered dozens of presentations and webinars on supply chain management, written hundreds of articles and blogs, and is frequently quoted in business and industry media. He was awarded the Global Logistics Person of the Year, as well as Innovator of the Year by Information Management. Gene has a BS from the University of Maryland and his MBA and DBA from the George Washington University.

Wolfgang Partsch

 Dr. Partsch is one of the originators of, and a pioneer in, the supply chain management concept, an internationally recognized thought leader, and has codeveloped many innovative supply chain concepts. He has substantial experience in integrating and coordinating the global supply chain for several leading companies and achieving world-class results.

He was chairman of the Global Supply Chain Network of Ernst & Young and a coauthor of the bestselling book *Supercharging Supply Chains*, published in 1998. He has been a trusted advisor for many presidents and CEOs, who are seeking his views and judgments on complex operational issues within the entire E2E supply chain. Since 2000 he has developed advanced solutions in supply chain security and supply chain risk management.

He is member of several advisory boards and partner of companies dealing with supply chain management and green and alternative energy solutions in Europe, the United States, and Asia-Pacific. He holds a PhD in physics from the University of Vienna in Austria.

Eleftherios Iakovou

Dr. Eleftherios "Lefteris" Iakovou is the Harvey Hubbell Professor of Industrial Distribution at Texas A&M University, where he also leads the supply chain management initiatives for several institutes and programs. He is a globally recognized supply chain management academic scholar and leader, a successful fundraiser, and a strategic thinker with transformational impacts on the organizations that he has served.

He has developed large-scale supply chain institutes, initiatives, and consortia funded by corporations and governmental agencies alike, in the United States and the European Union.

Lefteris has published hundreds of peer-reviewed scientific papers, coauthored three books, authored three textbooks, and contributed to more than 100 events as a keynote or invited speaker. He can move across professional fields and academic disciplines having in-depth experience in engineering, management, policy-making, logistics, and operations and is a well-sought expert by international bodies, governments, industry, and the media. He holds a five-year diploma in Mechanical Engineering from the Aristotle University of Thessaloniki, and an MS and PhD in Operations Research and Industrial Engineering from Cornell University.